NORTHBROOK PUBLIC LIBRARY
1201 CEDAR LANE
NORTHBROOK, ILL 60062

BARRON'S

MATH WORKBOOK FOR THE

GED® TEST

4TH EDITION

Johanna Holm
Teacher of Mathematics
Kanawha County Schools
Charleston, West Virginia

Writer and Editor,
American Council on Education

GED® is a registered trademark of the American Council on Education (ACE) and administered exclusively by GED Testing Service LLC under license. This material is not endorsed or approved by ACE or GED Testing Service.

SEP 2 1 2016

© Copyright 2015 by Barron's Educational Series, Inc.
© Copyright 2009, 2003, 1997 by Barron's Educational Series, Inc., under the title *GED Math Workbook*.

All rights reserved.
No part of this publication may be reproduced in any form, or by
any means without the written permission of the copyright owner.

All inquiries should be addressed to:
Barron's Educational Series, Inc.
250 Wireless Boulevard
Hauppauge, New York 11788
www.barronseduc.com

Library of Congress Control No. 2014958693

ISBN: 978-1-4380-0571-3

10%
**POST-CONSUMER
WASTE**
Paper contains a minimum
of 10% post-consumer
waste (PCW). Paper used
in this book was derived
from certified, sustainable
forestlands.

PRINTED IN THE UNITED STATES OF AMERICA

9 8 7 6 5 4 3 2 1

CONTENTS

Introduction to the GED® Test

1

The GED® test is the test of General Educational Development and is given to adults who did not graduate from high school. When you pass the GED® test, you will be awarded a certificate that is the equivalent of a high school diploma. Like the diploma, it is regarded as the entry key to the workplace and to higher education.

If you could visit with GED® test graduates, you would hear stories that bring tears to your eyes, stories that make you want to applaud, and stories full of courage, strength, and goals fulfilled. These successful graduates are like you. They used their life experiences, their determination, and their hard work to move on with their lives by taking this all-important first step. Your passing the GED® test will open doors for you that have been closed. We wish you the very best on your journey!

HISTORY

The GED® test was established in an effort to help military personnel who were returning from the battlefields of World War II. These were people whose education had been interrupted by war and who were trying now to pick up the pieces of their lives and careers. From those beginnings, the GED® program has offered a golden opportunity for tens of thousands for whom the regular high school setting was just not the right plan. The list of GED® program graduates contains every success story you could think of: small business owners, college graduates, writers, doctors, computer technicians, repair specialists—productive individuals all across the country. For you, just as it was for them, passing the GED® test will truly be the first day of the rest of your life.

INTENT

It is the intent of this book to be very user friendly. Use it as a road map to get you from where you are today to your successful completion of the GED® test. Even if reading is not your favorite activity, think about this: Every word in this book is there to help you. Every word has a purpose. If you find a word you don't know, look it up.

It is true that everything you know is something you taught yourself. Someone else may have explained it, but you were the one who took it in and made it yours. You taught yourself. This book is carefully designed not only to help you teach yourself enough math to pass the GED® test but also to help you gain skills that you can use on the job, in your home, in the marketplace, in your life.

LAYOUT

The layout of this book is modeled after the actual GED® test. The exam covers the categories of measurement, geometry, algebra, number relations, and data analysis. This book has chapters that include each of these topics. Each chapter contains the topics you are likely to see on the GED® test within that area. They are developed in the most straightforward manner possible. The variety of activities for you to do as you teach yourself is meant to involve your mind so that the learning will be easier. At the end of each of the review chapters, you will find GED® test-style questions. Taking these tests and checking your answers with those provided will let you evaluate your progress. There are explanations given with the answers to enhance your understanding.

In addition to these instructional chapters, there are two chapters for self-testing. Chapter 2 contains a diagnostic test set up so that you can evaluate your math strengths and weaknesses. A chart at the end of the chapter will allow you to see where you need to concentrate your efforts. The final chapter of the book contains four practice exams modeled after the actual GED® test. Taking these tests will allow you to determine how effective your study has been and to see if additional review of some topics is necessary.

THE GED® TEST

The GED® test is made up of four separate tests, as shown in the chart below. Some states require that you take all tests on the same day. In other states you may spread the testing over several days.

Test	Content Areas	Items	Time Limit
Reasoning Through Language Arts	Writing, interpreting, grammar, reading comprehension.	54	150 minutes
Mathematical Reasoning	Number operations, geometry, data, algebra.	46	115 minutes
Social Studies	Geography, history, economics, civics, analysis.	35	90 minutes
Science	Life science, earth science, physical science, interpretation, analysis.	34	90 minutes

Mathematical Reasoning Test Organization

Quantitative Problem Solving

45% of the test
Contains problems that involve whole numbers, positive and negative numbers, decimals, fractions, percent, ratios, data analysis, and geometry.

Algebraic Problem Solving

55% of the test
Contains problems that are about equations, inequalities, graphs, quadratic equations, functions, and patterns.

The math part of the GED® test will have approximately 46 questions. The first five must be done without a calculator. After you finish these problems, you may not return to them. For the rest of the test, a calculator may be used.

The Computer and the GED® Test

The GED® test must be taken on a computer at an official GED® Testing Center. If you need help to feel comfortable using a computer, taking a class or getting some kind of instruction would be a big help. Many public libraries have such classes.

You will have two calculator choices when you take the GED® exam. The computer you will be using has a calculator that you can access by clicking the computer mouse on the calculator icon. The other choice is to bring you own calculator to the test. This calculator MUST be the TI-30XS. You will NOT be allowed to share or borrow a calculator. To increase your calculator expertise, it would be an excellent investment to purchase and practice with the TI-30XS. Detailed instruction for using this calculator begins on page 50.

Mathematical Reasoning Test Question Types

MULTIPLE-CHOICE QUESTIONS

In answering multiple-choice questions, you will use the computer mouse to select the correct answer and then click on it.

DROP LIST QUESTIONS

After you read the question, you will see | Choice 1 ▼ |

The only choice you will be able to see is choice 1. Use the mouse to take the cursor to the triangle and click there. As you continue to click, the other choices are revealed. Click on the one you have decided is correct.

DRAG-AND-DROP QUESTIONS

In the drag-and-drop style questions, you will be asked to move numbers to a new location. For example, a test question could ask you to place these fractions in the correct box.

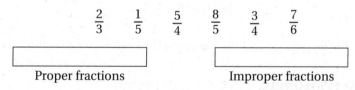

$$\frac{2}{3} \quad \frac{1}{5} \quad \frac{5}{4} \quad \frac{8}{5} \quad \frac{3}{4} \quad \frac{7}{6}$$

Proper fractions   Improper fractions

You know that a proper fraction is one in which the denominator is larger than the numerator. So, the $\frac{2}{3}$ is a proper fraction and goes in the left box. Use the mouse to put the cursor on the $\frac{2}{3}$ and drag it to the left box. Continue with the other fractions until the screen looks like this.

$$\frac{2}{3} \quad \frac{1}{5} \quad \frac{3}{4} \qquad\qquad \frac{5}{4} \quad \frac{8}{5} \quad \frac{7}{6}$$

Proper fractions   Improper fractions

SHORT-ANSWER QUESTIONS

Some questions are set up so that you have to come up with an answer and then use the keyboard to enter that answer in the space provided.

HOT SPOT QUESTIONS

Some questions will ask that you move the cursor to the answer and click on that.

WHITE BOARD

The test center will provide you with a white board and marker that you can use to make diagrams, do scratch work, and whatever else will help you. The white board is not part of the test.

Sample Test Questions

ARITHMETIC: NUMBER RELATIONS

Number sense and number relations involve evaluating how one number relates to another. Within this area you will find the concepts of ratio, percent, and proportion.

➡ EXAMPLE _____

Suppose a store is advertising that they are having a special sale, and that every pair of shoes in stock will be 25% off. What would be the selling price of a pair of shoes that cost $60 before the sale?

(A) $45
(B) $30
(C) $25
(D) $20

Answer: (A)

Explanation: To say 25% means to multiply by 0.25.

$$\$60 \times 0.25 = \$15$$

The price would be reduced by $15. The new selling price would be $60 – $15 = $45.

ARITHMETIC: DATA ANALYSIS

Data analysis is the part of the test that requires that you be able to read and interpret graphs, tables, and charts. You will also see questions relating to probability, averages, mode, and median.

➡ EXAMPLE

Suppose your state requires either a minimum grade of 150 on each of the four GED® tests or an average of 165 when you consider all the tests. What would your average be if your test results were as follows?

Test	Your Score	Possible Score
Language Arts	140	200
Social Studies	180	200
Science	170	200
Mathematics	150	200

(A) 160
(B) 200
(C) 360
(D) 640

Answer: (A)

Explanation: To find an average, first add all the scores. Then divide by 4 because 4 is the number of scores that you added together. In this case, 640 is the total of all the scores. Then divide 640 by 4. The number 200 is not needed to answer the question.

ARITHMETIC: MEASUREMENT (NUMBER OPERATIONS AND NUMBER SENSE)

Measurement questions address your ability to evaluate diagrams and to apply measuring skills to such topics as perimeter, area, volume, time, and space.

➡ EXAMPLE

Suppose you were taking a pre-employment test and one of the questions said to give the number the arrow is pointing to in the diagram below. Which of the following responses is correct?

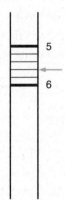

(A) 5.3
(B) 5.4
(C) 5.6
(D) 6.2

Answer: (C)

Explanation: First, you should notice that the arrow lies between 5 and 6, so the answer should be 5 decimal point something. Then you should find that each mark represents 0.2. If you had decided each represents 0.1, you would see that there are not enough marks to get from 5 to 6. In starting at the 5 and counting downward, the first mark would be 5.2, then 5.4, and 5.6 at the arrow.

ALGEBRA

The algebra questions on the test will address ideas that include writing and solving equations, using formulas, factoring, and using exponents and ratios.

➡ EXAMPLE

One of the formulas that will be available to you on a separate formula page of the GED® test is $d = rt$. This is an algebraic way of saying that distance is equal to rate times time. Use this formula to find out how fast you would have to drive in order to cover a distance of 200 miles in exactly 3.5 hours. Which of these choices gives you the correct answer?

(A) $r = \dfrac{200}{3.5}$

(B) $r = 200 \times 3.5$

(C) $r = 3.5 \times 200$

(D) $r = \dfrac{3.5}{200}$

Answer: (A)

Explanation: Because $d = rt$, 200 miles = rate × 3.5 hours. To find the rate, divide both sides of the equation by 3.5 hours.

This results in $\dfrac{200}{3.5}$ = rate.

GEOMETRY

The geometry-based questions on the GED® test will ask that you deal with lines, angles, and formulas as they relate to circles, squares, rectangles, triangles, and cylinders. Formulas for area, volume, and perimeter are provided on the formula page.

➡ EXAMPLE_____

Observe the diagram below and calculate the area it shows.

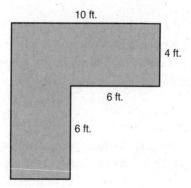

(A) 20 sq. ft.
(B) 40 sq. ft.
(C) 60 sq. ft.
(D) 64 sq. ft.

Answer: (D)

Explanation: The area of a rectangle can be found by multiplying the length of the rectangle by its width. If you were to split the figure into two separate rectangles as shown below, the area of each rectangle could be calculated. Rectangle #1 has an area of $10 \times 4 = 40$ square feet, while the area of rectangle #2 is $4 \times 6 = 24$ square feet. Adding these two rectangles together gives an area of $24 + 40 = 64$ square feet.

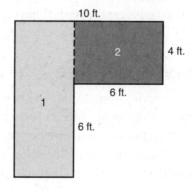

The Anatomy of a Question

Each question on the mathematical reasoning test of the GED® test is built around an every-day application of math, and contains a short descriptive passage, a graph, or a table. Some problems require the use of a formula. A page of formulas will be provided, both on the GED® test and in this book. In this book's algebra chapter, there is an instructional section on the use of formulas, followed by practice with answers and explanations.

As you evaluate the answer choices provided for a question, remember that some problems include more information than you need.

The mathematical reasoning GED® test is divided into two parts. On the first part, you are not allowed to use a calculator. On the second part of the test, you will be allowed to use a calculator. At the end of Chapter 3, there are instructions in the use of this calculator. Calculator icons are used throughout the book to mark problems particularly suitable for calculator use. The TI-30XS calculator is a fairly inexpensive calculator, costing about $20, so its purchase would be a good study aid.

You will be instructed by the test administrator to use a white board, which will be provided, and to enter just the answers in the computer.

In addition to the multiple-choice type of questions, some of the questions on the GED® test will require that you calculate the answer and then enter your answer.

➡ EXAMPLE

If your car gets 20 miles to the gallon of gas, how many gallons will you need to go from your home to Oak Grove and back, if Oak Grove is 150 miles away?

(A) 3
(B) 7.5
(C) 15
(D) 30

Answer: (C)

Explanation: The distance traveled will be 300 miles, since it is a round trip of 150 miles each way. Three hundred miles divided by 20 miles for one gallon gives 15 gallons.

This type of algebraic solution will be covered in depth in the chapter on algebra.

TEST-TAKING TIPS

You will not be penalized for wrong answers, so you should answer every question.

In general, if you answer 50 to 60 percent of the test questions correctly, you will pass the test.

WHERE THE GED® TEST IS OFFERED

The location of the GED® testing varies from community to community. It will be offered at one or more of these locations: a public library, board of education, community college, adult education center, or a continuing education center. When you contact the appropriate location for your community, you will find out about the testing schedule, identification you will need, fees, and what to bring to the test.

TEST-TAKING STRATEGIES

When you go to take the GED® test, it is important that you be comfortable and relaxed. A good night's sleep and a good breakfast will help you to operate efficiently. Comfortable clothing, including a sweater or jacket in case the room is chilly, is a real must. Be certain to provide yourself with tissues, mints, or whatever you can anticipate that you would like to have. Photo identification is usually required.

Try not to be nervous about the test. If you should happen not to do well, you can always take the test again. Some states have a waiting period between tests, which offers you the opportunity for more practice. It should help to know that you have additional chances to do well.

Read all parts of the test carefully, especially the directions. Read each question twice: the first time for a general idea of what the problem is about, and the second time in order to decide how to solve the problem. Read all answer choices, even if you think you know the answer. Once you have read all the choices, you may see one that is better than your original idea.

If you have difficulty with a problem, go on to the next question, making a note to return if time permits. If you cannot determine the correct answer to a problem, try to eliminate any responses that you can. Even if you can eliminate only two responses, you have improved your odds of choosing the correct answer.

Wear a watch and pace yourself, knowing that you have 115 minutes for approximately 46 questions. Although you will be busy while taking the test, it is not designed to be an unreasonable amount of work to accomplish in the time allotted. Remember that the GED® testing program exists to provide opportunity!

STUDY SKILLS

Your successful performance on the GED® exam depends on the quality of your preparation. It has been said that you are not really serious about a goal until you have a written plan. Make yourself a calendar of the time between today and the date you plan to be ready to take the exam. Use the table of contents to help you decide how long you can spend with each chapter. Some chapters may come to you more easily than others, so build in a little extra time for a safety net. You can revise your plan later if need be, but now that you have your calendar designed, jump right in—today!

When you learn something new, your brain needs time to "digest" it. Set aside some time each day to prepare for the GED® test. Even if you can normally spare only 45 minutes a day, make yourself be very faithful to using that 45 minutes well. As you whittle away at your preparation, you will be surprised at the progress you are making. You may also be surprised that 45 minutes will stretch into longer work times as you get hooked on your progress. Usually, getting started is the hardest part.

Your study efficiency will be improved by your study surroundings. You will need a quiet place where you can work without interruption. You will certainly use your time well if you can keep all your study materials together and therefore minimize the time you will need to assemble your books and papers each day.

It will be helpful to make a set of study cards as you work your way through this book. Use index cards, or pieces of paper that you have cut to a convenient size to carry with you. On one side of the card, write the term or idea you want to remember and on the other side draw a picture or use a few words to remind yourself of the meaning. You will never be asked for a definition on the GED® test, but you will need to be comfortable with ideas. The stack of cards that you make will expand your study time by a surprising number of minutes per day. Just making the cards will improve your understanding of the material. Take the cards with you—in the car, in the kitchen, with you all the time. There are bits of time in every day that you can use for learning.

You can get a feel for the test by doing what the test writers do. They keep their eyes and minds open to ideas while in the supermarket, while on the highway, while in the garage, the kitchen, the yard. Learning to look at life around you in this way will certainly improve your preparation. Remember that the GED® test has opened doors to millions, and you could be next in line! Now is a marvelous time to begin.

Diagnostic Test

The mathematics part of the GED® test is allocated 115 minutes. The first five questions are to be answered without the use of a calculator. For the remaining questions on the test, a calculator will be available as an online feature of the computer you will be using for the test. You are also permitted to bring your own TI-30XS. The diagnostic test in this chapter is designed to give you a way to evaluate your own strengths and weaknesses. The answers are provided after the test questions. After you have finished the test and checked your answers, look at the table that helps you to see which chapters and topics are best for you and which ones you need to work on.

ANSWER SHEET
Diagnostic Test

Mathematical Reasoning

Part 1

1. Ⓐ Ⓑ Ⓒ Ⓓ
2. Ⓐ Ⓑ Ⓒ Ⓓ
3. [   ]
4. Ⓐ Ⓑ Ⓒ Ⓓ
5. Ⓐ Ⓑ Ⓒ Ⓓ

Part 2

6. Ⓐ Ⓑ Ⓒ Ⓓ
7. [   ]
8. Ⓐ Ⓑ Ⓒ Ⓓ
9. Ⓐ Ⓑ Ⓒ Ⓓ
10. Ⓐ Ⓑ Ⓒ Ⓓ
11. Ⓐ Ⓑ Ⓒ Ⓓ
12. Ⓐ Ⓑ Ⓒ Ⓓ
13. Ⓐ Ⓑ Ⓒ Ⓓ
14. Ⓐ Ⓑ Ⓒ Ⓓ
15. Ⓐ Ⓑ Ⓒ Ⓓ
16. Ⓐ Ⓑ Ⓒ Ⓓ
17. Ⓐ Ⓑ Ⓒ Ⓓ
18. Ⓐ Ⓑ Ⓒ Ⓓ
19. Ⓐ Ⓑ Ⓒ Ⓓ
20. Ⓐ Ⓑ Ⓒ Ⓓ

21. Ⓐ Ⓑ Ⓒ Ⓓ
22. Ⓐ Ⓑ Ⓒ Ⓓ
23. Ⓐ Ⓑ Ⓒ Ⓓ
24. Ⓐ Ⓑ Ⓒ Ⓓ
25. Ⓐ Ⓑ Ⓒ Ⓓ
26.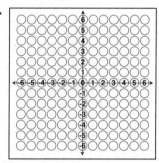
27. Ⓐ Ⓑ Ⓒ Ⓓ
28. Ⓐ Ⓑ Ⓒ Ⓓ
29. [   ]
30. Ⓐ Ⓑ Ⓒ Ⓓ
31. Ⓐ Ⓑ Ⓒ Ⓓ
32. Ⓐ Ⓑ Ⓒ Ⓓ
33. Ⓐ Ⓑ Ⓒ Ⓓ
34. Ⓐ Ⓑ Ⓒ Ⓓ
35. Ⓐ Ⓑ Ⓒ Ⓓ
36. Ⓐ Ⓑ Ⓒ Ⓓ

37. Ⓐ Ⓑ Ⓒ Ⓓ
38. Ⓐ Ⓑ Ⓒ Ⓓ
39. Ⓐ Ⓑ Ⓒ Ⓓ
40. Ⓐ Ⓑ Ⓒ Ⓓ
41. Ⓐ Ⓑ Ⓒ Ⓓ
42. Ⓐ Ⓑ Ⓒ Ⓓ
43. [   ]
44. Ⓐ Ⓑ Ⓒ Ⓓ
45. [   ]
46. Ⓐ Ⓑ Ⓒ Ⓓ
47. Ⓐ Ⓑ Ⓒ Ⓓ
48. Ⓐ Ⓑ Ⓒ Ⓓ
49. Ⓐ Ⓑ Ⓒ Ⓓ
50. Ⓐ Ⓑ Ⓒ Ⓓ

Mathematics Formula Sheet & Explanation

The 2014 GED® Mathematical Reasoning test contains a formula sheet, which displays formulas relating to geometric measurement and certain algebra concepts. Formulas are provided to test-takers so that they may focus on *application*, rather than the *memorization*, of formulas.

Area of a:

square	$A = s^2$
rectangle	$A = lw$
parallelogram	$A = bh$
triangle	$A = \frac{1}{2} bh$
trapezoid	$A = \frac{1}{2} h(b_1 + b_2)$
circle	$A = \pi r^2$

Perimeter of a:

square	$P = 4s$
rectangle	$P = 2l + 2w$
triangle	$P = s_1 + s_2 + s_3$
Circumference of a circle	$C = 2\pi r$ OR $C = \pi d$; $\pi \approx 3.14$

Surface area and volume of a:

rectangular/right prism	$SA = ph + 2B$	$V = Bh$
cylinder	$SA = 2\pi rh + 2\pi r^2$	$V = \pi r^2 h$
pyramid	$SA = \frac{1}{2} ps + B$	$V = \frac{1}{3} Bh$
cone	$SA = \pi rs + \pi r^2$	$V = \frac{1}{3} \pi r^2 h$
sphere	$SA = 4\pi r^2$	$V = \frac{4}{3} \pi r^3$

(p = perimeter of base with area B; $\pi \approx 3.14$)

Data

mean	mean is equal to the total of the values of a data set, divided by the number of elements in the data set
median	median is the middle value in an odd number of ordered values of a data set, or the mean of the two middle values in an even number of ordered values in a data set

Algebra

slope of a line	$m = \dfrac{y_2 - y_1}{x_2 - x_1}$
slope-intercept form of the equation of a line	$y = mx + b$
point-slope form of the equation of a line	$y - y_1 = m(x - x_1)$
standard form of a quadratic equation	$y = ax^2 + bx + c$
quadratic formula	$x = \dfrac{-b \pm \sqrt{b^2 - 4ac}}{2a}$
Pythagorean theorem	$a^2 + b^2 = c^2$
simple interest	$I = Prt$ (I = interest, P = principal, r = rate, t = time)
distance formula	$d = rt$
total cost	total cost = (number of units) × (price per unit)

© Copyright 2014 GED Testing Service. All rights reserved. GED® and GED Testing Service® are registered trademarks of the American Council on Education (ACE). They may not be used or reproduced without the express written permission of ACE or GED Testing Service. The GED® and GED Testing Service® brands are administered by GED Testing Service LLC under license from the American Council on Education.

DIAGNOSTIC TEST

Part 1

Directions: You will have 115 minutes to complete this test. For the first five questions (Part 1), you will NOT be allowed to use a calculator. For the remainder of the test (Part 2), you may use either your own TI-30XB calculator or the calculator that is in the computer.

1. It is often necessary to read a tire pressure gauge. Properly inflated tires not only improve safety, but also save gasoline. How many pounds of pressure are in the tire if the gauge looks like the one in the diagram below?

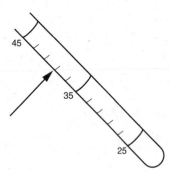

(A) 35.2
(B) 36
(C) 37
(D) 39

TIP

On the computerized test, a question like this would have you drag and drop the arrow to the correct location rather than give you number choices.

2. At the charter high school, the enrollment figures show that there are 565 boys and 385 girls. What is the ratio of boys to girls, rounded to the nearest tenth?

(A) 1 to 0.6
(B) 1 to 0.7
(C) 1 to 1.4
(D) 1 to 1.5

3. Reducing caloric intake causes weight loss. One pound of fat will be lost for every 3,500 calories removed from the normal intake. If a dieter eliminates one canned soda (150 calories) every day, how many pounds will be lost in one year?

[Fill in the blank box on your answer sheet.]

4. The pie graph below shows where the federal government spends money. Which of these statements is an accurate analysis of the graph?

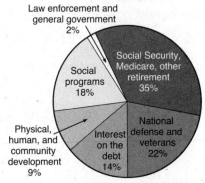

U.S. Outlay of Federal Money

(A) Social Security and social programs are equally expensive.
(B) The United States pays seven times as much on interest as on law enforcement and general government.
(C) The nation's defense requires more than half of the nation's money.
(D) For every dollar taken in, the government spends 20 cents on law enforcement.

5. In triangle ABC below, $\overline{AD}$ is a straight line. What is the sum of the degrees in $\angle x$ and $\angle y$?

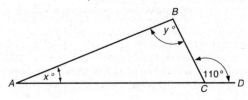

(A) 60
(B) 85
(C) 90
(D) 110

GO ON TO THE NEXT PAGE

Part 2

6. The euro (€) is the primary unit of currency in Europe. It is similar to the U.S. dollar (USD), but they are not exactly equal. Suppose that the euro is equal to $1.25 in U.S. dollars. From the list below, select the equation that would allow you to convert the euro to dollars.

   (A) USD = € + 0.25
   (B) USD = €/4 + €
   (C) USD = 3/4 €
   (D) USD = USD + €

7. Jean drives an average of 30,000 miles per year. Her car gets 25 miles to the gallon. If she trades for a car getting 40 miles per gallon, how many gallons of gasoline will she save per year?

   [Fill in the blank box on your answer sheet.]

8. Suppose that your dog, Daisy, weighed 122 pounds on her last visit to the veterinarian. Since Daisy is not as active as she used to be, you want to watch her diet so she will not get fat. The label below provides feeding information. How many cans of food should Daisy get each day?

DOG WEIGHT LBS.	UP TO 5	UP TO 10	UP TO 20	UP TO 50	UP TO 90	OVER 90
AMOUNT TO FEED—374 g/13.2 oz. CANS						
LESS ACTIVE	UP TO ¾	UP TO 1¼	UP TO 2	UP TO 4	UP TO 6	6 PLUS 1 CAN FOR EACH 16 LBS. OVER 90 LBS.
WEIGHT LOSS	UP TO ½	UP TO ¾	UP TO 1½	UP TO 3	UP TO 4½	4½ PLUS 1 CAN FOR EACH 21 LBS. OVER 90 LBS.

   (A) $5\frac{1}{2}$
   (B) 6
   (C) 7
   (D) 8

9. The square root of 50 lies between which pair of numbers?

   (A) 7 and 8
   (B) 8 and 9
   (C) 49 and 50
   (D) 50 and 51

10. Suppose that a notice appears in the newspaper that states that homeowners with trees taller than 50 feet will have to pay an assessment. In order to determine the height of your trees, you recall the idea of similar triangles, and make a diagram as shown below. How tall is the tree?

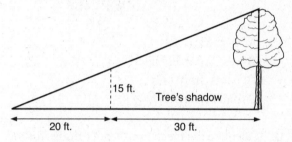

   (A) $\dfrac{15(50)}{20}$
   (B) $15(50)(20)$
   (C) $\dfrac{15(20)}{50}$
   (D) $\dfrac{50(20)}{15}$

GO ON TO THE NEXT PAGE

DIAGNOSTIC TEST

11. The laws of many states require that hunters wear a minimum of 400 square inches of blaze orange when in the woods in order to improve hunter safety. Study the diagram below. Which choice would provide the hunter with closest to the minimum 400 square inches?

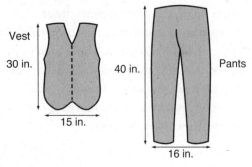

(A) vest, front only
(B) vest, front and back
(C) pants, front only
(D) pants, front and back

12. Calculate the mean number of calories for the first four days of Sandy's diet.

Day one:	1,145 calories
Day two:	1,395 calories
Day three:	1,205 calories
Day four:	1,715 calories

(A) 1,115
(B) 1,340
(C) 1,365
(D) 1,390

13. Airplane pilots must consider the fact that they will need more feet of runway for landing when the outside temperature is hot than when it is cold. This is because hot air is less dense than cold air and so does not provide as much resistance to the plane's movement. Which of the following graphs best represents this idea?

(A)   (B)

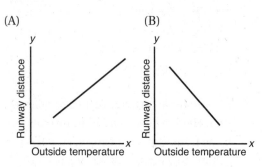

(C)   (D)

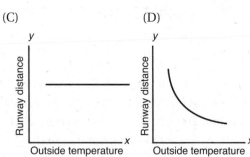

14. Find the value of the following expression if $x = 5$ and $y = -3$:

$$4xy - 3x + y$$

(A) −78
(B) −66
(C) −48
(D) 42

GO ON TO THE NEXT PAGE

15. Men's hat sizes are based on the measurement of the circumference of the head. The average man's head is about 23 inches in circumference. If you divide this number by the value for pi of 3.14, you will get about $7\frac{3}{8}$, a common hat size. From the formulas that apply to circles, which of these conclusions can be drawn?

    (A) The hat size is the approximate radius of the head.
    (B) The hat size is the approximate diameter of the head.
    (C) The hat size is the approximate area of the head.
    (D) The hat size is the approximate volume of the head.

16. What is the widest sheet of plywood (in inches) that can be fitted through the tailgate of the SUV in the diagram below?

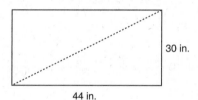

30 in.

44 in.

    (A) 30
    (B) 44
    (C) $44^2 + 30^2$
    (D) $\sqrt{44^2 + 30^2}$

17. Sam makes $5,000 per month. If he gets a $6\frac{1}{2}$ % raise, what will his monthly salary become?

    (A) $5,065
    (B) $5,325
    (C) $5,650
    (D) $8,250

18. A national ice cream chain creates an ice cream "pizza" and cuts it into eight sections as shown in the diagram below. It then sells the pizza either by the slice or as an entire pizza. Which of the following statements most accurately analyzes this information?

$9.99
One polar pizza
(8 slices)

99¢
Each slice

    (A) The highest cost per slice occurs with the purchase of the whole pizza.
    (B) The highest cost per slice occurs with the purchase of pizza by the slice.
    (C) The individual slices are larger than the slices in the whole pizza.
    (D) The individual slices are smaller than the slices in the whole pizza.

19. What are the factors of $12x^2 + x - 6$?

    (A) $(2x + 1)(6x - 6)$
    (B) $(6x - 3)(2x + 2)$
    (C) $(3x + 2)(4x - 3)$
    (D) $(3x - 2)(4x + 3)$

20. For which value of x is the inequality $3x > -12$ true?

    (A) –9
    (B) –5
    (C) –4
    (D) 5

21. Which number has the same value as 1×10^{-5}?

    (A) –0.000001
    (B) –0.00001
    (C) 0.000001
    (D) 0.00001

GO ON TO THE NEXT PAGE

DIAGNOSTIC TEST

22. In order to fence a field, you need a measure of its perimeter. To measure the perimeter of a field shaped as in the diagram below, you make a measuring roller as shown. If the wheel goes around 1,000 times, what is the perimeter of the field?

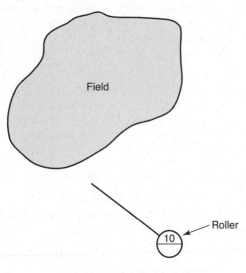

Field

Roller

10

(A) 1,000(3.14)(5)
(B) 1,000(3.14)(10)
(C) 1,000(3.14)(25)
(D) 1,000(3.14)(100)

23. Current health information suggests that a healthy diet is one in which fat provides less than 20% of the calories you eat each day. Each gram of fat provides 9 calories. One of your favorite foods has 15 grams of fat. Which choice gives the percent of fat that this food represents if your daily intake is 2,000 calories?

(A) 9(15)(2,000)

(B) $\dfrac{9(15)(100)}{2,000}$

(C) 9(2,000)(15)

(D) 9(20%)(15)

24. A 50% antifreeze solution is recommended to best protect the radiator of cars. According-ing to the table below, if you were to create a 50% antifreeze solution by using 6 quarts of antifreeze for a 12 quart cooling system, to what temperature would your car be protected from winter's cold?

Cooling System Capacity (Quarts)	Quarts of Antifreeze Required							
	4	5	6	7	8	9	10	
8	−34	−70						
9		−50	−82					
10		−34	−62	−84				
11			−47	−76				
12			−34	−57	−82			
13				−45	−66	−84		
14				−34	−54	−76		
15					−43	−62	−82	
16					−34	−52	−70	

(A) −34°
(B) −50°
(C) −70°
(D) −82°

25. Simplify: $3x - (15 - x) - 3$

(A) $-14x$
(B) $2x + 12$
(C) $2x - 18$
(D) $4x - 18$

26. Using the coordinate grid on your answer sheet, mark the correct location of the point whose coordinates are (−2, 3).

  TIP

On the computerized test, this would be a hot spot question. You would click on the grid to indicate your answer.

GO ON TO THE NEXT PAGE

27. A landscaper wants to plant shrubs around the pond shown below. How many shrubs would be needed in order for them to be 8 feet apart?

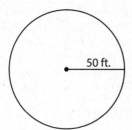

50 ft.

   (A) $\pi\,(100)/8$
   (B) $\pi\,(50)/8$
   (C) $\pi\,(100)(8)$
   (D) $\pi\,(50)(8)$

28. Solve the equation for a

$$5a - 2 = a + 6$$

   (A) -2
   (B) 1 and $\frac{1}{3}$
   (C) 2
   (D) $\frac{2}{3}$

29. Inspect the tax rate schedule below and calculate the amount of tax owed on $28,000. Round your answer to the nearest dollar.

Less than $5,000 .... 3% of the taxable income		
At least–	But less than–	
$ 5,000	$12,500 .... $ 150.00 plus 4%	of excess over $5,000
$12,500	$20,000 .... $ 450.00 plus 4.5%	of excess over $12,500
$20,000	$30,000 .... $ 787.50 plus 6%	of excess over $20,000
$30,000	.... $1,387.50 plus 6.5%	of excess over $30,000

[Fill in the blank box on your answer sheet.]

30. For the quadratic equation

$$x^2 - 7x + 10 = 0$$

What are the two values for x?

   (A) 2 and 5
   (B) –2 and –5
   (C) 2 and –5
   (D) –2 and 5

31. Solve the following inequality:

$$5x - 10 < 7x + 4$$

   (A) $x > \frac{1}{7}$
   (B) $x < -\frac{1}{7}$
   (C) $x < -7$
   (D) $x > -7$

TIP

On the computerized test, questions like this would have you choose from a drop-down list of the choices above.

32. On the thermometer shown below, how many degrees are shown at the arrow?

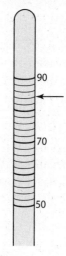

90

70

50

   (A) 77 degrees
   (B) 80.2 degrees
   (C) 82 degrees
   (D) 84 degrees

GO ON TO THE NEXT PAGE

33. The owner's manual for a string trimmer says that a 16:1 ratio of gasoline to 2-cycle oil must be used for its fuel. How many gallons of gasoline would be needed to go with an 8 ounce packet of the oil, if 1 gallon is equal to 128 ounces?

    (A) 8
    (B) 4
    (C) 2
    (D) 1

34. A leaky faucet can be expensive. Suppose you put a measuring cup under a leak and collect a half cup of water from 8 A.M. to 4 P.M. How many gallons would this amount to in a day if there are 16 cups in a gallon?

    (A) $16(3)\left(\frac{1}{2}\right)$

    (B) $\dfrac{3\left(\frac{1}{2}\right)}{16}$

    (C) $\dfrac{16\left(\frac{1}{2}\right)}{3}$

    (D) $\dfrac{16(3)}{\left(\frac{1}{2}\right)}$

35. The plastic line for string trimmers is available in sizes of 0.080, 0.065, 0.105, and 0.095. These numbers are the diameters of the line in inches. Arrange these string trimmer line sizes from thinnest to thickest.

    (A) 0.105, 0.095, 0.080, 0.065
    (B) 0.065, 0.080, 0.095, 0.105
    (C) 0.080, 0.065, 0.095, 0.105
    (D) 0.105, 0.095, 0.065, 0.080

36. If you were to divide the difference between 28 and 4 by 3 and multiply the result by 2, which of these equations would express these operations?

    (A) $\dfrac{28-4}{3(2)}$

    (B) $2\left(\dfrac{28-4}{3}\right)$

    (C) $\left(\dfrac{28+4}{3}\right)2$

    (D) Not enough information is given.

37. In order to keep a chain link gate from sagging, a rod can be installed on the diagonal as shown in the diagram below. How long should the rod be?

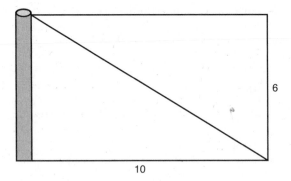

    (A) $\sqrt{6^2+10^2}$
    (B) 36 + 100
    (C) $6(10)\left(\dfrac{1}{2}\right)$

    (D) $\dfrac{1}{2}(6+10)$

GO ON TO THE NEXT PAGE

38. Express 20,900 in scientific notation.

    (A) 2.09×10^{-4}
    (B) 0.20900
    (C) 2.09×10^{2}
    (D) 2.09×10^{4}

39. You already know that hot air expands. A hot air balloon works in this way. Which of the graphs below shows the relationship that as temperature increases, volume increases?

    (A)
    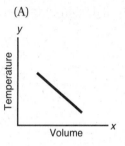

    (B)
    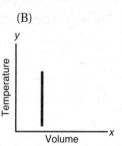

    (C)
    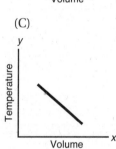

    (D)
    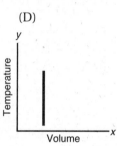

40. A stroke patient's blood thinning medicine was changed from 2.5 milligrams to 2.0 milligrams. What percent change is this?

    (A) 0.5%
    (B) 2.5%
    (C) 5.0%
    (D) 20.0%

41. Based on the graph below, which of the following conclusions can you draw?

    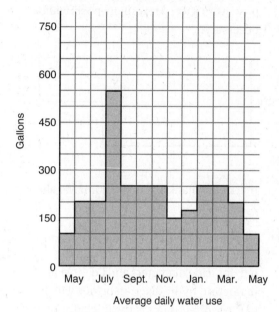

    Average daily water use

    (A) The daily average use in March was 250 gallons.
    (B) Heavy August usage was caused by a drought.
    (C) May is the month with the heaviest rainfall.
    (D) Water use increases steadily after the first of the year.

42. Which of the following is the correct set of factors for the equation:

    $$x^2 - 4x - 12 = 0$$

    (A) $(x - 6)(x - 2) = 0$
    (B) $(x - 6)(x + 2) = 0$
    (C) $(x - 4)(x + 3) = 0$
    (D) $(x + 1)(x - 12) = 0$

GO ON TO THE NEXT PAGE

DIAGNOSTIC TEST

43. In buying fence posts for the field shown below, the fencing regulations call for a post every 8 feet. How many posts will be necessary?

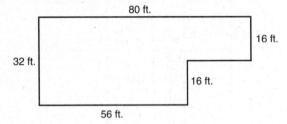

[Fill in the blank box on your answer sheet.]

44. Hose and tubing are sold with two dimensions listed. These are called o.d. (outside diameter) and i.d. (inside diameter). In the diagram below, which of these dimensions is the thickness of the wall of the hose?

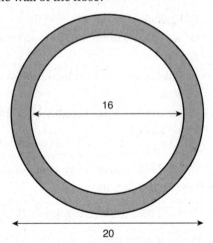

(A) 8
(B) 6
(C) 4
(D) 2

45. The Internal Revenue Service encourages you to round all amounts to the nearest dollar. On your income tax return, how would you record a deduction of $998.48?

[Fill in the blank box on your answer sheet.]

46. Carnival prizes are awarded to participants who draw either a yellow or a green ball out of a barrel. If the barrel holds 80 red balls, 10 blue balls, 8 green balls, and 2 yellow balls, what is the probability of drawing a winner?

(A) 1 in 1
(B) 2 in 10
(C) 8 in 100
(D) 10 in 100

47. Simplify : $3x^2 + 4x - 2x(x - 12) + 3x$

(A) $x^2 + 31x$
(B) $3x^2 + 6x - 12$
(C) $x^2 - 17x - 12$
(D) $5x^2 + 31x$

GO ON TO THE NEXT PAGE

48. A hillside will eventually slip if the slope of that hillside is too steep. The slope formula is given in the list of formulas. Use it to calculate the slope shown in the diagram below.

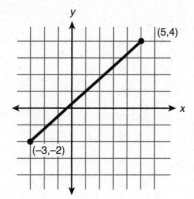

(A) $-\dfrac{3}{4}$

(B) $\dfrac{3}{4}$

(C) $\dfrac{4}{3}$

(D) $-\dfrac{4}{3}$

49. Hospitalization insurance is set up so that the patient pays the first dollars, called "the deductible," and then the insurance pays 80% of the remaining bill. Bob's deductible is $50 and his hospital bill was $6400. How much more will he be required to pay?

(A) $1,270
(B) $1,280
(C) $1,300
(D) $1,320

50. Which of the following is the correct equation for the graph shown below?

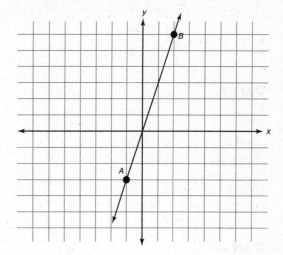

(A) $y = 3$
(B) $y = 3x$
(C) $y = 3x + 6$
(D) $y = 6$

END OF EXAMINATION

DIAGNOSTIC TEST

Part 1

1. **D**
2. **B**
3. **15.64**
4. **B**
5. **D**

Part 2

6. **B**
7. **450**
8. **D**
9. **A**
10. **A**
11. **A**
12. **C**
13. **A**
14. **A**
15. **B**
16. **D**
17. **B**
18. **A**
19. **D**
20. **D**
21. **D**
22. **B**
23. **B**
24. **A**
25. **D**
26.

27. **A**
28. **C**
29. **1,268**
30. **D**
31. **D**
32. **D**
33. **D**
34. **B**
35. **B**
36. **B**
37. **A**
38. **D**
39. **C**
40. **D**
41. **B**
42. **B**
43. **28**
44. **D**
45. **998**
46. **D**
47. **A**
48. **B**
49. **D**
50. **B**

SELF-ANALYSIS

Did you get at least 35 correct answers? If not, you need more practice for the Mathematical Reasoning Test. You can improve your performance to Good or Excellent by analyzing your errors. To determine the areas in which you need further study, review the chart below. The question numbers from the Diagnostic Test appear in the column to the left. Circle the questions you answered incorrectly. (Unsolved problems are counted as incorrect.) Refer to the Chapter and Chapter Section indicated for each question for additional review.

WHAT'S YOUR SCORE?

Your rating	Number of correct answers	Equivalent GED® score
Outstanding	45–50	180–200
Excellent	40–44	160–179
Good	35–39	140–159
Fair	30–34	120–139
Passing (min.)*	25–29	100–119

*The acceptable passing score varies with each state. Your state GED® test sites can provide this information. If your score is low on this practice test, the explanation of the correct answers that follows will help you. You may obtain additional help by reviewing the self-analysis chart below.

SELF-ANALYSIS CHART

Question	Chapter	Topic
Part I		
1.	5	Measurement
2.	4	Ratio and proportions
3.	3	Set-up style
4.	7	Circle graph
5.	6	Angles
Part II		
6.	4	Modeling
7.	3	Multiplication/subtraction
8.	7	Charts
9.	3	Square root; calculator
10.	6	Similar triangles
11.	6	Area
12.	7	Average
13.	7	Line graphs
14.	4	Substitution
15.	6	Circles
16.	6	Area
17.	4	Percent
18.	6	Circles
19.	4	Factoring

Question	Chapter	Topic
20.	4	Inequalities
21.	4	Scientific notation
22.	6	Perimeter
23.	3	Set-up styles
24.	7	Charts
25.	4	Order of operations
26.	6	Coordinate grid
27.	6	Circles
28.	4	Solving equations
29.	4	Percent
30.	3	Multiplication/addition
31.	4	Inequalities
32.	5	Measurement
33.	4	Proportions
34.	3	Set-up style
35.	3	Sequencing
36.	4	Quadratic equations
37.	6	Pythagorean relationship
38.	4	Scientific notation
39.	7	Line graph
40.	4	Percent
41.	7	Bar graphs
42.	4	Factoring
43.	6	Perimeter
44.	6	Circles
45.	3	Rounding
46.	7	Probability
47.	4	Equations
48.	6	Slope
49.	4	Percent
50.	4	Solving equations

ANSWERS EXPLAINED

Part 1

1. **D** When checking the scale, the first thing you need to do is to find the value of each of the marks. Here every mark has a value of 2. You can test this by counting from 35 to 45 using the marks. Because each mark is worth 2, start at 35, counting by 2's. This gives 37, 39, 41, 43, 45, which agrees with the numbers on the gauge.

2. **B** To find the ratio of boys to girls, divide both by the number of boys, since boys are what the girls are to be compared to. Boys $\frac{565}{565} = 1$, Girls $= \frac{385}{565} = 0.6814\ldots$, rounded to tenths $= 0.7$.

3. **15.64**

$$\frac{1 \text{ pound}}{3500 \text{ calories}} \left(\frac{150 \text{ calories}}{1 \text{ can}} \right) 365 \text{ cans}$$

This strategy is explained in detail in the algebra chapter.

4. **B** When you multiply the 2% spent on law enforcement by 7, you get 14%, which is the percent paid in interest.

5. **D** Since $\overline{AD}$ is a straight line, the angle beside the 110° is 180° − 110° = 70°. Then, since the total of the angles in a triangle equals 180°, the sum $x + y$ is 180° − 70° = 110°.

Part 2

6. **B** This equation is the same as saying one euro plus $\frac{1}{4}$ of a euro.

7. **450** 30,000 miles/25 mpg = 1,200 gallons of gas. 30,000 miles/40 mpg = 750 gallons of gas. 1,200 − 750 = 450 gallons of gas that would be saved each year.

8. **D** Daisy is 32 pounds over the 90 pounds shown on the chart. These 32 pounds allow Daisy to have 2 cans over the 6 shown on the chart for a 90 pound dog. The total cans allowed is 6 + 2 = 8.

9. **A** You can solve this by the process of elimination. The 6 times 7 gives 42, which is too small, but is close. The 8 times 9 is 72, which is too big. Therefore the answer lies between the two numbers.

10. **A** This is a similar triangles problem, so use a proportion. The tree height is to 15 as the big triangle's base of 50 is to the smaller triangle's base of 20.

This gives the proportion $\frac{x}{15} = \frac{50}{20}$, so $x = \frac{15(50)}{20}$.

11. **A** Square inches is a measure of area. The area of a rectangle is the length times the width. The vest's approximate dimensions of 30 by 15 give an area of 450 square inches. Since the vest is the smaller of the two garments, you need to look no further because any other combination will give a number bigger than 450.

12. **C** When you add the four calorie values, you get 5,460. Dividing this by 4 gives an average of 1,365 calories.

13. **A** You are looking for a graph that shows both variables increasing. Choice (1) is the only graph that shows this.

14. **A** Substituting gives the expression $4(5)(-3) - 3(5) - 3$, which simplifies to -78.

15. **B** From the formula Circumference = (pi)(diameter), if you substitute the values you know, you get $23 = (3.14)(\text{diameter})$. To solve for diameter, you divide 23 by 3.14, giving an answer in the range of 7.

16. **D** This is a Pythagorean theorem problem in which you will need to find the hypotenuse (the dotted line). Let the dotted line be x. Then x^2 equals the sum of 44^2 and 30^2, or $x = \sqrt{44^2 + 30^2}$. Solve for x to get x = the square root of the sum 44^2 plus 30^2.

17. **B** To find $6\frac{1}{2}$ % of $5,000, multiply $5,000 \times 0.065 = 325$. This is the amount of the monthly raise, so you would add it to the $5,000, giving $5,325 as the new salary.

18. **A** There are two issues here. One is slice size. You can see that there is no indication that the slice size differs when buying a whole pizza or pizza by the slice. The second issue is price. The whole pizza is cut into 8 pieces, so the price of each can be determined by dividing the whole price ($9.99) by 8. Even easier, look at the price of the individual slice at $.99. If you were to multiply this by 8 to get enough slices to make a whole pizza, you would have nearly $8, which is considerably cheaper than a whole pizza for almost $10.

19. **D** A system that works is to multiply the two expressions in parentheses to see when you get the right answer. This is an algebraic process called FOIL, which is explained in the algebra chapter.

20. **D** You can substitute the various choices and see which works.

21. **D** The negative 5 exponent means to move the decimal point five places in the negative (left) direction.

22. **B** When a wheel rolls, it rolls on its circumference. If the wheel goes around 1,000 times, you have 1,000 circumferences. Since circumference is pi times diameter, Circumference = $(3.14)(10)$. A thousand circumferences equals $3.14(10)(1,000)$.

23. **B** A convenient way to think of percent is that it is part times 100 divided by whole. The whole diet is 2,000 calories. The part from the favorite food is 15 grams times 9 calories per gram.

24. **A** The -34 is the value you get from following the row for a 12 quart cooling system over to the column for 6 quarts of antifreeze.

25. **D** When you remove the parentheses, you get $3x - 15 + x - 3$. The x's sum to $4x$, and the numbers sum to -18.

26. **(-2, 3)** Remember that the x-value is first and the y-value is second. The x-value is -2 and the y-value is 3.

27. **A** The formula for the distance around the pond is $C = \pi d$. Then divide this distance by 8.

28. **C** $5a - 2 = a + 6$

$$\underline{-a \qquad -a}$$
$$4a - 2 = 0 + 6$$
$$\underline{\quad +2 \qquad +2}$$
$$\frac{4a}{4} = \frac{8}{4}$$
$$a = 2$$

29. **1,268** For $28,000, the taxpayer would owe $787.50 plus 6% of $8,000 (the excess over $20,000). This would be $787.50 plus $480 = $1,267.50. Rounding this number to the nearest dollar would result in $1,268 because amounts of 50 cents and above go to the next higher dollar.

30. **D** $x^2 = 7x + 10 = 0$
    $(x - 5)(x - 2) = 0$

31. **D** Remember to turn the inequality sign when multiplying or dividing by a negative.

32. **D** The darker line midway between the 70 and the 90 would be 80. Since there are five spaces for the 10 degrees between the 80 and the 90, each of these spaces would be 2 degrees each. Going up two spaces from the 80 would result in 4 degrees, so the reading is 84 degrees.

33. **D** Set up the proportion $\frac{1}{16} = \frac{8}{x}$, knowing that x will be in ounces because the 8 is in ounces. Solving for x gives $x = 8(16) = 128$ ounces. Since one gallon is 128 ounces, one gallon is the answer.

34. **B** In one day (24 hours) there are 3 of the 8 hour segments. Since the answer must be in gallons, the cups must be changed to gallons by dividing by 16, the number of cups in a gallon.

35. **B** A system that makes dealing with these numbers easier is to move the decimal point (in your mind) three places to the right for every number. Then you can see that the order from smallest to largest is 65, 80, 95, 105.

36. **B** The word "difference" means to subtract, so look for a subtraction of 28 and 4. Then look for a representation of "divide by 3." So far, it looks like it could be any of the first three choices. The final idea, that of multiplying the result by 2, gives you only the possibility of (2). In case (1), only the divisor, 3, is multiplied by 2, and in case (3), only the 4 is multiplied by 2.

37. **A** Check the formula page for the Pythagorean relationship. This problem is an application of that relationship, in which the length of the rod is the hypotenuse (the side across from the right angle). The length of the rod squared is equal to the sum of the squares of the other two sides of the triangle. In order to find the length of the rod, you must take the square root, which is choice (1).

38. **D** In using scientific notation, the decimal must be placed between the first two digits, so begin with 2.09 (it is not necessary to use the rest of the zeroes). To decide what exponent to use, start with the new location of the decimal and count how many spaces you would have to move to get to the end of the original number. In this case, you would

move four spaces. Because you are moving to the right (the positive direction), the 4 is positive.

39. **C** Experiment with the graphs by making an imaginary starting point somewhere on the line. Then put another imaginary point on the line at a spot where the temperature would be more than the first point. See what happens to the volume and you will know if you made the right selection.

40. **D** Percent can be written: $\frac{\text{Part} \times 100}{\text{Whole}}$. The part that is changed is $2.5 - 2.0 = 0.5$.

    The whole is the original, 2.5, so $\frac{0.5 \times 100}{2.5} = 20\%$.

41. **B** As you start working your way through the choices, you need go no further than choice (2) before you encounter the right answer. The only thing that you have to do is to analyze the scale on the left to see that 250 gallons matches March's water use.

42. **B** Perform FOIL on the answer possibilities to see which gives the original equation.

43. **28** The most graphic solution to this problem is to use the diagram and put a dot for every post. As you think of how many dots to place, remember that the space between dots represents 8 feet. For example, on a section of the fence that is 32 feet long, there will be dots (posts) at the ends of the section and then dots at 8, 16, and 24 feet.

44. **D** The total diameter of the walls is the difference between 20 and 16, which is 4. Then divide by 2 because there is a wall on the left and a wall on the right.

45. **$998** To round to the nearest dollar, look at the cents part. If the cents part is 50 or bigger, add a dollar and round to $999. But the cents portion is less than 50 cents, so you just "throw it away" and make no adjustment, giving you the answer of $998.

46. **D** Probability is the number of good choices out of the number of total choices. In this case the good choices (the blue ones) number 10 and the total choices number 100 (all the balls). When you reduce 10 out of 100, you get 1 out of 10.

47. **A** The first step is to take care of the parentheses, which would give

    $$3x^2 + 4x - 2x^2 + 24x + 3x.$$

    Then remember that x^2 terms cannot be combined with x terms, to give $x^2 + 31x$.

48. **B** Use of the slope formula (see formula page), gives a slope of $\frac{-2-4}{-3-5}$.
    So, slope $= \frac{-6}{-8} = \frac{3}{4}$.

49. **D** Take the $50 deductible from the $6,400, leaving $6,350. Bob will be responsible for 20% of that: $0.20 \times 6,350 = \$1,270$.

50. **B** Recall the $y = mx + b$ equation for a straight line. Eliminate choices (A) and (D) since they would be horizontal lines. Eliminate choice (C) since the y-intercept is 0.

Skill Building, Number Operations, and Number Sense

3

Most of the difficulty with math is usually not the "how" part, but the "when" part. For example, you know how to multiply and how to divide, but for some problems, you do not know which should be done. This chapter is designed to sharpen your math skills (the "how" part), while the additional chapters are set up to improve your ability to diagnose and solve problems (the "when" part). The chapter is set up so that you have explanations followed by practice. Because practice works only if you have the chance to see if your responses are right, the answers are given at the end of the chapter.

The following topics will be covered in this chapter, followed by practice for the entire chapter.

Calculation Skills
 Arithmetic Operations
 Estimation
 Shortcuts

How to Read a Math Problem
 Symbols
 Vocabulary
 Choosing the Correct Answer
 Set-up Style Answers

Types of Problems
 Word Problems
 Whole Number Problems
 Fraction Problems
 Decimals
 Sequencing

CALCULATION SKILLS

Arithmetic Operations

The first step in developing your math ability is to practice the fundamentals. The GED® test provides a calculator for all but the first five questions. You will be asked to add, subtract, multiply, and divide. Some practice is offered here, and other practice is located in the decimal and fraction parts of this chapter, as well as throughout the book.

Practice

Add the following:

1. 1,009
   + 54

2. 45
   + 8

3. 24,023
   + 250

4. 546
   + 2,349

5. 20,075 + 3,672

6. 46 + 3,070

Subtract the following:

7. 7,652
   − 842

8. 9,008
   − 599

9. 140
   − 78

10. 25
    −16

11. 457 − 274

12. 2,235 − 902

Multiply the following:

13. 703
    × 25

14. 48
    × 25

15. 2,074
    × 123

16. 400
    × 20

17. 28,003 × 560

18. 354 × 6,721

Long division is frequently an operation needing extra instruction.

➡ **EXAMPLE** _____

$\dfrac{343}{7}$ (This is said, "343 divided by 7.")

Step #1 How many times will 7 go into 3? Zero times, so go on to asking how many times 7 will go into 34? Four times, so

$$\begin{array}{r} 4 \\ 7\overline{)343} \end{array}$$

Step #2 Multiply $4 \times 7 = 28$, and put the 28 under the 34 and subtract.

$$\begin{array}{r} 4 \\ 7\overline{)343} \\ -28 \\ \hline 6 \end{array}$$

Step #3 Bring down the next digit, which is the second 3.

$$\begin{array}{r} 4 \\ 7\overline{)343} \\ -28\downarrow \\ \hline 63 \end{array}$$

Step #4 How many times will 7 go into 63? Nine times, so 9 goes on top.

$$\begin{array}{r} 49 \\ 7\overline{)343} \\ -28 \\ \hline 63 \end{array}$$

To check your answer, multiply 7 times 49 and see if it equals 343. It does, which means that your answer is correct.

Division is shown in a variety of ways, all meaning the same thing.

$$343/7 \qquad 7\overline{)343} \qquad \dfrac{343}{7} \qquad 343 \div 7$$

If you are using a calculator with a division problem, it is important that you enter the correct number first into the calculator. In the problem above, the 343 is entered first.

Divide the following:

19. $45 \div 9$

20. $50\overline{)3{,}050}$

21. $\dfrac{7{,}875}{63}$

22. $\dfrac{20{,}400}{150}$

23. $7{,}800 \div 50$

24. $855 \div 19$

If you find that you need additional practice, set up problems for yourself and check your answers with a calculator. Educational research shows that creating problems helps your understanding.

ANSWERS

1. 1,063	9. 62	17. 15,681,680
2. 53	10. 9	18. 2,379,234
3. 24,273	11. 183	19. 5
4. 2,895	12. 1,333	20. 61
5. 23,747	13. 17,575	21. 125
6. 3,116	14. 1,200	22. 136
7. 6,810	15. 255,102	23. 156
8. 8,409	16. 8,000	24. 45

Estimation

Estimation is an operation, usually done in your head, to avoid making errors. An example of estimation looks like this.

- Look at the problem 21×32
- Change to easy, close numbers 20×30
- Figure answer in your head   600

So, if your answer to the original 21×32 isn't close to 600, look for a mistake.

Practice

25. 22 times 735 is equal to *about* what number?

26. 13,864 divided by 42 is equal to *about* what number?

ANSWERS

25. 14,000
26. 350

Shortcuts

When multiplying by 10, 100, 1,000 or any other power of 10, just move the decimal point.

$$1.55 \times 10 = 15.5$$
$$1.55 \times 100 = 155$$
$$1.55 \times 1,000 = 1,550$$

> **RULE:** Move the decimal to the right the same number of spaces as the number of zeros in the power of ten number.

Dividing by a power of 10 is different only in that you move the decimal to the left.

$$\frac{256}{10} = 0.256$$

$$\frac{2.56}{100} = 0.0256 \text{ (adding zeros may be necessary)}$$

$$\frac{2.56}{1,000} = 0.00256$$

➡ EXAMPLES

Find 0.35 times 1,000.

The decimal point moves three places to the right. The answer is 350.

Find 125 divided by 100.

The decimal point moves two places to the left. The answer is 1.25.

Find 20.9 times 100.

The decimal point moves two places to the right. The answer is 2,090.

Practice

Perform the indicated operation:

27. $36,726 \times 10,000$

28. $\dfrac{5,647}{100}$

29. $63 \div 1,000$

30. $24 \times 10,000$

ANSWERS

27. 367,260,000   29. 0.063

28. 56.47   30. 240,000

HOW TO READ A MATH PROBLEM

Symbols

Math is a symbolic language. It is more than numbers. Following are symbols that you need to know because they will not be provided on the GED® exam. Any symbols that are unusual, however, will be explained in the test itself.

$-\left(\text{as in } \dfrac{12}{4}\right)$ means "divide"

$\div$ (as in $12 \div 4$) means "divide"

In both cases, divide the first number by the second number.

➡ **EXAMPLES** _____

$\dfrac{24}{3}$ means to divide 24 by 3, so $\dfrac{24}{3} = 8$.

$24 \div 6$ means to divide 24 by 6, so $24 \div 6 = 4$

( )   means "do this part first"

➡ **EXAMPLES** _____

$(4 + 3) - (2 + 1)$ means to add 4 and 3 to get 7; then add 2 and 1 to get 3; then subtract 3 from 7 to arrive at your answer, 4.

$(8 - 2) \times (10 \div 5)$ means to subtract 2 from 8 to get 6; then divide 10 by 5 to get 2; then multiply 6 by 2 to get your answer, 12.

Vocabulary

The words in math are very important. Often, every word is important to the meaning, so you do not want to skip even one. Just remember that the words are there to help you with your understanding and are not intended to make things difficult for you. As you read problems and instructions, try reading the entire problem or a section quickly one time just to see in general what it's about. Then you can go back and read more carefully.

"of" can mean to multiply. For example, 20% *of* $500 means to multiply $500 by 20%.

"per" means to divide. For example, if you wanted to find the cost per ounce of shampoo, you would divide the price by the ounces of shampoo in the bottle.

Choosing the Correct Answer

The most common form of the GED® test questions has four possible answers, from which you will choose one. The incorrect answers have been calculated so they will include the most common errors that test takers make. For example, if the correct way to solve a problem were to multiply and then subtract, one of the possible answers would be the result if you subtracted and then multiplied.

The best system for choosing the right answer is to do your own calculation of the answer and then to look at the possibilities to see if it is there. If there is a problem for which this does not work for you, try to narrow your choices to just two. At that point, you have at least a 50–50 shot at the right answer. You have no doubt heard that your first impression of the right answer is the best. Once you have narrowed the choices to two, go with your first "gut feeling" about which one of those two to select.

Set-up Style Answers

Some test questions ask you to show *how* you would solve a problem. In these cases, your answer choice would be the one that shows the correct *approach* to the problem.

➥ EXAMPLE

Sam worked for 10 hours this week at $5.50 per hour, and also worked 8 hours at $6.00 per hour. Which of the following describes Sam's earnings for the week?

(A) 10 + 5.50 + 8 + 6.00
(B) 10(5.50 + 6.00) + 8
(C) 10(5.50) + 8(6.00)
(D) 10(5.50) × 8(6.00)

Answer: (C)

Explanation: As you approach the problem, look first at the 10 hours of work. For this time period the earnings are 10 times $5.50. Then look at the 8 hours of work. Multiplying 8 hours times the $6.00 rate gives these earnings. The final answer is the sum of the two amounts.

TYPES OF PROBLEMS

Word Problems

Word problems may seem less threatening if you think of them as life stories. Many of the math questions tell a story, so you cannot just skip this topic. One of the goals of this book is to make you feel comfortable with stories and word problems.

The following word problems are ones for which you already have the necessary skills. Jump right in and see what you can do with them.

Practice

31. The odometer on Fred's car showed 8,914 miles when he pulled in to buy gas. He filled the tank, drove for a few days, and filled the tank again. It took 8.3 gallons and the odometer now read 9,100 miles. How many miles per gallon does Fred's car get?

32. Suppose that you get in a taxi and you see the following fare schedule:

$2.30 plus $0.50 per mile

How much will you pay to go ten miles?

33. A bowling handicap is a number you add to your score so you can compete fairly with more experienced bowlers. To find your handicap, subtract your average score for the last three games from 200. Then multiply that number by 0.80. The result is your bowling handicap. Suppose your average for the last three games was 110. Calculate your handicap.

ANSWERS

31. As you plan how to solve this, you'll need to know gallons (8.3) and miles driven (9,100 − 8,914 = 186). Finally, to find miles per gallon, you would divide gallons into miles. (Recall that per means divide.) So, 186 miles divided by 8.3 gallons equals 22.4 miles per gallon for Fred's car.
32. The taxi ride costs $7.30 based on adding $2.30 to $5.00. To find the $5.00, multiply ten miles by the $0.50 cost per mile.
33. The bowling handicap is 72. When you subtract 110 from 200, you get 90. Multiplying the 90 by 0.8 gives 72.

Whole Number Problems

Most of the problems on the GED® test use whole numbers. For this reason, most of the instruction and practice in this book use only whole numbers.

Fraction Problems

It is hoped that this fraction instruction section will help you to master the basics so that you do well when you see fractions on the GED® exam.

There are essentially two types of fraction work that you must be able to do:

Type one: Multiplication and division
Type two: Addition and subtraction

A fraction is a way of splitting something up so you can see the relationship between the parts. The fraction $\frac{1}{2}$ is the most familiar of fractions, and you already have an idea of what it represents.

Every fraction is made up of two parts, the numerator and the denominator. The numerator is the top of the fraction. The denominator is the bottom of the fraction. For example, in the fraction $\frac{3}{4}$, the numerator is 3 and the denominator is 4.

You can think of the numerator as the "part," while the denominator is the "whole." For example, if you say that $\frac{1}{2}$ of your money goes for rent, you are saying that for every two dollars that you have, one of these dollars goes for rent. Two dollars is the whole amount of money, and one dollar is the part that goes for rent.

Practice

34. Stock prices are given in fractions. The stock market report says that Super Sporting Goods is selling at $24\frac{1}{2}$ up $\frac{1}{4}$.

    The fractions are fractional parts of a dollar. In dollars and cents, what is the selling price of Super Sporting Goods stock? In dollars and cents, how much has it gone up? What was the previous selling price? Stock prices also are given in eighths. How many cents is an eighth of a dollar?

ANSWERS

34. The selling price is $24.50 (since half of a dollar is 50 cents). The stock has gone up 25 cents (a quarter of a dollar). The previous selling price was $24.25. Because $24.50 is a quarter higher than the price used to be, subtract a quarter to obtain $24.25. An eighth of a dollar is $12\frac{1}{2}$ cents. To find this, divide $1.00 by 8 or divide $\frac{1}{4}$ dollar ($0.25) by 2.

MULTIPLICATION AND DIVISION OF FRACTIONS

These two operations are the easiest fraction operations, and they work basically alike.

Multiplication

Step One: Multiply the numerators.
Step Two: Multiply the denominators.
Step Three: Reduce the resulting fraction if possible.

$$\frac{1}{4} \times \frac{2}{5} = \frac{2}{20} = \frac{1}{10}$$

$$\frac{1}{3} \times \frac{3}{4} = \frac{3}{12} = \frac{1}{4}$$

Practice

Multiply the following fractions. Reduce answers where possible.

35. $\frac{3}{5} \times \frac{2}{3}$ 38. $\frac{1}{3} \times \frac{1}{4}$

36. $\frac{1}{4} \times \frac{3}{4}$ 39. $\frac{5}{9} \times \frac{3}{10}$

37. $\frac{5}{7} \times \frac{1}{3}$ 40. $\frac{7}{8} \times \frac{2}{3}$

ANSWERS

35. $\frac{2}{5}$ 36. $\frac{3}{16}$ 37. $\frac{5}{21}$ 38. $\frac{1}{12}$ 39. $\frac{\overset{1}{\cancel{5}}}{\underset{3}{\cancel{9}}} \times \frac{\overset{1}{\cancel{3}}}{\underset{2}{\cancel{10}}} = \frac{1}{6}$ 40. $\frac{7}{\underset{4}{\cancel{8}}} \times \frac{\overset{1}{\cancel{2}}}{3} = \frac{7}{12}$

Division

To divide fractions, first take the second fraction (the divisor) and turn it upside down. This process is called inverting the fraction. Then multiply the two fractions, just like before.

➡ **EXAMPLE** _____

What is $\frac{1}{8}$ divided by $\frac{3}{4}$?

$\frac{1}{8} \div \frac{3}{4} = \frac{1}{8} \times \frac{4}{3}$ (This is the "invert and multiply" step.)

The numerator is $1 \times 4 = 4$.
The denominator is $8 \times 3 = 24$.

The new fraction is $\frac{4}{24}$.

Both 4 and 24 can be divided by 4 (reduced), so the answer is $\frac{1}{6}$.

Practice

41. $\frac{2}{3} \div \frac{1}{3}$ 42. $\frac{3}{4} \div \frac{1}{5}$ 43. $\frac{4}{5} \div \frac{2}{3}$ 44. $\frac{5}{9} \div \frac{2}{3}$

ANSWERS

41. 2   42. $\frac{15}{4}$ 43. $\frac{6}{5}$ 44. $\frac{5}{6}$

ADDITION AND SUBTRACTION OF FRACTIONS

The reason that adding and subtracting are more difficult than multiplying and dividing is that there is often an extra step before you can add or subtract. This initial step is to change both of the fractions so that they have the same, or common, denominator. There are several ways to do this, but the most reliable way is to multiply the existing denominators together to get the new one.

 **EXAMPLE**

What is $\frac{1}{5} + \frac{1}{3}$?

The new denominator is 5(3) = 15.

The way to find the new numerator of each fraction is to divide the original denominator into the new denominator, and then multiply the result by the old numerator.

$$15 \div 5 = 3, \text{ so } \frac{1}{5} = \frac{3(1)}{15} = \frac{3}{15}$$

$$15 \div 3 = 5, \text{ so } \frac{1}{3} = \frac{5(1)}{15} = \frac{5}{15}$$

After you have rewritten both fractions so that they each have the same denominator, the problem is easy. You add (or subtract) the numerators and leave the denominators alone.

$$\frac{1}{5} + \frac{1}{3} = \frac{3}{15} + \frac{5}{15} = \frac{3+5}{15} = \frac{8}{15}$$

Practice

Add or subtract the following fractions. Remember to change them first so that they have the same denominator.

45. $\frac{5}{6} + \frac{2}{3}$ 46. $\frac{2}{3} - \frac{1}{8}$ 47. $\frac{7}{8} + \frac{3}{4}$ 48. $\frac{6}{7} - \frac{1}{3}$

ANSWERS

45. $\frac{3}{2}$ 46. $\frac{13}{24}$ 47. $\frac{13}{8}$ 48. $\frac{11}{21}$

Two additional topics complete the skills needed for fraction problems.

SUBTRACTION WITH BORROWING

It sometimes happens that subtraction is not possible without a change called borrowing.

➡ EXAMPLE _____

$4\frac{1}{4}$ Since the 3 cannot be subtracted from the 1, a whole number will have to be

$-1\frac{3}{4}$ borrowed from the 4, making it a 3, and allowing $\frac{4}{4}$ to be added to the $\frac{1}{4}$.

Now, the problem looks like this and can be solved by the usual method.

$3\frac{5}{4}$

$-1\frac{3}{4}$

$2\frac{2}{4}$ reduced to give $2\frac{1}{2}$

If the denominators do not start out being the same, then you must use the least common denominator approach reviewed earlier.

Practice

49. $4\frac{1}{3} - 2\frac{2}{3}$ 51. $3\frac{2}{5} - 1\frac{3}{5}$ 53. $6\frac{3}{8} - 2\frac{5}{6}$

50. $7\frac{5}{8} - 3\frac{7}{8}$ 52. $2\frac{1}{2} - 1\frac{5}{8}$

ANSWERS

49. $1\frac{2}{3}$ 50. $3\frac{3}{4}$ 51. $1\frac{4}{5}$ 52. $\frac{7}{8}$ 53. $3\frac{13}{24}$

MIXED NUMBERS

Mixed numbers are those that are made up of both a whole number and a fraction. Examples of mixed numbers are $3\frac{1}{2}$ and $23\frac{1}{4}$. In performing any of the operations (add, subtract, multiply, or divide) on mixed numbers, the first step is always to change the mixed number into an improper fraction (one in which the numerator is larger than the denominator).

EXAMPLES

The mixed number $3\frac{1}{2}$ is changed into an improper fraction by multiplying the 3 by the 2 to get 6, and then adding the 1 to get 7. This 7 is then placed over the original denominator of 2 to produce the improper fraction $\frac{7}{2}$.

Other mixed number examples include:

$$23\frac{1}{4} = \frac{4\times23+1}{4} = \frac{93}{4}$$

$$8\frac{2}{3} = \frac{8\times3+2}{3} = \frac{26}{3}$$

These improper fractions can then be used in just the same way as proper (regular) fractions in any problem.

Practice

Change the following mixed numbers into improper fractions.

54. $5\frac{2}{3}$ 55. $8\frac{5}{8}$ 56. $11\frac{3}{4}$ 57. $20\frac{2}{5}$ 58. $1\frac{5}{6}$

ANSWERS

54. $\frac{17}{3}$ 55. $\frac{69}{8}$ 56. $\frac{47}{4}$ 57. $\frac{102}{5}$ 58. $\frac{11}{6}$

IMPROPER FRACTIONS

Sometimes a fraction has a numerator that is greater than the denominator. This is called an improper fraction. Improper fractions should be rewritten as a mixed number (a whole number plus a proper fraction). To do this, divide the denominator into the numerator, and then write this number followed by the remainder placed over the original denominator. Reduce if possible.

EXAMPLE

Write $\frac{15}{12}$ as a mixed number.

You can tell that it is improper because the top is greater than the bottom.

The first step is to see if the fraction can be reduced. Since both numbers can be divided by 3, the fraction reduces to $\frac{5}{4}$.

Dividing the 4 into the 5 gives 1 with 1 left over, so $\frac{15}{12} = \frac{5}{4} = 1\frac{1}{4}$.

Practice

Change the following improper fractions into mixed numbers:

59. $\dfrac{11}{9}$ 60. $\dfrac{9}{8}$ 61. $\dfrac{27}{8}$ 62. $\dfrac{18}{7}$

ANSWERS

59. $1\dfrac{2}{9}$ 60. $1\dfrac{1}{8}$ 61. $3\dfrac{3}{8}$ 62. $2\dfrac{4}{7}$

Decimals

Decimals are nearly as easy to deal with as are whole numbers.

ADDITION AND SUBTRACTION OF DECIMALS

When adding or subtracting decimals, line up the problems so that the decimal points are in a straight line. Then, go about the problem just as you would do if there were no decimals. The decimal point in the answer goes straight below the decimal points in the problem.

➡ EXAMPLE _____

What is 34.765 – 2.33?

Line up the problem like this: 34.765
Then subtract, bringing the   – 2.33
decimal point straight down.   32.435

Practice

Add or subtract the following decimals:

63. 4.005 + 98.8

64. 1.23 – 0.9

65. 1002.15 – 3.4

66. 17.67 + 5.0004

ANSWERS

63. 102.805
64. 0.33
65. 998.75
66. 22.6704

MULTIPLICATION OF DECIMALS

When multiplying decimal numbers, multiply as though there were no decimals. To determine where the decimal point goes in the answer, first count the number of places to the right of the decimal point in both of the numbers you are multiplying. Then find the sum of these decimal places, and position the decimal point that many places in from the right-hand end of the product (the answer in multiplication).

➡ **EXAMPLE** _____

What is 23.004×3.45?

When you multiply as if there were no decimals, you get 7936380.

$$
\begin{array}{r}
23.004 \\
\times \quad 3.45 \\
\hline
115020 \\
920160 \\
6901200 \\
\hline
7936380 \\
\end{array}
$$

In all, there are five decimal places to the right of the decimal, so move the decimal point in five places from the right-hand end, giving 79.36380.

Practice

Multiply the following decimal numbers:

67. 23.55×14.1

68. 1.333×25.002

69. 0.0044×35.4

70. $20,000 \times 0.005$

ANSWERS

67. 332.055
68. 33.327666
69. 0.15576
70. 100

DIVISION OF DECIMALS

When you divide and there are decimal numbers involved, look at the divisor (the 3.45 in the example below) and move the decimal point to the right however many places necessary for the divisor to be a whole number. Then move the decimal point in the dividend (the 150.9375 in the example) the same number of places that you moved the other decimal point. Next, divide as if there were no decimals. Finally, place the decimal point in the quotient (the answer line) directly above the decimal point in the dividend.

➡ **EXAMPLE** _____

What is 150.9375 ÷ 3.45?

You must move the decimal point two places to make 3.45 the whole number 345, so move the decimal point in 150.9375 two places to the right also, and then divide.

$$
\begin{array}{r}
43.75 \\
345\overline{)15093.75} \\
1380 \\
\hline
129375 \\
1035 \\
\hline
25875 \\
2415 \\
\hline
1725 \\
1725 \\
\hline
0
\end{array}
$$

Practice

Divide the following decimal numbers:

71. 198.34 ÷ 8.44

72. 1.4 ÷ 0.0056

73. 2.0091 ÷ 2,009.1

74. 69.084 ÷ 34.2

ANSWERS

71. 23.5
72. 250
73. 0.001
74. 2.02

Sequencing

There will be questions on the GED® exam that ask you to arrange numbers in order from smallest to largest or from largest to smallest.

SEQUENCING OF FRACTIONS

If the denominators (bottoms) are the same, then the sequencing is just what you would imagine. That is, in placing the fractions $\frac{2}{7}$, $\frac{6}{7}$, and $\frac{4}{7}$ in order from smallest to largest, the smallest is $\frac{2}{7}$, the next is $\frac{4}{7}$, and the last is $\frac{6}{7}$.

If the denominators are not the same, then you must first rewrite all of the fractions so that their denominators are the same. To do this, follow the same process that you practiced in the addition of fractions section earlier in this chapter.

➡ **EXAMPLE** _____

Arrange the fractions $\frac{5}{8}$, $\frac{3}{4}$, and $\frac{2}{3}$ in sequence from smallest to largest.

To find a common denominator, multiply the denominators 8 and 3 to obtain 24. In this case, you don't have to multiply by the denominator 4 because it will divide into any denominator into which 8 divides.

$$\frac{5}{8} = \frac{15}{24} \qquad \frac{3}{4} = \frac{18}{24} \qquad \frac{2}{3} = \frac{16}{24}$$

Placing these numbers in order gives $\frac{15}{24}$, $\frac{16}{24}$, $\frac{18}{24}$, so the original fractions in order are $\frac{5}{8}$, $\frac{2}{3}$, and $\frac{3}{4}$.

SEQUENCING OF DECIMALS

Decimals are easier to sequence than are fractions. To do so, add enough zeros so that every number has the same number of digits to the right of the decimal point. Then you can mentally remove the decimal point.

➡ **EXAMPLE** _____

Organize the numbers 0.004, 0.15, 0.22, and 0.05 from smallest to largest.

Adding zeros to give every number the same number of digits to the right of the decimal point gives the following:

0.004 0.150 0.220 0.050

When you mentally remove the decimal point, you can see that the numbers fit into sequence as follows:

0.004 0.050 0.150 0.220

Practice

Arrange the following numbers in sequence from smallest to largest:

75. $\frac{3}{8}$ $\frac{2}{5}$ $\frac{1}{2}$

76. 0.0335   0.120   0.0055

77. $\frac{7}{8}$ $\frac{3}{4}$ $\frac{11}{16}$

78. 0.002   0.004   0.010

ANSWERS

75. $\frac{3}{8}, \frac{2}{5}, \frac{1}{2}$ (They are in order.)

76. 0.0055, 0.0335, 0.120

77. $\frac{11}{16}, \frac{3}{4}, \frac{7}{8}$

78. 0.002, 0.004, 0.010 (They are in order.)

USING THE CALCULATOR

The calculator that will be available to you is an on-screen version of the TI-30XS. It will look the same as the hand-held calculator, but instead of using keys, you will be using the mouse to click on the appropriate key. Since so much of your test outcome depends on your expertise with the calculator, it would be advisable for you to purchase or borrow the calculator for practice.

Calculator Instruction

The on key is at the lower left of the keyboard. The off key is the same key, but to use it you have to first use the 2nd key on the top left of the keyboard. This 2nd key makes all the gray keys do whatever it says directly above that key. When you have finished with a computation, use the clear key to erase the screen. To find the result of the keys you have used, press the enter key. You are already familiar with add, subtract, multiply, and divide functions.

SQUARE ROOT

There will be questions on the test involving something called the square root, ($\sqrt{\ }$). Finding a square root is the opposite of squaring a number. When you square a number, you multiply it by itself. For example, 3^2 means $3 \times 3 = 9$. To find the square root ($\sqrt{\ }$) of 9, locate the square root key on the calculator. Notice that the square root symbol is in green and that it is above another key (the one with the x^2). This means that you must use the green second function key (2nd) to get to it.

For example, to find the square root of 9:

| 2nd | | x^2 | | 9 | | enter | The answer will be 3.

If you ever get a screen message that says "syntax error," that means that the keystrokes have been done in the wrong order.

FRACTIONS

Locate the | < $\overset{\wedge}{_\vee}$ > | on the right side of the calculator that allows you to go up, down, and to the side.

Locate the key | $\frac{n}{d}$ |, which means numerator divided by denominator. These are the keystrokes for entering a fraction, say 2/3. | $\frac{n}{d}$ | | 2 | Use the | ↓ | key to go down so that the next number will be in the denominator and enter | 3 |. Now the screen will show 2/3. You can now do something else with the 2/3, like adding another fraction by going through the same steps.

TOGGLE KEY

The toggle key is the next to last key on the bottom right of the key pad. This key allows you to go back and forth between fractions and decimals. To try this out, press the keys for 0.75; then press enter. If you press the right side of the toggle switch, you will get the fraction equivalent of 0.75 which is 3/4. Pressing the left side of the toggle switch goes back to the decimal form.

Other uses of the calculator, such as scientific notation, percent, and negative numbers will be explained in the appropriate chapter.

The computer provides not only the test questions but also the calculator and a system of marking questions so you can come back to them later. These resources are not displayed on the computer screen until you "ask" the computer for them. The way you do this is by clicking on the appropriate icon on the computer screen. To ask for the calculator, use the mouse to move the cursor to the icon that looks like a calculator, and click on it. As you take the test, some questions will be easy for you. You may want to skip the hard questions temporarily and come back to them later. The way you do this is to click on the "mark" question icon. Whenever you want to return to that question, click on the "attempt marked "question icon. This test-taking strategy can help you manage your time. The computer screen displays a running clock on the upper right.

Mathematics Test Question Types

MULTIPLE-CHOICE QUESTIONS

In answering multiple-choice questions, you will use the computer mouse to select the correct answer and then click on it.

DROP LIST QUESTIONS

After you read the question, you will see | Choice 1 ▼ |

The only choice you will be able to see is choice 1. Use the mouse to take the cursor to the triangle and click there. As you continue to click the other choices are revealed. Click on the one you have decided is correct.

DRAG-AND-DROP QUESTIONS

In the drag-and-drop-style questions, you will be asked to move numbers to a new location. For example, a test question could ask you to place these fractions in the correct box.

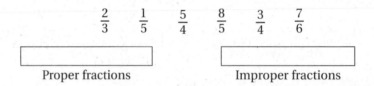

$$\frac{2}{3} \quad \frac{1}{5} \quad \frac{5}{4} \quad \frac{8}{5} \quad \frac{3}{4} \quad \frac{7}{6}$$

| Proper fractions | Improper fractions |

You know that a proper fraction is one in which the denominator is larger than the numerator. So, the $\frac{2}{3}$ is a proper fraction and goes in the left box. Use the mouse to put the cursor on the $\frac{2}{3}$ and drag it to the left box. Continue with the other fractions until the screen looks like this.

| $\frac{2}{3} \quad \frac{1}{5} \quad \frac{3}{4}$ | $\frac{5}{4} \quad \frac{8}{5} \quad \frac{7}{6}$ |

Proper fractions   Improper fractions

SHORT-ANSWER QUESTIONS

Some questions are set up so that you have to come up with an answer and then use the keyboard to enter that answer in the space that will be provided for it.

HOT SPOT QUESTIONS

Some questions will ask that you click on points on coordinate grids, number lines, or dot plots.

SIGNED NUMBERS

Locate the (–) key on the calculator. Use it when any number is a negative. The keystroke plan is to enter the (–) first and then enter the number.

Problem #7 $-14 \times 23 =$

Keystrokes: | – | 1 | 4 | × | 2 | 3 | enter |

(See pages 65–66 for signed number review.)

SCIENTIFIC NOTATION

The topic of scientific notation is taken up completely in the algebra chapter. The calculator can be used in the following way.

Problem #8 $2.4 \times 10^5 =$

Keystrokes: | 2 | . | 4 | × | 2nd | log | 5 | enter |

Problem #9 $3.3 \times 10^{-2} =$

Keystrokes: | 3 | . | 3 | × | 2nd | log | – | 2 | enter |

> Note: If the exponent is so large that the answer will not fit on the calculator display, then the answer display will be in exponential form.

Problem #10 $5.1 \times 10^{12} =$

Keystrokes: | 5 | . | 1 | × | 2nd | log | 12 | enter |

PI

The value of pi is usually rounded off to be 3.14, but this value can be accessed by the calculator. There is a π key. If you want it in decimal form, use the toggle key .

Problem #11 $3.3 \times \pi =$

Keystrokes: | 3 | . | 3 | × | π | enter |

PERCENT

Look at the (key on the calculator. Written above this key is %. It is accessed by the 2nd key.

Problem #12   Find 15% of 300 =

Keystrokes: | 1 | | 5 | | 2nd | | (| | × | | 3 | | 0 | | 0 | | enter |

Throughout this book you will find a calculator icon beside problems that are suitable for calculator practice.

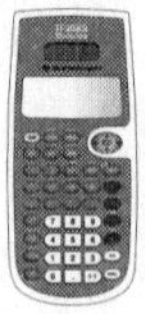

FRACTIONS

The calculator can be used to solve fraction problems. Locate the $\boxed{\frac{n}{d}}$ key. This key can be used to enter a fraction. Use the following keystrokes to enter the fraction $\frac{2}{3}$.

| 2 | | $\frac{n}{d}$ | | 3 | The display on the screen will look like 2 n/d 3. This is the calculator's way of saying $\frac{2}{3}$.

➥ EXAMPLES _____

Addition

$\frac{3}{4} + \frac{5}{8} =$

Keystrokes: | $\frac{n}{d}$ | | 3 | | ↓ | | 4 | | ↑ | | enter | | + | | $\frac{n}{d}$ | | 5 | | ↓ | | 8 | | ↑ | | enter |

Display: $\frac{11}{8}$

Subtraction

$\frac{5}{6} - \frac{1}{3} =$

Keystrokes: | $\frac{n}{d}$ | | 5 | | ↓ | | 6 | | ↑ | | enter | | − | | $\frac{n}{d}$ | | 1 | | ↓ | | 3 | | ↑ | | enter |

Display: $\frac{1}{2}$

Multiplication

$\frac{3}{4} \times 2 =$

Keystrokes: | $\frac{n}{d}$ | | 3 | | ↓ | | 4 | | ↑ | | × | | 2 | | enter |

Display: $\frac{3}{2}$

Division

$$\frac{1}{2} \div \frac{1}{3} =$$

Keystrokes: $\boxed{\frac{n}{d}}$ $\boxed{1}$ $\boxed{\downarrow}$ $\boxed{2}$ $\boxed{\uparrow}$ $\boxed{\text{enter}}$ $\boxed{\div}$ $\boxed{\frac{n}{d}}$ $\boxed{1}$ $\boxed{\downarrow}$ $\boxed{3}$ $\boxed{\uparrow}$ $\boxed{\text{enter}}$

Display: $\frac{3}{2}$ which means $1\frac{1}{2}$

The GED® test is a timed test, so you will want to use your time well. In the section of the test that allows for the use of a calculator, there will be times when using a calculator is not a good idea. For example, look at the kind of answer that the question requires. If the answers are in set-up form, then a calculator is not going to be of any help.

The algebra questions may require that the answers be in the form of letter/number combinations, such as $2a + 3b$, and therefore a calculator is not going to be of any assistance.

A calculator will be especially helpful for questions about money and for questions involving large numbers. The section of the test allowing for the use of calculators is not different from the section that does not allow for their use, so you need not assume that the calculator section problems are more difficult.

THE COORDINATE GRID

In using the coordinate grid,
• The coordinates are always given in *x, y* order.
• The *x*-axis is positive to the right of zero, and negative to the left of zero.
• The *y*-axis is positive up from zero and negative down from zero.

This coordinate grid is the one that will be given on the GED® test for recording some of your answers.

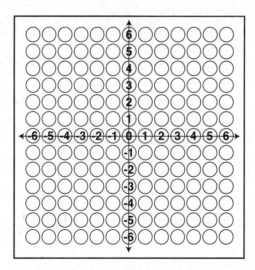

This coordinate grid has been labeled to show when *x* and *y* are positive and negative.

1. (−1, 2)

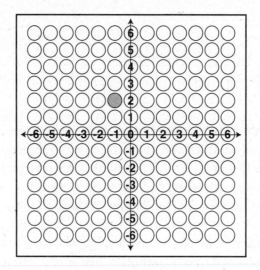

2. (4, −3)

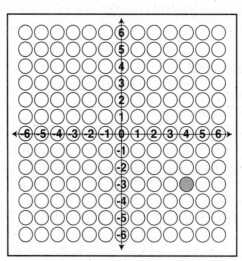

3. (−4, −5)

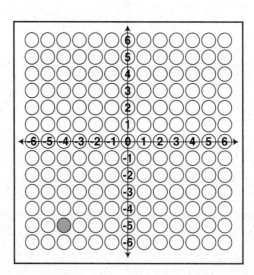

4. (3, 5)

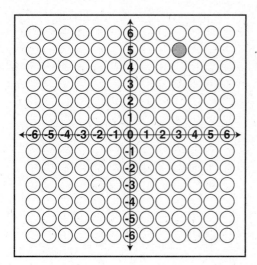

Practice

Enter the following coordinates on the coordinate grids provided.

79. (4, 5)

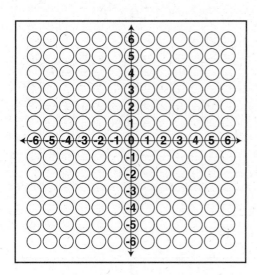

80. (−5, 2)

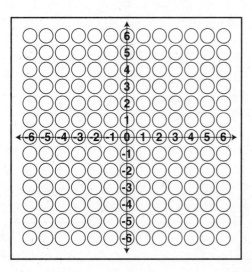

81. (2, –4)

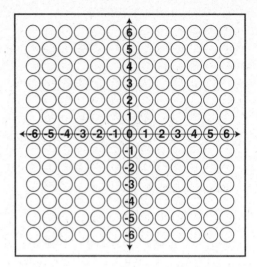

82. (–1, –6)

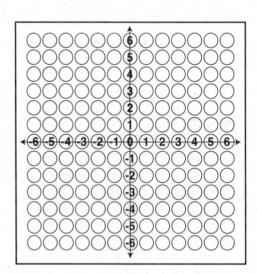

ANSWERS

79.

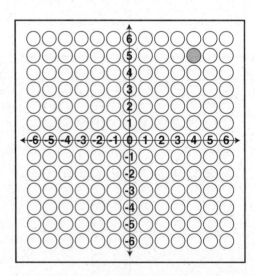

80.

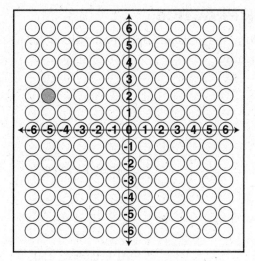

81.

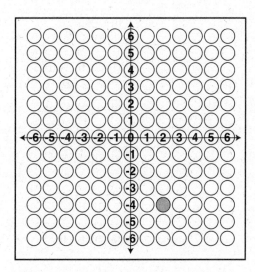

82.

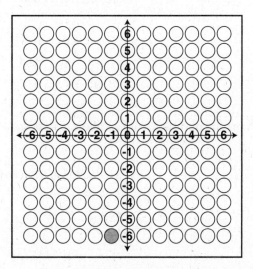

Remember that your answer sheet will be machine scored. All circles must be filled in completely, and your marks should not stray outside the circle.

END OF CHAPTER PRACTICE

For problems 1–28, perform the indicated operation. Hint: Solve first with paper and pencil; then solve with the calculator.

1. 23×105

2. $\dfrac{1}{2} + \dfrac{3}{8}$

3. $405 + 1{,}009$

4. $\dfrac{458.67}{100}$

5. $\dfrac{3}{8} \times \dfrac{2}{3}$

6. $\dfrac{5}{8} \div \dfrac{1}{2}$

7. $\dfrac{625}{25}$

8. $\dfrac{1}{2} - \dfrac{1}{3}$

9. $51 - 19$

10. 203×500

11. 1.01×3.5

12. $\dfrac{2}{3} + \dfrac{1}{6}$

13. $\dfrac{135}{9}$

14. $29.13 + 19.005$

15. 3.275×100

16. $130 - 0.095$

17. $20 + 159{,}917$

18. $\dfrac{7}{8} \div \dfrac{1}{3}$

19. 0.005×150

20. $\dfrac{3}{4} - \dfrac{3}{8}$

21. 75.05×0.15

22. $13 \times 1{,}000$

23. $\dfrac{5}{8} \times \dfrac{3}{4}$

24. $\dfrac{3}{4} \div \dfrac{1}{2}$

25. $95.6 - 0.75$

26. $34{,}974 \div 1{,}000$

27. $23{,}000 - 651$

28. $15.015 + 3.9$

For problems 29–32, arrange the numbers from smallest to largest:

29. $\dfrac{1}{4}, \dfrac{1}{3}, \dfrac{1}{6}$

30. $0.05, 0.005, 0.15$

31. $0.0005, 0.02, 0.001$

32. $\dfrac{5}{8}, \dfrac{2}{3}, \dfrac{3}{4}$

For problems 33–38, perform the indicated operation:

33. $\frac{34.97}{6.3}$ = round answer to the hundredth place

34. Do not solve, but rather estimate the value of 110×532.

35. One-third of 12 is what number?

36. If you drive 70 miles in 2 hours, what is your average speed in miles per hour?

37. Change the improper fraction $\frac{38}{12}$ into a mixed number.

38. What would you do to change 4.5 inches into feet?

Answers

1. 2,415

2. $\frac{7}{8}$

3. 1,414

4. 4.5867

5. $\frac{1}{4}$

6. $\frac{5}{4}$, or $1\frac{1}{4}$

7. 25

8. $\frac{1}{6}$

9. 32

10. 101,500

11. 3.535

12. $\frac{5}{6}$

13. 15

14. 48.135

15. 327.5

16. 129.905

17. 159,937

18. $\frac{21}{8}$, or $2\frac{5}{8}$

19. 0.75

20. $\frac{3}{8}$

21. 11.2575

22. 13,000

23. $\frac{15}{32}$

24. $\frac{3}{2}$, or $1\frac{1}{2}$

25. 94.85

26. 34.974

27. 22,349

28. 18.915

29. $\frac{1}{6}, \frac{1}{4}, \frac{1}{3}$

30. 0.005, 0.05, 0.15

31. 0.0005, 0.001, 0.02

32. $\frac{5}{8}, \frac{2}{3}, \frac{3}{4}$ (They are already in order.)

33. 5.55

34. 50,000

35. 4

36. 35 miles per hour

37. $3\frac{1}{6}$

38. divide by 12

Algebra, Functions, and Patterns

4

Algebra uses a combination of numbers and letters. The letters are called "unknowns," and you may use any letter you like. Commonly used letters are x, y, a, and b.

$2a$	means 2 times a
$2(a)$	also means 2 times a
$2 \times a$	also means 2 times a
$3 + y$	means 3 plus y
$2/y$	means 2 divided by y
$2/4$	means 2 divided by 4
$2(x + 5)$	means 2 times the sum of x and 5
a^2	means a squared or $a \times a$ or $(a)(a)$

Practice

Write each of these in algebraic form.

1. A number decreased by 14.

2. A number doubled plus its square.

3. Twenty-three divided by three times some number.

4. Four times the sum of a number and five.

5. The product of a number and 5 less than that number. (Remember that product is the result of multiplication.)

6. The difference of twice the square of a number and fifteen.

7. The sum of three times a number, eight and the number less seven.

8. The sum of twelve and y, divided by 5.

9. Nine minus the square of x.

10. Three divided into the sum of twelve and x.

ANSWERS

1. $x - 14$ 6. $2x^2 - 15$

2. $2x + x^2$ 7. $3x + 8 + x - 7$

3. $23/3x$ 8. $\dfrac{12 + y}{5}$

4. $4(x + 5)$ 9. $9 - x^2$

5. $x(x - 5)$ 10. $\dfrac{12 + x}{3}$

ALGEBRA EQUATIONS

In an algebraic equation there is an equal sign.

➡ **EXAMPLE** _____

If you let x be the number of hours that you work in a week, you could write an algebraic equation to describe how much you would make in a week at a wage of $10 an hour.

$$\$10x = \text{weekly earnings}$$

Then if you worked 28 hours in a week, your income would be:

$$\$10(28) = \$280$$

Parentheses are used to show multiplication.
An algebra equation works for all values of x. For instance, if you worked 37.5 hours in another week, your income would be

$$\$10(37.5) = \$375$$

In algebra you will be doing two things: writing equations and solving equations. In the example above:

Writing the equation was

$$\$10x = \text{weekly earnings}$$
$$\text{where } x = \text{hours worked}$$

Solving the equation was

$$\$10(37.5) = \$375 \text{ weekly earnings}$$

The remainder of this algebra chapter will be about solving equations.

SIGNED NUMBERS

Numbers are either positive or negative. Some examples of negative numbers are an overdrawn bank account, a cold snap with temperatures below zero, and elevations below sea level.

Positive numbers include the amount of money that dinner costs, the measurement of a carpet, or your shoe size. Many people find that the idea of signed numbers can best be understood by thinking of a number line, as shown below.

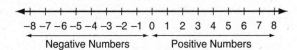

Notice that the positive numbers get larger as you move to the right of zero. The negative numbers also get larger as you move to the right toward zero. For example, a temperature of −3 is larger than a temperature of −20.

Using Signed Numbers

ADDITION

You can picture solving the equation −3 + 4 = ? by looking at the number line below.

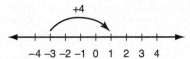

Start at the location of −3 and go 4 spaces in the positive direction, because adding a positive number means to go in the positive direction. You will land at the location marked 1, so the solution is −3 + 4 = 1.

SUBTRACTION

If you saw the subtraction problem 1 − (−4) = ?, you could use this easy system:

An odd number of minuses multiplied together is a minus.

An even number of minuses multiplied together is a plus.

So, the problem becomes 1 + 4 = 5.

Now that you have dealt with the multiplication of negative numbers (minuses), you are ready to move along the number line. Start at 1 and move 4 spaces in the positive direction. You are now at 5, your answer.

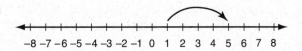

Practice

Solve.

11. $5 + (-2)$

12. $6 - (-2)$

13. $9 - (4)$

14. $-7 - 7$

15. $-12 + 1$

16. $6 - (-3)$

17. $-5 - (-1)$

18. $0 - (-9)$

ANSWERS

11. 3	13. 5	15. −11	17. −4
12. 8	14. −14	16. 9	18. 9

MULTIPLICATION AND DIVISION

To multiply or divide two signed numbers, just do the operation as though there were no pluses or minuses present. Then use the following rules:

The sign of the answer will be + if the signs are the same.

The sign of the answer will be − if the signs are different.

➡ EXAMPLES _____

$(6)(4) = 24$
$(6)(-4) = -24$
$(-6)(-4) = 24$

Practice

19. $(-5)(-3)$

20. $\dfrac{12}{-6}$

21. $\dfrac{-15}{5}$

22. $(-6)(-12)$

23. $(-4)(2)$

24. $\dfrac{(8)}{-2}$

25. $\dfrac{(-4)}{(-4)}$

26. $(8)(-2)$

ANSWERS

19. 15	21. −3	23. −8	25. 1
20. −2	22. 72	24. −4	26. −16

EXPONENTS

In the expression a^2, the 2 is called an exponent. It tells you how many times to multiply a by *itself* (not by 2). For example, 2^3 means:

$$2 \times 2 \times 2 = 8$$

➡ EXAMPLES _____

$a^2 = (a)(a)$
$x^3 = (x)(x)(x)$
$3^4 = (3)(3)(3)(3) = 81$

Practice

Find the following answers:

27. 2^5 28. 4^3

Write each of the following without an exponent:

29. x^4 30. c^6

ANSWERS

27. 32   29. $(x)(x)(x)(x)$
28. 64   30. $(c)(c)(c)(c)(c)(c)$

Using Exponents When Multiplying

When there are exponents involved in multiplying numbers or variables that are alike, add the exponents.

➡ EXAMPLES _____

$(a^2)(a^3) = a^{2+3} = a^5$
$(x)(x^2) = x^{1+2} = x^3$
$(2b)(3b^2) = 2(3)(b)(b^2) = 6b^{1+2} = 6b^3$
Note: $3b^2 \neq (3b)^2$

Using Exponents When Dividing

The process used when dividing numbers or variables with exponents is like multiplying, but you subtract the exponents instead of adding them. Always subtract the denominator exponent from the numerator exponent.

➡ **EXAMPLES** _____

$$\frac{a^5}{a^2} = a^{5-2} = a^3$$

$$\frac{a^3}{a^5} = a^{3-5} = a^{-2}$$

$$\frac{6x^3}{2x} = \frac{6}{2}\,\frac{x^3}{x} = 3x^{3-1} = 3x^2$$

Using Exponents When Adding and Subtracting

The only time you can add or subtract when using exponents is when the letters or numbers that have the exponents are alike, and the exponents are the same.

That is, because $2x^2$ and $3x^2$ both have the exponent 2 applied to x, you can add them:

$$2x^2 + 3x^2 = (2+3)x^2 = 5x^2$$

Notice that the x^2 does not change.

This is rather like adding 2 apples and 3 apples. You add the numbers, and the word apples does not change.

But you *cannot* do the following addition:

$$2x^3 + 3x^2$$

You cannot add because the exponents differ.

➡ **EXAMPLES** _____

$$5x^3 - 2x^3 = 3x^3$$

Since the letters and their exponents are the same, any addition or subtraction can be done, keeping the letter and exponents unchanged in the answer.

$$3y^5 + 4y^5 = 7y^5$$

Once again, the letters and their exponents are the same, so the operation can be done.

$$4a^4 - 2a^2 = \text{cannot be subtracted}$$

Although the letters are the same, the exponents are different, so nothing more can be done.

If the variables (the letters) are different, such as x and y, then their exponents cannot be combined.

For example: $(x^3)(y^2)$ does not equal $(xy)^5$. The x^3y^2 is as far as you can go.

Another example: $(x^4)(y^3)(x^2) = x^6y^3$ The x exponents can be added, but the y cannot be included.

Practice

31. $(x^2)(x^4)$

32. $2y^3 - 5y^3$

33. $\dfrac{(x^5)}{(x^2)}$

34. $(4x)(3x^3)$

35. $\dfrac{(18y^3)}{(6y)}$

36. $6x^5 - 2x^5$

37. $7a^2 + a^3$

38. $\dfrac{5d^2}{5d^7}$

39. $(-2x^3)(5y)(x) =$

40. $(4a^2)(3a^3)/2a^2 =$

41. $3a^2 + 2b - a^2 - 5b^2 =$

42. $(7x^5)(6x)/3x^2 =$

43. $4x^3 - 2x^2 + 1 =$

ANSWERS

31. x^6
32. $-3y^3$
33. x^3
34. $12x^4$
35. $3y^2$
36. $4x^5$
37. Cannot be simplified further. Remember that you can add or subtract only when the exponents are the same.
38. d^{-5}
39. $-10x^4y$
40. $6a^3$
41. $2a^2 - 5b^2 + 2b$
42. $14x^4$
43. Cannot be simplified further.

SCIENTIFIC NOTATION

Scientific notation is a way of writing numbers that looks like this.

A number with just one digit to the left of the decimal point times 10 to a power.

For example, the number 5,280 could be written in scientific notation as:

$$5.280 \times 10^3$$

The exponent is 3 because $10^3 = 1,000$.

$$1,000 \times 5.280 = 5,280$$

595	=	5.95	×	10^2
88,500	=	8.85	×	10^4
0.1590	=	1.590	×	10^{-1}

The exponent is negative since the decimal will have to go to the left to get it back to its original location.

| 0.000039 | = | 3.9 | × | 10^{-4} |

Practice

Write the following numbers in scientific notation:

44. 795

46. 90,845

48. 0.00091

45. 46

47. 0.082

49. 1,003

Write the following scientific notation numbers in ordinary form:

50. 4.05×10^3

52. 8.04×10^5

54. 3.75×10^4

51. 7.96×10^{-1}

53. 9.00×10^{-2}

Follow the directions in the questions below.

55. The distance from Earth to the Sun is 93,000,000 miles. Write this distance in scientific notation.

56. The diameter of a flu virus is approximately 0.00006047 inches. Write this diameter in scientific notation.

57. The planet Venus is 1.208×10^4 kilometers across. Write this in standard number form.

58. The new library has 5.5×10^6 books. Write this in standard number form.

59. The width of some human hair is 1.2×10^{-8} inches. Write this in standard number form.

44. 7.95×10^2	52. 804,000
45. 4.6×10	53. 0.0900
46. 9.0845×10^4	54. 37,500
47. 8.2×10^{-2}	55. 9.3×10^7
48. 9.1×10^{-4}	56. 6.047×10^{-5}
49. 1.003×10^3	57. 12,080
50. 4,050	58. 5,500,000
51. 0.796	59. 0.000000012

ORDER OF OPERATIONS

When working math problems of any kind, there is a certain order of operations. This means that there is a sequence that you must follow in order to get the correct answer. The proper sequence follows:

PEMDAS

P	=	parentheses
E	=	exponents
M	=	multiplication
D	=	division
A	=	addition
S	=	subtraction

➡ EXAMPLE

Use PEMDAS to solve the following:

$$5 \times 9 + 3^2 - 2 + (5 - 3)$$

Parentheses first:	$5 \times 9 + 3^2 - 2 + 2$
Exponent next:	$5 \times 9 + 9 - 2 + 2$
Multiplication next:	$45 + 9 - 2 + 2$
Addition next:	$56 - 2$
Subtraction last:	54

➡ EXAMPLES

1. $5 + 3 \times 12 + (16 - 4)$ =
   $5 + 3 \times 12 + 12$ =
   $5 + 36 + 12$ =
   $41 + 12$ = 53

2. $18 - 3^2 + (2^2 + 6)/5$ =
   $18 - 3^2 + (4 + 6)/5$ =
   $18 - 3^2 + 10/5$ =
   $18 - 9 + 10/5$ =
   $18 - 9 + 2$ =
   $9 + 2$ = 11

Practice

Find each of the following using the order of operations:

60. $5 + 9 \times 3 + 7$

61. $12 \div 3 + 4 \times 6$

62. $4(9 + 3) - 6 \times 7$

63. $18 - 9 + 5 \times 2$

64. $20 \div 4 - 6 + (3 - 1)$

65. $(144 \div 3)(4 - 6)$

66. $20 - 3 + 3^2 \times 2$

67. $2 \times 50 - (9 - 4)^2 + (3 - 1)$

ANSWERS

60. 39
61. 28
62. 6
63. 19

64. 1
65. −96
66. 35
67. 77

SOLVING EQUATIONS

To solve an equation means to get the variable (like x) on one side of the equal sign and everything else on the other side of the equal sign. In order to do this, you have to move numbers around. Remember this rule:

> **RULE:** Whatever operation is performed on one side of the equal sign must be performed on the other side of the equal sign. For example, if 3 is added to the left of the equal sign, then 3 must be added to the right of the equal sign.

For example, look below at the solution of the equation $x + 7 = 3$:

$$\begin{array}{r} x + 7 = 3 \\ \underline{-7 = -7} \\ x = -4 \end{array}$$

The 7 was subtracted in order to get the x to be alone. The 7 was subtracted from both sides because of the rule above.

> **Hint:** Whenever you have to "move" a number in an equation, you are actually canceling out the number. To do this, you have to perform the opposite operation. For example, if the problem says to add, you must subtract; if it says to subtract, you add. If the problem says to multiply, you divide; and if it says to divide, you multiply.

As you study the examples, try to see how the variable is isolated in each case.

➠ EXAMPLE _____

$3x = 15$ In this case, $3x$ means that 3 is multiplied by x. In order to get x by itself, you would divide by 3. Remember that you have to divide both sides by 3.

$$\frac{3x}{3} = \frac{15}{3}$$

$x = 5$ The solution is $x = 5$; that is, the original equation is true when x is 5.

➠ EXAMPLE _____

$x + 15 = 60$ In order to isolate x, you need to get rid of the 15. Since it has an addition sign in front of it, the reverse or opposite is subtraction, so subtract 15 from both sides.

$$\begin{array}{r} x + 15 = 60 \\ -15 = -15 \\ \hline x = 45 \end{array}$$

   The solution is $x = 45$; that is, the original equation is true when x is 45.

➠ EXAMPLE _____

Sometimes solving an equation is a two-step process.

$$\begin{array}{r} 2x + 5 = 23 \\ -5 = -5 \\ \hline 2x = 18 \end{array}$$

   The first step is to get rid of the number (5) that is not with the x.

$$\frac{2x}{2} = \frac{18}{2}$$ The second step is to divide both sides by 2 to get x by itself.

$x = 9$ The original equation is true when $x = 9$.

Practice

For each of the following equations, find the value of the letter (variable):

68. $x + 15 = 32$

69. $5x + 6 = 10$

70. $120 = 2x + x$

71. $3x + 4x - 5 = 23$

72. $2x - 4 = -12$

73. $3(x + 2) = 15$

74. $12(c - 12) = 10 + c$

75. $15 = \dfrac{t}{5}$

68. 17

69. $\frac{4}{5}$

70. 40; Your first step in any solution is to combine what you can. In this case that would be to add the $2x$ and x to get $120 = 3x$.

71. 4

72. -4

73. 3

74. 14

75. 75

PERCENT

The idea of percent logically follows solving equations.

The basic percent equation looks like this:

$$\% = \frac{\text{part} \times 100}{\text{whole}}$$

Since there are three unknown quantities in this equation (%, part, and whole), the unknown can go in any one of these three positions. Any percent problem will then fit one of these formats:

When looking for %:

$$x = \frac{\text{part}(100)}{\text{whole}}$$

When looking for the part:

$$\% = \frac{(x)(100)}{\text{whole}}$$

When looking for the whole:

$$\% = \frac{\text{part}(100)}{x}$$

➡ **EXAMPLE (%)** _____

If you scored 60 out of a possible 80 on a test, what is your percent score?

$\% = \dfrac{\text{part} \times 100}{\text{whole}}$

$\% = \dfrac{60 \times 100}{80}$

$\% = 75$

Your percent score is 75%.

EXAMPLE (WHOLE)

Stan paid 5% sales tax on an audio system for his house. The sales tax was $60. What was the purchase price of the sound system?

$$5\% = \frac{\$60 \times 100}{\text{price of whole system}}$$

$$(5)(\text{price}) = 6{,}000$$

$$\frac{(5)(\text{price})}{5} = \frac{6{,}000}{5}$$

$$\text{price} = \frac{6{,}000}{5}$$

$$\text{price} = 1200$$

The purchase price was $1,200.

EXAMPLE (PART)

If a car dealer requires a 15% down payment, what would that cost you on a $20,000 car?

$$\% = \frac{\text{part} \times 100}{\text{whole}}$$

$$15\% = \frac{x \text{ dollars} \times 100}{\$20{,}000}$$

$$\frac{(15)(20{,}000)}{1} = \frac{(x)(100)}{20{,}000}\left(\frac{20{,}000}{1}\right)$$

$$(15)(20{,}000) = 100x$$

$$300{,}000 = 100x$$

$$\frac{300{,}000}{100} = \frac{100x}{100}$$

$$3{,}000 = x$$

You must make a $3,000 down payment.

Practice

76. What is 30% of 1,200?

77. What percent is 12 out of 15?

78. If 5% of your salary is $60, how much is your salary?

79. If you finished 4 hours of your 12 hour work shift, what % is finished?

80. Jane gets an 8% good driver discount on car insurance. If her insurance is normally $1,000 a year, how much is the discount?

81. A freeze-damaged fruit shipment has 200 bad grapefruit. If 10% of the fruit was damaged, how many grapefruit were there before the freeze?

ANSWERS

76. 360	78. $1,200	80. $80
77. 80%	79. $33\frac{1}{3}$ %	81. 2,000

Percent Increase and Decrease

If prices increase by 15% what would be the new price of a $30 pair of slacks?

Step 1:   Change % to decimal.

$15\% = 0.15$

Step 2:   Multiply decimal by original price.

$0.15 \times \$30.00 = \$4.50$

Step 3:   Add to original price.

$\$4.50 + \$30.00 = \$34.50 =$ new price

Percent Decrease

Carla's new car cost $25,000. A new car loses 18% of its value in its first year. How much will her car be worth after a year?

Step 1:   Change % to decimal.

$18\% = 0.18$

Step 2:   Multiply the decimal by the original amount.

$0.18 \times 25,000 = \$4,500$

Step 3:   Subtract this amount from the original amount.

$\$25,000 - \$4,500 = \$20,500$ value of the car after a year

Practice

82. A 5% increase in the natural gas price is expected. For a customer who paid $3,500 last year, what will be the new price?

83. Joe's doctor tells him that a 10% weight loss would help his health. Joe weighs 225 pounds now. What would he weigh if he followed the doctor's orders?

84. Sam makes $50,000 a year. If he gets a 6% pay raise, what will be his new annual salary?

85. A leading airline announces that 11% of its 1,200 daily flights are being eliminated. How many flights will remain after this cut?

ANSWERS

82. $0.05 \times \$3,500 = \$175$
$\$175 + \$3,500 = \$3,675$

83. $0.10 \times 225 = 22.5$
$225 - 22.5 = 202.5$

84. $0.06 \times \$50,000 = \$3,000$
$\$50,000 + \$3,000 = \$53,000$

85. $0.11 \times 1,200 = 132$
$1,200 - 132 = 1,068$

PROPORTION

Ratio and Proportion

A ratio is a relationship between numbers.

➡ **EXAMPLE** _____

A cheese sandwich is made of 2 slices of bread and 1 slice of cheese.

Ratios:

$$\frac{1 \text{ slice cheese}}{2 \text{ slices bread}} \qquad \frac{1 \text{ sandwich}}{1 \text{ slice cheese}} \qquad \frac{2 \text{ slices bread}}{1 \text{ slice cheese}}$$

There are other sandwich ratios you could write. The only necessity is that the numerator and the denominator must be true for any one sandwich.

Ratios have a special usefulness. They can be used to create what is called a proportion. Proportions have a four part format.

$$\frac{A}{B} = \frac{C}{D}$$

From the sandwich example, the A and the B are about one sandwich. The C and D are about larger quantities of sandwiches.

The A and the C have to be about the same part of the sandwich (the bread, the cheese, or the sandwich itself).

The B and the D also have to be about the same sandwich part.

➡ **EXAMPLE** _____

Let A and B be about cheese (A) and bread (B). How many slices of cheese would be needed if there are 34 slices of bread? Solve by creating a proportion:

$$\frac{1}{2} = \frac{x}{34}$$

The solving of a proportion is done by a technique called cross multiplying.

Cross Multiplying

The process called cross multiplying can help you solve proportions quickly. To cross multiply, you multiply and equate the parts of the proportion that are diagonally opposite. Look at the following proportion:

$$\frac{A}{B} \diagup \kern-1.2em \diagdown \frac{C}{D}$$

Because A and D are diagonally opposite and B and C are diagonally opposite, multiply and equate each pair:

$$AD = BC$$

You can then solve as before for whatever quantity that you want to find.

➡ **EXAMPLE** _____

Solve the equation for x.

$$\frac{12}{4} = \frac{9}{x}$$

Cross multiply to solve for x:

$12x = (9)(4)$

$12x = 36$

$x = 3$ (Divide both sides by 12.)

Practice

Solve each of the following equations for the variable (letter):

86. $\dfrac{x}{15} = \dfrac{2}{5}$

87. $\dfrac{3}{4} = \dfrac{6}{a}$

88. $\dfrac{7}{3b} = \dfrac{3}{9}$

89. $\dfrac{2}{5} = \dfrac{c}{41}$

90. $\dfrac{x}{-3} = \dfrac{12}{4}$

91. $\dfrac{12}{2y} = \dfrac{-3}{5}$

ANSWERS

86. 6   87. 7   88. $16\dfrac{2}{5}$ 89. –9   90. –10   91. 8

Setting Up a Proportion

Suppose that you are mixing lemonade mix and water for a large group. You know that your usual recipe is to use 3 scoops of lemonade mix for each quart of water. If you want to know how many scoops you need for 12 quarts, you can set up the following proportions:

$$\frac{3 \text{ scoops}}{1 \text{ quart}} = \frac{x \text{ scoops}}{12 \text{ quarts}}$$

Notice that in setting up the proportion there is a logical order. Both numerators are about scoops. Both denominators are about quarts. The left side of the equation is about your usual recipe. The right side of the equation is about the larger recipe. When you set up proportions, use this type of logic.

Using the cross multiplying technique to solve this proportion gives:

$$(3)(12) = (1)(x)$$
$$36 = x$$

Another format for the same process looks like this:

$$3 : 1 = x : 12$$

This is read "3 is to 1 as x is to 12."

Solving involves the same plan:

$$(3)(12) = (x)(1)$$
$$36 = x$$

Practice

For each of the following problems, set up a proportion and then solve for the unknown:

92. If you are supposed to give 5 milligrams of antibiotic to a 15 pound dog, how many milligrams would you give to a 51 pound dog?

93. If you drive at a constant speed and can travel 100 miles in 2 hours, how many miles can you travel in $3\frac{1}{2}$ hours?

94. Your neighbor gets nice results by using 3 bags of grass seed on his 10,000 square feet of lawn. How many bags would you need for a 15,000 square foot lawn?

95. Rick used 20 gallons of gasoline for a 710 mile trip. At that same rate, how many gallons will it take for a 500 mile trip?

96. Don's friend joined an investment club. He invested $5,000 and earned a profit of $800 the first year. Don would like to invest $12,000. What would his profit be at the same rate?

ANSWERS

92. $\dfrac{5 \text{ mg}}{15 \text{ lb}} = \dfrac{x \text{ mg}}{51 \text{ lb}}$; 17

95. $\dfrac{20 \text{ gal}}{710 \text{ mi}} = \dfrac{x \text{ gal}}{500 \text{ mi}}$; 14.08

93. $\dfrac{100 \text{ mi}}{2 \text{ h}} = \dfrac{x \text{ mi}}{3\frac{1}{2} \text{ h}}$; 175

96. $\dfrac{\$800}{\$5,000} = \dfrac{\$x}{\$12,000}$; $1,920

94. $\dfrac{3 \text{ bags}}{10,000 \text{ sq ft}} = \dfrac{x \text{ bags}}{15,000 \text{ sq ft}}$; 4.5

FORMULAS

A formula is a way of describing how things are related to each other. For example, here is a formula you might use when driving a car:

$$\text{Distance} = \text{Rate times Time}$$
$$\text{or}$$
$$D = R \times T$$

How to Work Formula Problems

Step 1: Write the formula.

Step 2: Directly under each letter, write a number for that letter, if you know one. If you do not know, write the letter itself. This will be the unknown for which you will be solving.

Step 3: Solve the equation that you have now written.

➡ EXAMPLE

How long would it take to drive 600 miles at an average speed of 50 miles per hour?

Step 1: Distance = Rate × Time

Step 2: $600 = 50 \times T$

Step 3: Solve for T.

$$600 = 50T$$

$$\dfrac{600}{50} = \dfrac{50T}{50}$$

$$12 = T$$

It would take 12 hours.

Practice

97. How much interest will you pay to borrow $15,000 for a year at a rate of 9% ? (Remember that 9% will become 0.09 when you use it in a problem.)

$$\text{Principal} \times \text{Rate} = \text{Interest}$$
$$\text{or}$$
$$P \times R = I$$

98. If you had a Christmas tree lot, what price would you need to charge for each tree if you had 75 trees to sell and wanted to make $3,000? The business formula is shown below.

$$\text{income} = \text{number} \times \text{price}$$

99. Using the formula for the area of a triangle ($A = \frac{1}{2} bh$), find the area of a triangle whose base is 12 feet long and whose height is 5 feet.

ANSWERS

97. $1,350
98. $40
99. 30 sq. ft.

SUBSTITUTION

Substitution is like working with a formula, because you are writing numbers to replace letters. A number next to a letter indicates multiplication, and variables next to each other indicate multiplication.

➡ **EXAMPLE** _____

Solve $2a^2 + b - 3c$, if you know that $a = 3$, $b = 4$, and $c = 2$.

As in the formula problem, write known numbers for the letters and then simplify.

$$2a^2 + b - 3c = 2(3)^2 + 4 - 3(2)$$
$$= 2(9) + 4 - 6$$
$$= 18 + 4 - 6$$
$$= 22 - 6$$
$$= 16$$

Practice

100. What is the value of $2a^2 b^3$ if: $a = 2$ and $b = 3$?

101. What is the value of $2(x^2 - y^2) + 3z$ if $x = 5$, $y = 4$, and $z = 3$?

ANSWERS

100. 216   101. 27

FACTORING

You already know how to factor, though you may not have called it that. For example, when you think of the numbers that you can multiply to get 12 and you come up with 3 and 4, you have just factored. That is, you have decided that 3 and 4 are factors of 12 because they multiply together to get 12. If you were asked for another set of factors for 12, you could come up with 6 and 2 or 12 and 1.

➡ **EXAMPLE** _____

Factor $6x^2$.

One possible factorization is $(3x)(2x)$, since $(3x)(2x) = 6x^2$.
Another possible factorization is $(6x)(x)$, whose product is also $6x^2$.

➡ **EXAMPLE** _____

Factor $18a^3$.

One posssible factorization is $(9a^2)(2a)$, since $(9a^2)(2a) = 18a^3$.
Two other factorizations are $(6a^2)(3a)$ and $(6a)(3a^2)$. There are also other factorizations that give the product $18a^3$.

Practice

Find at least one set of two factors for each of the following expressions:

102. $16a^2$ 104. $21x^2 y$

103. $9r^3$ 105. $15x^2$

ANSWERS

102. $(8a)(2a)$; Other possibilities include $(4a)(4a)$ and $(16a)(a)$.
103. $(3r)(3r^2)$; Other possibilities include $(9r)(r^2)$ and $(9r^2)(r)$.
104. $(7x)(3xy)$; Other possibilities include $(3x^2)(7y)$ and $(7x^2)(3y)$.
105. $(5x)(3x)$; Other possibilities include $(15x)(x)$ and $(3)(5x^2)$.

FOIL and Factoring

THE FOIL METHOD

The FOIL method allows you to multiply expressions like $(x + 2)(x - 1)$ or $(2 - 3a)(1 + a)$ quickly. The word FOIL comes from the first letters of four words:

$$F = \text{First}$$
$$O = \text{Outside}$$
$$I = \text{Inside}$$
$$L = \text{Last}$$

These words are position words. For example, look at the problem $(3a + 2)(4a - 5)$.

First: The $3a$ and the $4a$ are first in each set of parentheses.
Outside: The $3a$ and the -5 are the two outside terms.
Inside: The 2 and the $4a$ are the two inside (middle) terms.
Last: The 2 and the -5 are last in each set of parentheses.

FOIL can be used only when multiplying binomials.

Here is how the FOIL system works: Suppose a problem says to multiply $(3a + 2)(4a - 5)$. The FOIL steps are the following:

F: $(3a)(4a) = 12a^2$
O: $(3a)(-5) = -15a$
I: $(2)(4a) = 8a$
L: $(2)(-5) = -10$

The only ones of these four expressions that can be added are the $-15a$ and the $8a$. In general, you can combine the "O" and "I" expressions by addition. In this case their sum is $-7a$. The whole answer is written as $12a^2 - 7a - 10$.

➡ **EXAMPLE** _____

Multiply $(2x + 4)(5x + 3)$ using FOIL.

F: $(2x)(5x) = 10x^2$
O: $(2x)(3) = 6x$
I: $(4)(5x) = 20x$
L: $(4)(3) = 12$

Combining the $6x$ and $20x$ gives $6x + 20x = 26x$.
The final answer is $10x^2 + 26x + 12$.

➡ **EXAMPLE** _____

Multiply $(3x + 7)(2x - 3)$ using FOIL.

> **Hint:** Try covering the rest of this example and doing the FOIL steps by yourself. Then show yourself the answers so you can see how you are doing.

F: $(3x)(2x) = 6x^2$

O: $(3x)(-3) = -9x$

I: $(7)(2x) = 14x$

L: $(7)(-3) = -21$

Combining the $-9x$ and $14x$ gives $-9x + 14x = 5x$.

The final answer is $6x^2 + 5x - 21$.

Practice

Multiply each of the following:

106. $(x + 5)(2x + 7)$

107. $(3a + 7)(2a - 2)$

108. $(4t - 3)(t + 5)$

109. $(b - 9)(2b - 4)$

110. $(4x - 1)(3x - 2) =$

111. $(2.5a - 1)(3a + 8) =$

112. $(2z + 5)(11z - 3) =$

ANSWERS

106. $2x^2 + 17x + 35$

107. $6a^2 + 8a - 14$

108. $4t^2 + 17t - 15$

109. $2b^2 - 22b + 36$

110. $12x^2 - 11x + 2$

111. $7.5a^2 + 17a - 8$

112. $22z^2 + 49z - 15$

USING FOIL IN FACTORING

To see the relationship between FOIL and factoring remember this:

FOIL means multiplying.

FOIL: $(3a + 2)(4a - 5) = 12a^2 - 7a - 10$

Factoring means "unmultiplying."

Factoring: $12a^2 - 7a - 10 = (3a + 2)(4a - 5)$

So, when you factor expressions with three terms like $12a^2 - 7a - 10$, you are basically "un-FOIL-ing." If you think you have found a factorization, you can check yourself by using FOIL on your answer to see if it gives you the original expression. If it does not, then your solution is not correct, and so you should try again.

When looking for factors for $x^2 + 8x + 15$, first set up a pair of parentheses.

$$(\ )(\ )$$

Then, look at the first term, the x^2. What two things would multiply to give the x^2? The answer is x and x.

$$(x)(x)$$

Now, what would multiply together to give 15? It could be 5 and 3, so try that.

$$(x\,5)(x\,3)$$

To decide what the signs need to be, look at the signs in the original equation. Since the 15 is positive, that means both signs have to be the same. Since the $8x$ is positive, that means both signs have to be positive.

$$(x + 5)(x + 3)$$

To check your work, perform the FOIL operation. You will get the equation that you began with. If you do not get the beginning question, then there is an error somewhere.

➡ EXAMPLES

Each of the following has been factored. (Notice that you can perform the FOIL operation on the answer and it will return you to the original problem.)

1. $x^2 + 8x + 15$ factors into $(x + 5)(x + 3)$
2. $x^2 - 5x - 14$ factors into $(x - 7)(x + 2)$
3. $x^2 - 7x + 12$ factors into $(x - 3)(x - 4)$
4. $2x^2 + x - 3$ factors into $(2x + 3)(x - 1)$
5. $6x^2 - 7x + 2$ factors into $(2x - 1)(3x - 2)$

Practice

For each of the following find at least one set of factors:

113. $x^2 + 6x + 8$

118. $2x^2 + x - 10$

114. $10x^2 + 19x + 6$

119. $6y^2 - 11y - 10$

115. $6a^2 + 8a + 2$

120. $14x^2 - 20x + 6$

116. $3b^2 - 10b - 8$

121. $10x^2 + x - 24$

117. $5c^2 + 8c + 3$

ANSWERS

113. $(x + 4)(x + 2)$
114. $(5x + 2)(2x + 3)$
115. $(3a + 1)(2a + 2)$ or $(6a + 2)(a + 1)$
116. $(3b + 2)(b - 4)$
117. $(5c + 3)(c + 1)$

118. $(x - 2)(2x + 5)$
119. $(3y + 2)(2y - 5)$
120. $(7x - 3)(2x - 2)$
121. $(2x - 3)(5x + 8)$

QUADRATIC EQUATIONS

The equations you have just been working with are called quadratic equations. All quadratic equations have a square term, such as x^2. Solving a quadratic equation involves the skills you have just learned, called factoring.

How to Solve a Quadratic Equation

Step 1:   Factor.

$$x^2 + 8x + 15 = 0$$
$$(x + 5)(x + 3) = 0$$

Step 2:   Set each factor equal to zero.

$$x + 5 = 0 \qquad\qquad x + 3 = 0$$

Step 3:   Solve each of these two equations.

$$
\begin{array}{ll}
x + 5 = 0 & x + 3 = 0 \\
\underline{-5\ -5} & \underline{-3\ -3} \\
x\ \ = -5 & x\ \ = -3
\end{array}
$$

Step 4:   The −5 and the −3 are the two numbers that are the solution to the quadratic equation that you started with.

Here is another example of how to solve a quadratic equation:

$2x^2 - 15x + 18 = 0$	This is the equation for which you are trying to find two answers.
$(2x - 3)(x - 6) = 0$	Factor the equation.
$2x - 3 = 0$ and $x - 6 = 0$	Write each factor equal to zero.
$2x - 3 = 0 \qquad x - 6 = 0$	Solve each equation separately.
$2x = 3 \qquad\qquad x = 6$	
$x = 3/2 \qquad\quad\ x = 6$	These are the two solutions for the quadratic equation.

Practice

Solve each of these quadratic equations. There will be two answers for each.

122. $x^2 + 5x + 4 = 0$

124. $x^2 + 2x - 3 = 0$

123. $x^2 - 4x - 12 = 0$

125. $x^2 - x - 20 = 0$

ANSWERS

	Factors	Values for x
122.	$(x+1)(x+4)$	−1 and −4
123.	$(x+2)(x-6)$	−2 and +6
124.	$(x-1)(x+3)$	+1 and −3
125.	$(x+4)(x-5)$	−4 and +5

INEQUALITIES

Suppose you wanted to describe the relationship between 7 and 5. You could say that 7 is greater than 5. An algebraic way of saying this is to write 7 > 5. The > means "greater than." There is also a < symbol, which means "less than." Just remember that the little end of the symbol points to the smaller value.

You can combine each of these symbols with an equals sign. The symbol ≤ means "less than or equal to." The symbol ≥ means "greater than or equal to."

➡ EXAMPLE

Sometimes insurance companies reward good students by offering a discount if their grade point average (GPA) is a B (3.0) or better. Express this as an inequality.

The GPA must be at least 3.0, which means that it must be greater than or equal to 3.0, so use the ≥ symbol. The answer is GPA ≥ 3.0.

Inequality Graphing

A number line is often used to picture the idea of inequality, as shown below.

The way to read this graph is to say it represents values greater than −2. The fact that the circle at the −2 location is an open (not shaded in) circle is important. This means that the value of −2 is not itself included.

As you look at the number line below, notice that the circle is shaded. This means that the value of the circle itself is included. This graph represents values greater than or equal to −3.

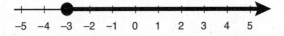

A number line can also show a range of values that is bounded on both ends. For example, if your ideal weight lies in the range from 165 to 170 pounds, you can write the range as $165 \leq w \leq 170$, and can graph it like this:

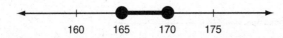

ALGEBRA, FUNCTIONS, AND PATTERNS 87

Practice

For each of the following inequalities, make a number line graph:

126. $x > 8$

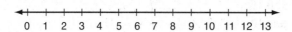

127. $a \leq -3$

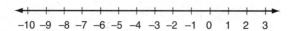

128. $t > -1$

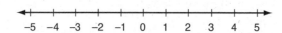

129. $x \leq 2$

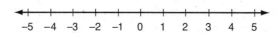

130. $1 < t < 4$

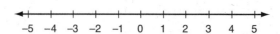

For each of the following graphs, write an inequality:

131.

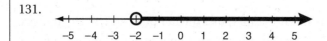

132.

133.

134.

135.

136.

ANSWERS

126.

```
  +--+--+--+--+--+--+--+--⊕--+--+--+--+--+
  0  1  2  3  4  5  6  7  8  9 10 11 12 13
```

127.

```
◄━━━━━━━━━━━━━━━━●--+--+--+--+--+--+
 -10 -9 -8 -7 -6 -5 -4 -3 -2 -1  0  1  2  3
```

128.

```
  +--+--+--⊕━━━━━━━━━━━━━━━━►
 -5 -4 -3 -2 -1  0  1  2  3  4  5
```

129.

```
◄━━━━━━━━━━━━━━●--+--+--+
 -5 -4 -3 -2 -1  0  1  2  3  4  5
```

130.

```
  +--+--+--+--⊕━━━━━━⊕--+
 -5 -4 -3 -2 -1  0  1  2  3  4  5
```

131. $x > -2$

132. $x < 3$

133. $x \geq 5$

134. $-2 < x < 1$

135. $x \leq -1$

136. $-7 \leq x \leq -4$

Solving Inequalities

You can solve inequalities in the same way that you solve regular equations—with one exception. This exception arises when you multiply or divide by a negative number. When this happens, you must turn the inequality sign around before solving as usual. That is, a > symbol becomes a < symbol, and so on.

➡ **EXAMPLE** _____

$2x + 3 > x + 5$ This is an inequality problem. To solve it, you want to isolate the x.

$\underline{-x \quad\quad -x}$ The first step is to subtract x from both sides.

$x + 3 > 5$

$x + 3 > +5$

$\underline{\quad -3 \quad -3}$ Subtract 3 from each side to isolate x.

$\quad\quad x > 2$ Notice that you did not multiply or divide by a negative number, so the inequality sign did not change.

The solution is all numbers that are greater than 2.

➡ EXAMPLE

$3x + 8 > 7x - 24$ This is an inequality problem. Subtract $7x$ from both sides so that

$\underline{-7x \qquad -7x}$ the variable x is on only one side.

$-4x + 8 > -24$

$-4x + 8 > -24$ Subtract 8 from both sides to isolate x further.

$\underline{\quad -8 \quad -8}$

$-4x > -32$

$x < 8$ Then divide by -4 to isolate x completely.

Dividing by a negative number causes the inequality sign to reverse.

Practice

Solve each of the following inequalities:

137. $x - 7 \leq 2x$ 140. $-13r \geq 91$ 143. $10 - 12a > -38$

138. $3x \leq -27$ 141. $2c + 5 < 3c$

139. $9x + 2 > 20$ 142. $7x - 27 \geq 4x$

ANSWERS

137. $-7 \leq x$ 140. $r \leq -7$ 143. $a < 4$

138. $x \leq -9$ 141. $5 < c$

139. $x > 2$ 142. $9 \leq x$

SLOPE

In the diagram below, you can see that line AB has a certain slope or tilt to it.

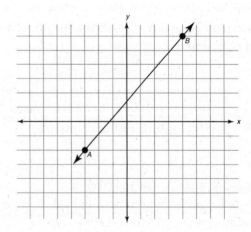

The slope of line AB is defined as $\dfrac{\text{rise}}{\text{run}}$. In order to find out what these numbers are, draw a dotted line like this:

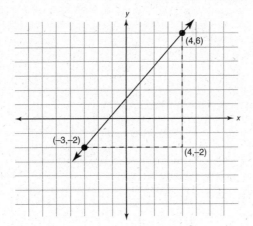

Now, to put numbers to the idea of $\dfrac{\text{rise}}{\text{run}}$, start at A and move to the right to the point where the dotted line starts to go up. As you did this, you went to the right 7 units, so the run is 7. It is a positive 7 because you headed in right, or the positive direction. Then to go up the dotted line, you go up 8 units. The 8 is also positive because you are moving up.

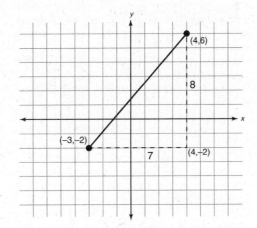

Use the numbers you have developed on the graph to calculate the slope.

$$\frac{\text{rise}}{\text{run}} = \frac{8}{7} = \text{slope}$$

Practice

Find the slope for each of the following graphs:

144.

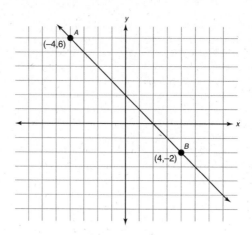

Slope =

145.

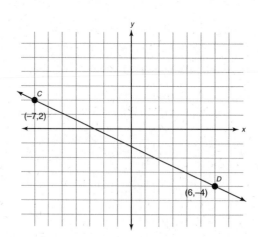

Slope =

146.

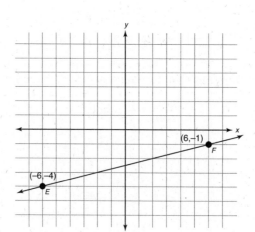

Slope =

Note, the numbers you have for rise and run may be different from those in the answer, but the value for the slope must be the same. The reason for this is that you may have drawn your dotted lines in a different way.

144. Rise = 8, run = –8,   slope = $\dfrac{8}{-8}$ = –1

145. Rise = 6, run = –13,   slope = $\dfrac{6}{-13}$ = $-\dfrac{6}{13}$

146. Rise = –3, run = 12,   slope = $\dfrac{-3}{12}$ = $-\dfrac{1}{4}$

From your earlier math lessons, you learned some things about zero. If you multiply anything by zero, the answer will always be zero. If you divide by zero, the answer is said to be undefined. These ideas apply to slope calculations.

As you look at line *AB*, what will its run be? _____

So, what will its slope be? _____

As you look at line *CD*, what will its rise be? _____

So, what will its slope be? _____

These lines are called "special cases." You will always be able to figure out which one is zero (horizontal) and which one is undefined (vertical), so you won't have to memorize.

Point-Slope Formula

Another way to find the slope of a line is to use what is called the point-slope formula. This formula will be available to you during the test.

Slope = $\dfrac{(y_2 - y_1)}{(x_2 - x_1)}$

The x_1 and y_1 are the coordinates for one point on the line.

The x_2 and y_2 are the coordinates for another point on the line.

➡ EXAMPLE

What is the slope of a line if two points on the line have the coordinates (4, –3) and (–3, 2)?

Slope = $\dfrac{(-3-2)}{(4-(-3))}$ = $\dfrac{-5}{7}$

Practice

147. Find the slope of the line that has one point at (–2, –3) and another point at (2, 3).

148. Find the slope of the line that has one point at (2, 5) and another point at (6, –2).

149. Find the slope of the line that has one point at (5, –1) and another point at (2, 8).

ANSWERS

147. $\dfrac{-6}{-4} = \dfrac{3}{2}$

148. $\dfrac{7}{-4} = -\dfrac{7}{4}$

149. $-\dfrac{9}{3} = -3$

END OF CHAPTER PRACTICE

1. Simplify $4a - 6a - 3a + a$.

   (A) $10a$
   (B) $4a$
   (C) $-4a$
   (D) $-6a$

2. What is 3.4×10^{-5} written in ordinary form?

   (A) 0.000034
   (B) 0.00034
   (C) 0.34
   (D) 340,000

3. What is the value of x if $\dfrac{4}{x} = \dfrac{12}{9}$?

   (A) 3
   (B) 7
   (C) 9
   (D) 18

4. A teacher requests that his annual salary be paid in 12 equal payments instead of 10. If each of the 10 payments is m dollars, how many dollars will each of the 12 payments be?

   (A) $\dfrac{6m}{5}$

   (B) $\dfrac{5m}{6}$

   (C) $10m - 12$
   (D) $12m - 10$

5. Solve $3x + 8 = -12 + x$ for x

   (A) -10
   (B) -2
   (C) 2
   (D) 5

6. Solve the following quadratic equation:

$$x^2 - 3x - 10 = 0$$

7. Tony's financial planner recommends a 2 to 3 ratio of stocks to bonds in Tony's portfolio. If Tony now has \$45,000 in bonds, how much does he have in stocks?

   (A) 5,000
   (B) 9,000
   (C) 30,000
   (D) 67,500

8. The standard aspirin dose for a 150 pound adult is 650 milligrams. To calculate the number of milligrams that would be appropriate for a 60 pound child, which of these proportions would be correct?

   (A) $\dfrac{150}{650} = \dfrac{60}{x}$

   (B) $\dfrac{150}{60} = \dfrac{x}{650}$

   (C) $\dfrac{x}{150} = \dfrac{650}{60}$

   (D) $\dfrac{150}{x} = \dfrac{60}{650}$

9. Some stores pay their employees what is called a "graduated commission." Suppose your commission is 3% on all sales up to $8,000 and 5% on all sales above $8,000. What would be your commission if your sales for the month amounted to $15,000?

(A) $590
(B) $750
(C) $4,066
(D) $5,900

10. Which is a factorization of $6a^2 - 7a - 24$?

(A) $(3a - 4)(2a + 6)$
(B) $(3a + 4)(2a - 6)$
(C) $(3a - 8)(2a + 3)$
(D) $(6a + 12)(a - 2)$

11. Jan's computer is 133 megahertz, or 133,000,000 hertz. Express the last number in scientific notation.

(A) 1.33×10^8
(B) 1.33×10^{-8}
(C) 13.3×10^{-8}
(D) 13.3×10^8

12. Rhonda wants to estimate how much she could save yearly by using coupons. Her yearly grocery bill is about $5,000. On a typical trip to the store, she spends $100 and uses $8 in coupons. Which equation will allow her to predict her yearly savings from coupons?

(A) $\dfrac{x}{5,000} = \dfrac{8}{100}$

(B) $\dfrac{x}{8} = \dfrac{100}{5,000}$

(C) $\dfrac{x}{100} = \dfrac{8}{5,000}$

(D) $\dfrac{100}{5,000} = \dfrac{x}{8}$

13. Find the value of x for $x = 3a(b - 2c)$ if $a = 5$, $b = 16$, and $c = 3$.

(A) 150
(B) 165
(C) 195
(D) 240

14. In mapping an undersea trench off the coast of South America, the geologist begins at a depth of 200 feet. From there the probe falls 50 feet, then rises 30 feet, then drops again 100 feet. How many feet under the ocean's surface is the probe?

    (A) –120
    (B) –280
    (C) –320
    (D) –380

15. Observe the order of operations to solve $48 \div (2 + 6) \times 2 - 1$.

    (A) 2
    (B) 8
    (C) 11
    (D) 36

16. Which of the following inequalities describes the graph?

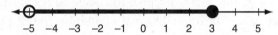

    (A) $-5 < x < 3$
    (B) $-5 < x < -3$
    (C) $-5 < x \leq 3$
    (D) $-5 \leq x \leq 3$

17. Find the slope of line AB in the diagram below.

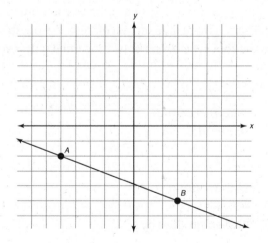

18. Find the slope of the line that has one of its points at (–5, –2) and another point at (2, 3). You may use the point-slope formula:

$$\text{Slope} = \frac{(y_2 - y_1)}{(x_2 - x_1)}$$

Answers

1. **C** Since every term in the expression $4a - 6a - 3a + a$ has the variable a, you can use the idea suggested in the signed number section of the chapter, in which you imagine that you are moving on a number line. You begin at the +4 position on the line, corresponding to the term $4a$. The next term is $-6a$, so you move 6 spaces to the left, putting you at –2. From this position you move 3 more spaces to the left because the next term is $-3a$. This move puts you at the –5 position on the number line. The last term in the problem is a, which is the same as $+1a$, so move l space in the positive direction. Your final position on the number line is therefore –4.

2. **A** The negative sign in the exponent tells you to move the decimal to the left because that is always the negative direction. The number 5 in the exponent means to move the decimal 5 spaces. Moving the decimal point in 3.4 to the left 5 spaces gives 0.000034.

3. **A** Whenever you see a problem that is set up in this manner, think of the cross multiply process. It does not matter which diagonal you begin with. One diagonal, containing the 4 and the 9, gives 36. The other diagonal, containing the 12 and the x, gives $12x$. Setting these equal to each other gives $12x = 36$. Dividing both sides by 12 gives $x = 3$.

4. **B** You can reason that if the teacher gets m dollars for 10 paychecks, then the total pay for the year is $10m$. Now take that yearly income and split it into 12 pieces. The result is $10m$ divided by 12, or $\dfrac{10m}{12}$.

    Remember to reduce to lowest terms, which gives $\dfrac{10m}{12} = \dfrac{5m}{6}$.

5. **A** Remember that when you are solving for a variable, you want to get the variable on one side by itself. There is more than one set of steps to work this problem, so if your steps vary from those shown here, do not be concerned unless you get the wrong answer.

$$3x + 8 = -12 + x$$
$$\underline{-8 \quad\; -8}\qquad \text{Subtract 8 from}$$
$$3x = -20 + x \qquad \text{both sides.}$$

$$3x = -20 + x$$
$$\underline{-x \qquad\quad -x}\qquad \text{Subtract } x \text{ from}$$
$$2x = -20 \qquad\quad \text{both sides.}$$
$$x = -10 \qquad\qquad \text{Divide both sides by 2.}$$

6. **–2, 5** The first step is to factor the equation into:

$$(x + 2)(x - 5) = 0$$

Next, set each factor equal to zero and solve each:

$$x + 2 = 0 \qquad\qquad x - 5 = 0$$
$$\underline{-2 \quad -2} \qquad\qquad \underline{+5 \;\; +5}$$
$$x \quad\;\; = -2 \qquad\qquad x \quad\; = +5$$

The two values for x are –2 and 5.

7. **C** $\dfrac{2 \text{ stocks}}{3 \text{ bonds}} = \dfrac{x \text{ stocks}}{45{,}000 \text{ bonds}}$

      $3x \qquad = \qquad 90{,}000$

      $x \qquad\; = \qquad 30{,}000$

8. **A** When you write a proportion, you must be consistent in positioning the values. Although there is more than one correct way to set up the proportion, the final answer will be the same. In the proportion that is the correct choice, notice that the first fraction is only about the adult and the second fraction is all about the child. Also, the numerators of both fractions give body weight and the denominators give milligrams of aspirin.

9. **A** The sales of $15,000 must be broken into two parts. These parts are the first $8,000 and the remainder, which is $7,000. To calculate the commission on the first $8,000 multiply it by 0.03 (which is 3%). This gives you $240. On the remainder (the $7,000), multiply by 0.05 (which is 5%) to get $350. The entire commission is the sum of $240 and $350, or $590.

10. **C** To determine which factorization is correct, multiply each set of possible factors using the FOIL technique. All of the choices give the correct answer for the product of the first terms and the last terms. Only choice 4, however, gives a sum of $-7a$ for the products of the outer and inner terms.

11. **A** When changing into scientific notation, the decimal must go between the first two digits. This will give the number 1.33 times 10 to some power. To decide on the power, count spaces from the new location of the decimal to the end of the number. This gives you 8 spaces. The only remaining part is to decide if the 8 is positive or negative. The sign will have to be positive. The reason for this is that you are moving the decimal in the positive direction when going from where the decimal is now to where the decimal was in the original problem.

12. **A** You might want to look back at Question 8 for another example of a proportion. In this problem, you can let the first fraction be about the yearly grocery bill and the second be about the typical trip to the store. Within each fraction, let the numerator be the coupon savings and the denominator be the whole price of the purchases.

13. **A** The first step in a substitution problem is to write the equation itself. Then, directly below each letter, write the number value for that letter.

$x = 3\,a\,(b - 2c)$
$x = 3(5)(16 - 2(3))$

Simplify using the order of operations.

$x = 3(5)(16 - 6)$
$x = 3(5)(10)$
$x = (15)(10)$
$x = 150$

14. **C** This is a number line problem with the number line vertical rather than horizontal. Imagine the probe starting at 200 feet under the water. The probe goes 50 feet farther down, leaving it 250 feet under the water. The probe then rises 30 feet,

making the new depth 220 feet. The 100 foot drop puts the probe 320 feet below the surface. Depths below the surface of the water register as negative numbers, so the answer is −320.

15. **C** As you recall (or look back in the chapter to) order of operations, you will see that you should deal with the contents of the parentheses first, giving you $48 \div 8 \times 2 - 1$. Next, do all of the multiplications and divisions in order. Dividing 48 by 8 gives 6. Multiplying 6 by 2 gives 12. Finally, subtracting 1 from 12 gives 11.

16. **C** The open circle at −5 tells you that −5 itself is not included. The closed circle at +3 tells you that +3 itself is included. The heavy line runs between these two numbers. Remember to put the equals part of the symbol with the +3 to show that the +3 is included.

17. $-\dfrac{3}{8}$ Slope $= \dfrac{\text{rise}}{\text{run}} = \dfrac{3}{-8} = -\dfrac{3}{8}$. Remember that your numbers might be different, but the slope has to be the same.

18. $\dfrac{5}{7}$ slope $= \dfrac{(y_2 - y_1)}{(x_2 - x_1)}$ slope $= \dfrac{(3-(-2))}{(2-(-5))} = \dfrac{5}{7}$

Measurement

Measurement is one of the most frequently used math skills. Measurement is the key to everyday activities such as reading a speedometer, using a recipe, calculating your pay, and making home improvements. Measuring requires the use of a device, whether it be a tape measure, a thermometer, a measuring cup, or a ruler. The first measurement step is to make certain that you understand the tool that you are using.

LINEAR MEASUREMENT

Look at the ruler shown below. The way to find out what each of the unmarked lines represents is to start by finding the halfway point between any two of the numbers. If you look at the ruler between 3 and 4, you can spot the halfway point. This tells you how many of the smallest spaces make a half inch. Count them to see that there are 8 spaces. Once you have figured out where ½ inch is on the ruler, ask yourself what would be half of a half. Because $\frac{1}{2} \times \frac{1}{2} = \frac{1}{4}$, you know where $\frac{1}{4}$ of an inch is and you can see that it takes 4 spaces to make $\frac{1}{4}$ of an inch. This same process will work for any measuring device.

Practice

1. On a sketch of the ruler shown below,

   place a letter "A" at $1\frac{3}{4}$.

   place a letter "B" at $3\frac{5}{8}$.

   place a letter "C" at $\frac{3}{16}$.

   place a letter "D" at $2\frac{7}{8}$.

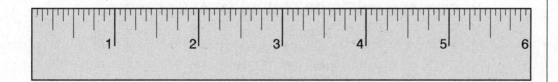

2. Use the barometer shown below to answer the following questions:

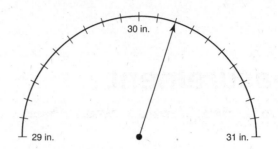

a. How much is each of the smallest spaces worth?

b. What is the reading at the arrow?

c. Place a mark where a reading of 29.8 inches would be.

ANSWERS

1.

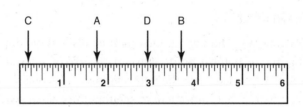

2a. Each of the smallest spaces is equal to 0.1 inch. As you look at the distance between 30 inches and 31 inches, you will see that there are 10 spaces. When you divide the 1 inch by 10, you get $\frac{1}{10}$, or 0.1.

2b. 30.2 inches

2c.

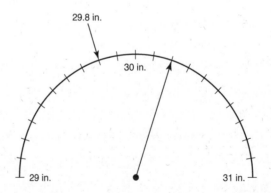

COMMON UNITS OF LINEAR MEASUREMENT

12 inches = 1 foot
3 feet = 1 yard
5,280 feet = 1 mile
1,760 yards = 1 mile

CHANGING UNITS

In order to solve problems involving units such as feet and inches, all the units have to be the same. The rules for changing units:

To go from a big unit to a smaller one, multiply.

To go from a small unit to a bigger one, divide.

Feet to Inches

Since a foot is bigger than an inch, going from feet to inches will result in a larger number, so you multiply.

 **EXAMPLE** _____

Change 2.5 feet to inches.

$$2.5 \text{ feet} \times 12 \text{ inches/foot} = 30 \text{ inches}$$

Inches to Feet

Since an inch is smaller than a foot, going from inches to feet will result in a smaller number, so you divide.

 **EXAMPLE** _____

Change 480 inches to feet.

$$480 \text{ inches}/12 \text{ inches per foot} = 40 \text{ feet}$$

Practice

3. How many feet are there in $3\frac{1}{2}$ miles?

4. How many yards are equal to 1,000 inches?

5. How many inches are there in 7.5 feet?

6. How many miles are there in 5,000 yards?

ANSWERS

3. $3\frac{1}{2}$ miles multiplied by 5,280 feet in one mile = 18,480 feet

4. 1,000 inches divided by 36 inches in one yard = 27.778 yards

5. 7.5 feet times 12 inches in one foot = 90 inches

6. 5,000 yards divided by 1,760 yards in one mile = 2.84 miles

MEASUREMENT OF TIME

> ### COMMON UNITS OF TIME
>
> 60 seconds = I minute
> 60 minutes = 1 hour
> 24 hours = I day
> 7 days = I week
> 52 weeks = 1 year
> 365 days = I year

Time Calculation

$$\begin{array}{lll} 1 \text{ hour} & \text{and} & 25 \text{ minutes} \\ + 2 \text{ hours} & \text{and} & 45 \text{ minutes} \\ \hline 3 \text{ hours} & \text{and} & 70 \text{ minutes} \end{array}$$

But 70 minutes is more than an hour.

$$\begin{array}{l} 70 \text{ minutes} \\ -60 \text{ minutes in one hour} \\ \hline 10 \text{ minutes and 1 hour} \end{array}$$

So, 3 hours and 70 minutes is 4 hours and 10 minutes.

Practice

7. Calculate the time Sally will be paid for this week if she works the following hours:

    Monday: 4 hours and 15 minutes

    Tuesday: 5 hours and 40 minutes

    Wednesday: 3 hours and 20 minutes

    Thursday: off

    Friday: 4 hours and 5 minutes

8. Calculate the number of minutes in one week.

9. If your daily commuting time is one hour and thirty-five minutes, how much time does commuting take for a five day workweek?

ANSWERS

7. The total time is 16 hours plus 80 minutes, or 17 hours and 20 minutes.

8. $1 \text{ week} \times \dfrac{7 \text{ days}}{1 \text{ week}} \times \dfrac{24 \text{ hours}}{1 \text{ day}} \times \dfrac{60 \text{ minutes}}{1 \text{ hour}} = 10{,}080 \text{ minutes}$

9. 5(1 hour and 35 minutes) = 5 hours and 175 minutes. To convert 175 minutes to hours, think of 2 hours as 120 minutes, which leaves 55 minutes. Then 5 hours plus 2 hours and 55 minutes equals 7 hours and 55 minutes.

WEIGHT MEASUREMENT

> ## COMMON UNITS OF WEIGHT
> 16 ounces = 1 pound
> 1,000 mg = 1 gram
> 2,000 pounds = 1 ton

Weight is a topic of interest for groceries, home improvement projects, recipes—even for workouts at the fitness center. The most common units of weight are the pound and the ounce. Medicinal weights are often given in milligrams and grams.

When working with weight problems, it is necessary that you make all of the units the same, so that you can compare better. For example, suppose that in shopping for laundry detergent you wanted to compare these two boxes:

Brand A   5 pounds 10 ounces
Brand B   100 ounces

Converting pounds to ounces is going from large to small, so you would multiply.

$$5 \text{ pounds} \times \frac{16 \text{ pounds}}{1 \text{ pound}} + 10 \text{ ounces} = 90 \text{ ounces}$$

Now it will be easier to see the relationship between Box A at 90 ounces and Box B at 100 ounces.

Practice

10. What will Joan's total amount of hamburger be if she bought the packages listed below?

    #1: 3 pounds 8 ounces
    #2: 2 pounds 9 ounces
    #3: 4 pounds 2 ounces

11. An elevator has a sign stating that it has a one ton capacity. How many people would this be if the average person weighs 200 pounds?

12. Prices for livestock are often given by the "hundred weight," that is, by the price for 100 pounds. What would be the price of a 750 pound cow if it were listed at $90 for a hundred weight?

ANSWERS

10. Add the pounds to get 9 pounds. When you add the ounces, you get 19 ounces. Recalling that there are 16 ounces in a pound, the 19 ounces is equal to 1 pound and 3 ounces. Add this to the 9 pounds, and the total weight is 10 pounds and 3 ounces.

11. One ton is 2000 pounds. Divide this by 200 pounds to get 10 persons.

12. A 750 pound cow is 7.5 hundred weight $\left(\frac{750}{100} = 7.5 \right)$. If the cost is $90 per hundred weight, you multiply the 90 by 7.5, getting $675.

LIQUID MEASUREMENT

> ### COMMON UNITS OF LIQUID MEASURE
> 8 ounces = 1 cup
> 2 cups = I pint
> 2 pints = 1 quart
> 4 quarts = 1 gallon

The measurement of liquids includes pumping gasoline, buying soft drinks, and mixing fuel for lawn equipment.

➡ **EXAMPLE** _____

How many quarts of antifreeze are equal to 2.5 gallons?

$$2.5 \text{ gallons} \times \frac{4 \text{ quarts}}{1 \text{ gallon}} = 10 \text{ quarts}$$

Here you are going to smaller units, so you would multiply.

Practice

13. How many cups are in 10 quarts?

14. How many quarts are in 10 cups?

15. How many pints are there in 3 gallons?

16. How many quarts of orange juice would you need to buy in order to have 30 gallons for the town pancake breakfast?

17. A case of motor oil contains 12 quarts. How many gallons is this?

ANSWERS

13. $10 \text{ quarts} \times \frac{4 \text{ cups}}{1 \text{ quart}} = 40 \text{ cups}$

14. $10 \text{ cups} \times \frac{1 \text{ quart}}{4 \text{ cups}} = 2.5 \text{ quarts}$

15. $3 \text{ gallons} \times \frac{4 \text{ quarts}}{1 \text{ gallon}} \times \frac{2 \text{ pints}}{1 \text{ quart}} = 24 \text{ pints}$

16. $30 \text{ gallons} \times \frac{4 \text{ quarts}}{1 \text{ gallon}} = 120 \text{ quarts}$

17. $12 \text{ quarts} \times \frac{1 \text{ gallon}}{4 \text{ quarts}} = 3 \text{ gallons}$

DRY MEASURE

COMMON UNITS OF DRY MEASURE

3 teaspoons = I tablespoon

4 tablespoons = $\frac{1}{4}$ cup

4 cups = 1 quart

2 pints = I quart

8 quarts = I peck

4 pecks = I bushel

Dry measure is a way to measure volume rather than weight. For example, a quart of blackberries tells you what size container will be filled with berries, but makes no claim about what those berries will weigh. Dry measure is a convenient way to measure things whose weight may vary. Berries, flour, sugar, and pasta are things that are often measured with the units shown above.

Practice

18. If you were preparing a recipe but you could not find your measuring cup, how many tablespoons would you use to get $\frac{3}{4}$ cup of sugar?

19. How many tablespoons are there in $1\frac{1}{2}$ cups?

20. If a case of strawberries contains 24 pints, how many quarts is that?

21. A recipe calling for $2\frac{1}{2}$ cups of ginger ale needs to be multiplied by 8 for a crowd. How many quarts would that be?

22. How many teaspoons are there in 6 tablespoons?

ANSWERS

18. $\frac{3}{4}$ cup $\times \dfrac{4 \text{ tablespoons}}{\frac{1}{4} \text{ cup}}$ = 12 tablespoons

19. $1\frac{1}{2}$ cups $\times$ 16 tablespoons in a cup = 24 tablespoons. (If there are 4 tablespoons in a $\frac{1}{4}$ cup, there would be four times that many in a cup, so 16 in a cup and 8 in a half cup = 24 in a cup and a half.)

20. 24 pints divided by 2 pints in a quart equals 12 quarts of strawberries.

21. $2\frac{1}{2}$ cups times 8 equals 20 cups of ginger ale needed. 20 cups divided by 4 cups in a quart equals 5 quarts of ginger ale for the larger recipe.

22. 6 tablespoons times 3 teaspoons in a tablespoon equals 18 teaspoons.

METRIC MEASURE

The metric system is based on prefixes whose meanings tell you about their size. The most common of these prefixes follow:

> milli = one thousandth
> centi = one hundredth
> deca = one tenth
> kilo = one thousand
> mega = one million (10^6)
> giga = one billion (10^9)

There are also common units. Grams are used for weight, meters for length, and liters for volume. Combining the common units with the prefixes allows you to find the sizes of various metric measurements.

For example, using the system above, you can see that a kilogram is 1,000 grams, since kilo means 1,000. Centimeter means one hundredth of a meter, or 0.01 meter.

> ### COMMON UNITS OF METRIC MEASURE
> 1 centimeter = 10 millimeters
> 1 meter = 100 centimeters
> 1 kilometer = 1,000 meters
> 1 milligram = 0.001 grams
> 1 kilogram = 1,000 grams
> 1 liter = 1,000 milliliters

The idea of *metric* scares many people. However, after they have worked with metric measures for awhile, they begin to see that it is really the easiest system of all. What makes it so easy is that moving around in the metric system is just a matter of moving the decimal point.

➡ **EXAMPLE**

How many millimeters (mm) equal 55 centimeters (cm)?

$$55 \text{ cm} \times \frac{10 \text{ mm}}{1 \text{ cm}} = 550 \text{ mm}$$

Changing from a big unit to a smaller one requires multiplication.

Practice

23. How many grams are there in 200 kilograms?

24. How many grams of aspirin are in a 325 milligram pill?

25. How many meters are equal to a 2.5 kilometer run?

ANSWERS

23. Going from the larger kilograms to smaller grams would require multiplication. 200 kilograms times 1,000 grams per kilogram equals 200,000 grams. Recall the earlier shortcut plan and move the decimal to the right three spaces.

24. $325 \text{ milligrams} \times \dfrac{1 \text{ gram}}{1,000 \text{ milligrams}} = 0.325 \text{ gram}$

25. $2.5 \text{ kilometer} \times \dfrac{1,000 \text{ meters}}{1 \text{ kilometer}} = 2,500 \text{ meters}$

CONVERSIONS USING PROPORTIONS

Proportions (from Chapter 4) can also be used to solve conversion problems.

Suppose you had a problem that asked:

$$87 \text{ cm} = ? \text{ mm}$$

A suitable proportion would be

$$\frac{x \text{ cm}}{87 \text{ cm}} = \frac{10 \text{ mm}}{1 \text{ cm}}$$

Notice two things:

1. Both numerators have the same units as do both denominators.
2. Left of equals is all about the problem itself. Right of equals is all about the relationship between mm and cm that is always true.

Following these two rules, you could come up with other, equally correct proportions. Examples are:

$$\frac{1 \text{ cm}}{10 \text{ mm}} = \frac{87 \text{ cm}}{x \text{ mm}}$$

$$\frac{10 \text{ mm}}{1 \text{ cm}} = \frac{x \text{ mm}}{87 \text{ cm}}$$

Each of these proportions yields the correct answer.

$$\frac{x \text{ mm}}{87 \text{ cm}} = \frac{10 \text{ mm}}{1 \text{ cm}}$$

Cross-multiply to get:

$$(x)(1) = 10(87)$$
$$x = 870 \text{ mm}$$

Practice

26. How many meters are equal to 45.2 cm?

27. How many inches are there in 100 yards?

28. How many pounds are equal to 30 ounces?

ANSWERS

26. $\dfrac{45.2 \text{ cm}}{x \text{ meters}} = \dfrac{100 \text{ cm}}{1 \text{ meter}}$

$$100x = 45.2$$
$$x = 0.452$$

Remember that you could have set up the proportion differently, but you must get 0.452 for your answer.

27. $\dfrac{100 \text{ yards}}{x \text{ inches}} = \dfrac{1 \text{ yard}}{36 \text{ inches}}$

$$100(36) = x(1)$$
$$3{,}600 \text{ inches} = x$$

28. $\dfrac{x \text{ pounds}}{30 \text{ ounces}} = \dfrac{1 \text{ pound}}{16 \text{ ounces}}$

$$16x = 30(1)$$
$$x = \frac{30}{16}$$
$$x = 1.875 \text{ pounds}$$

END OF CHAPTER PRACTICE

As you work your way through these measurement practice questions, remember that you are free to use the tables that are within the chapter that give the common units for measurements. These will also be available on the GED® exam.

1. The distance between the two marks on the dipstick shown below is 1 quart. If you only had access to a kitchen measuring cup, how many cupfuls would be needed to take the oil level from the add mark to the full mark.

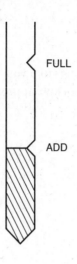

   (A) 2
   (B) 4
   (C) 6
   (D) 8

2. In a scene from an adventure film, the hero is shown grabbing up a sack filled with gold. The hero runs with the gold as if it were not hard to carry. How much does the gold weigh if gold weighs 19 grams per milliliter and the sack is a 2 liter sack?

   (A) $19 \times 2 \times 1{,}000$

   (B) $\dfrac{19}{2 \times 1{,}000}$

   (C) $\dfrac{2 \times 1{,}000}{19}$

   (D) $\dfrac{19 \times 2}{1{,}000}$

3. About how long do you need to bake a roast if it requires 28 minutes per pound and the roast weighs 5.3 pounds?

   (A) 1 hour 48 minutes
   (B) 2 hours 28 minutes
   (C) 2 hours 47 minutes
   (D) 2 hours 54 minutes

4. The following represents a time card, which records your times of arrival and departure at work for one day. What were your total hours of work for the day?

In: 8:50
Out: 11:45
In: 12:30
Out: 5:35

(A) 8 hours
(B) 8 hours 15 minutes
(C) 8 hours 35 minutes
(D) 8 hours 45 minutes

5. The owner's manual for your car states that your gas tank holds 15 gallons of gas. If the gauge looks like the one shown below, approximately how many gallons will be in the tank?

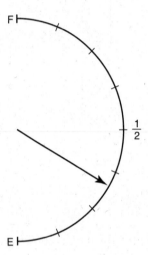

(A) 2 gallons
(B) 3 gallons
(C) 5 gallons
(D) 6 gallons

6. The recipe calls for $\frac{3}{4}$ cup of ketchup and $\frac{1}{4}$ cup of vinegar. If you have only $\frac{1}{2}$ cup of ketchup, how many cups of vinegar should you use?

(A) $\frac{1}{6}$

(B) $\frac{1}{5}$

(C) $\frac{1}{4}$

(D) $\frac{1}{3}$

7. A prescription medication for flea control in dogs calls for a tablet that is 204 milligrams for a 50 pound dog. Which of the ways of equally dividing the tablet shown below would be closest to the right dosage for a 10 pound dog?

(A)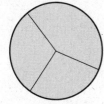

(B)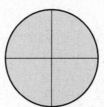

(C)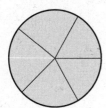

(D)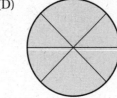

8. A catalog offers 950 milliliters of Diet Nectar for sale. In another catalog there is an ad for Diet Nectar, but it is given in liters. Which of the following shows how many liters would be comparable to the amount in the first catalog?

(A) 0.0950
(B) 0.950
(C) 95.0
(D) 950.0

9. Rita has selected drapery fabric whose width is perfect for her windows. She needs to buy enough fabric to make two panels, each 62" long with a 5" hem at the top and at the bottom. How many yards of fabric should she buy?

(A) 2
(B) 4
(C) 6
(D) 12

10. Each time zone in the United States is 1 hour different from each of its neighboring time zones. The most eastern zone (farthest on the right) is the latest of the zones shown on the map. When it is 8 P.M. in city A, what time is it in city B?

(A) 6 P.M.
(B) 7 P.M.
(C) 8 P.M.
(D) 9 P.M.

11. The label on a quart milk carton states that it contains 946 milliliters of milk. How many liters is this?

(A) 0.00946
(B) 0.0946
(C) 0.946
(D) 94,600

12. A bottle of vitamin C crystals states that there are 250 grams of crystals in the bottle and that 1 teaspoon equals 5,000 milligrams. How many teaspoonfuls are in the bottle?

(A) 10
(B) 20
(C) 50
(D) 100

13. A 1 pound box of chocolates contains 32 pieces of candy. How many calories are in each piece of candy if 1 ounce of candy has 100 calories?

(A) 25
(B) 50
(C) 75
(D) 100

14. An airplane flies at 30,000 feet. How many miles is this if there are 5,280 feet in one mile?

 (A) $(30,000)(5,280)$

 (B) $\dfrac{30,000}{5,280}$

 (C) $\dfrac{5,280}{30,000}$

 (D) $30,000 \times 1,760$

15. If gasoline prices go up 4 cents on the gallon, how much will that cost you yearly if you buy an average of 15 gallons of gasoline each week?

 (A) \$13.87
 (B) \$31.20
 (C) \$312.00
 (D) \$138.67

16. Stan reads the labels on pain killers:

 Regular strength:
     100 pills   \$5.00   325 mg

 Extra strength:
     100 pills   \$10.00   500 mg

 Which of these can you conclude from these labels?

 (A) Regular strength is the best buy.
 (B) Extra strength is the best buy.
 (C) They are the same value.
 (D) They cannot be compared.

17. Pineapple slices are stacked, one on top of the other, in the can. How many slices will fit in the can?

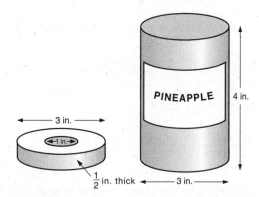

 (A) 6
 (B) 8
 (C) 10
 (D) 12

18. How many one quart containers would be needed to transport $2\frac{1}{2}$ gallons of gasoline?

(A) 5
(B) 7.5
(C) 10
(D) 15

19. A peanut butter label states the following:

2 tablespoons = 1 serving size
90 calories per serving

If your typical peanut butter sandwich has 2 teaspoons of peanut butter, how many calories of peanut butter is that?

(A) 30
(B) 60
(C) 90
(D) 120

Answers

1. **B** Since the distance is 1 quart, it would take 4 cups, as 4 cups are shown to equal 1 quart in the measurement table.

2. **A** The volume of the sack needs to be in milliliters, since the weight given for the gold has milliliters in it. Then the volume times the grams per volume gives the grams.

3. **B** 5.3 pounds $\times \dfrac{28 \text{ minutes}}{1 \text{ pound}} = 148$ minutes

   Because 120 minutes = 2 hours, 148 minutes equals 2 hours with 28 minutes left over.

4. **A** Working from 8:50 to 11:45 gives 2 hours 55 minutes, and working from 12:30 to 5:35 gives 5 hours 5 minutes, so the totoal is 7 hours 60 minutes, or 8 hours.

5. **C** There are 4 divisions in $\frac{1}{2}$ tank, so each mark represents $\frac{1}{8}$ tank. The amount is a little less than $\frac{3}{8}$ of 15, or about 5 gallons.

6. **A** You can use a proportion approach:

$$\frac{\frac{3}{4} \text{ cup ketchup}}{\frac{1}{4} \text{ cup vinegar}} = \frac{\frac{1}{2} \text{ cup ketchup}}{x \text{ cups vinegar}}$$

7. **C** Since 10 is $\frac{1}{5}$ of 50, the whole pill would need to be split into five parts.

8. **B** 950 milliliters $\times \dfrac{1 \text{ liter}}{1{,}000 \text{ milliliters}} = 0.950$ liters

9. **B** Each panel will need to be 72 inches long (the 62 inches of the drape plus 10 inches for the top and bottom hems). For two panels, that will mean 144 inches of fabric.

$$144 \text{ inches} \times \frac{1 \text{ yard}}{36 \text{ inches}} = 4 \text{ yards}$$

10. **A** The time zone for city B is 2 zones (hours) earlier than city A.

11. **C** $946 \text{ milliliters} \times \frac{1 \text{ liter}}{1{,}000 \text{ milliliters}} = 0.946 \text{ liters}$

12. **C** $250 \text{ grams} \times \frac{1{,}000 \text{ milligrams}}{1 \text{ gram}} \times \frac{1 \text{ teaspoon}}{5{,}000 \text{ mg}} = 50 \text{ teaspoons}$

13. **B** $\frac{1 \text{ box}}{32 \text{ pieces}} \times \frac{1 \text{ pound}}{1 \text{ box}} \times \frac{16 \text{ ounces}}{1 \text{ pound}} \times \frac{100 \text{ calories}}{1 \text{ ounce}} = 50 \text{ calories/piece}$

14. **B** $30{,}000 \text{ feet} \times \frac{1 \text{ mile}}{5{,}280 \text{ feet}}$

15. **B** $\frac{\$0.04}{1 \text{ gallon}} \times \frac{15 \text{ gallons}}{1 \text{ week}} \times \frac{52 \text{ weeks}}{1 \text{ year}} = \$31.20\text{/year}$

16. **A** You would have to pay twice as much for extra strength, but you would not get twice the milligrams. Since extra strength has no extra ingredients, just more of the painkiller, it is not as good a buy.

17. **B** Everything is information that you do not need except for two things—the thickness of the pineapple slice and the height of the can. You can fit 8 one-half inch slices into a four inch can.

18. **C** $2.5 \text{ gallons} \times \frac{4 \text{ quarts}}{1 \text{ gallon}} = 10 \text{ quarts}$

19. **A** $2 \text{ teaspoons} \times \frac{1 \text{ tablespoon}}{3 \text{ teaspoons}} \times \frac{90 \text{ calories}}{2 \text{ tablespoons}} = 30 \text{ calories}$

Geometry

6

On the GED® mathematics test, some of the questions will have a basis in geometry. The good news is that the test does not assume that you have done well in geometry in school, but rather that you can read about a situation, study a diagram about that situation, and come to correct conclusions. The focus of the GED® test is to see how well you can deal with everyday life situations that you will find at home, in the marketplace, and on the job.

The geometry ideas that you will need to be able to handle for the GED® exam are the following:

- lines and angles
- coordinates
- slope
- shapes, including rectangles, squares, triangles, circles, cubes, rectangular solids, and cylinders
- perimeter, area, and volume

LINES AND ANGLES

Everywhere you look, you see lines and angles. Lines define boundaries, mark highways, create pictures, form logos, make designs. Lines form angles in the corner of a room, the slope of the road, the direction the halfback runs with the ball.

Lines

The vocabulary of lines includes "horizontal," "vertical," and "parallel." If any of these words are unfamiliar to you, make index cards for them. The following diagram will help you to understand horizontal and vertical lines.

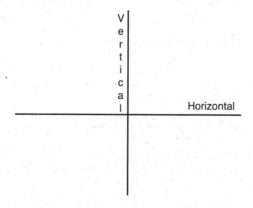

As you can see from the illustration above, a horizontal line is a line that runs across. You might remember it by relating it to the word "horizon," the line that is the boundary between Earth and sky. Since a vertical line runs up and down, you might link it in your mind to a basketball player's vertical leap.

Parallel lines are lines that are the same distance apart, no matter at which point they are measured. The yard markers on a football field are parallel lines. The 40-yard line is parallel to the 30-yard line; the 30-yard line is parallel to the goal line, and so on. It does not matter how far apart the lines are, as long as they would never meet, no matter how long they were extended.

In the rectangle below, the horizontal lines are parallel and the vertical lines are parallel. You will often see parallel lines designated this way:

$$AB \parallel CD$$
$$AC \parallel BD$$

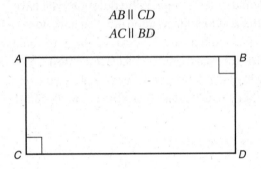

Practice

Examine the diagram and answer Questions 1–4.

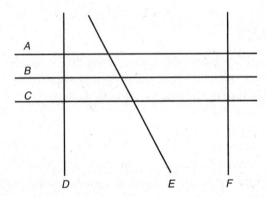

1. Which of the lettered lines are horizontal?

2. Which of the lettered lines are vertical?

3. Which of the lettered lines are parallel to line *B*?

4. Which of the lettered lines are parallel to line *F*?

5. Suppose that in giving directions, someone says that his home is on a road that runs parallel to the river. Which of the diagrams shown below reflects this statement?

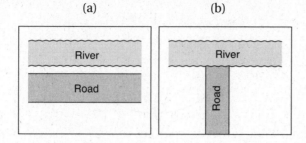

(a)   (b)

ANSWERS

1. *A, B, C*
2. *D, E*
3. *A, C*
4. *D*
5. (a)

Angles

Everywhere you look, angles come into view. Angles are formed where lines meet. The GED® test will not ask you to name angles, or to measure them, but rather to evaluate them and their relationship to everyday objects and events.

ANGLES AND THEIR MEASURE

Remembering that there are 360° (360 degrees) in a circle will help you picture various angles. Notice in the figure below that the circle is split into four parts, *A, B, C,* and *D*.

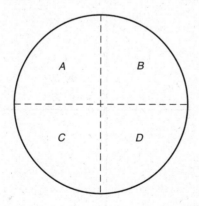

If you divide the 360° into four parts, you get four angles measuring 90° each.

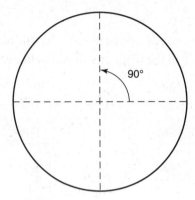

Once you can see a 90° angle in your mind, you can imagine a 45° angle by picturing half of the 90° angle.

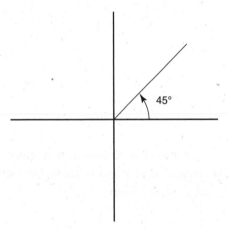

You can then picture a 30° angle and a 60° angle by imagining the 90° angle (also called a right angle) divided into thirds, as shown below.

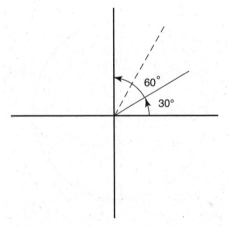

There is a special symbol, as shown below, to indicate a right angle.

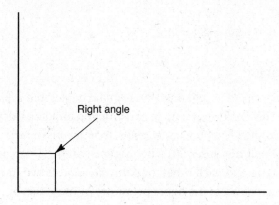

Right angle

As you learn more geometry, try to visualize the concepts. Whenever you can, draw a diagram to help you picture each relationship.

Practice

In each diagram below, there is an angle marked with an x. Find the number of degrees in each marked angle.

6.

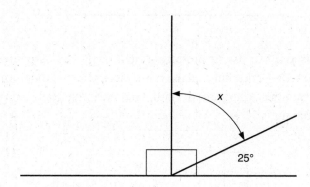

7.

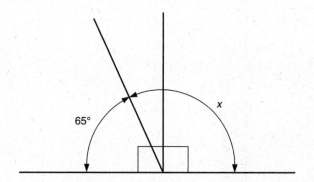

ANSWERS

6. 65°; 90° − 25° = 65°
7. 115°; 90° + (90° − 65°) = 90° + 25° = 115°

THE "SQUARE" ANGLE

There is a special angle, called a right angle or a square angle, that is especially important in the world around us. This angle shows up in constructing buildings, designing playing fields, making picture frames, and laying out street plans, to name just a few.

A right angle is one that measures 90°. The presence of the 90° angle makes the two lines that create the angle square to each other, or *perpendicular*. If two lines k and l are perpendicular to each other, as shown in the figure below, we indicate this by writing $k \perp l$.

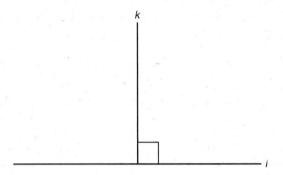

One of several tools you can use to produce a right angle is a carpenter's square, shown below, which is also called a framing square. It is a piece of metal that forms a 90° angle. It is handy for marking and measuring wood, cloth, floor covering, walls, and so on, and can be used to test for "squareness."

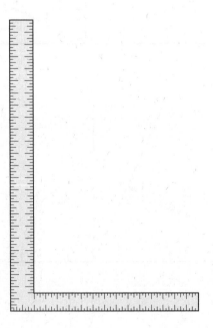

Practice

8. In the diagram below, the carpenter's square will guarantee that the door opening is square if all the corners are 90°. Draw what a corner would look like with the carpenter's square in it if the corner measured more than 90°, and therefore was not square.

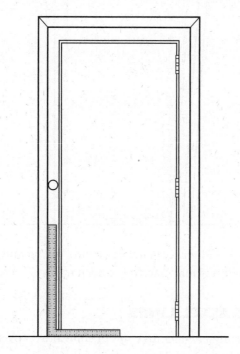

9. If a marching band were marching due east and their routine called for them to make three 90° turns in a clockwise direction, in which direction would they now be marching?

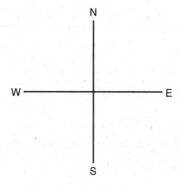

ANSWERS

8.

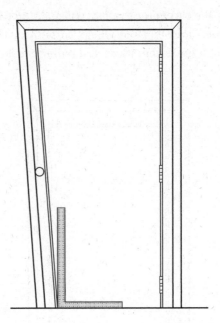

9. north; The first turn would make them head south; the second turn would make them head west; the third turn would make them head north

ANGLES AND PARALLEL LINES

If you were laying out a garden or a tennis court or some other space in which you wanted to have parallel lines, the idea illustrated below could help you.

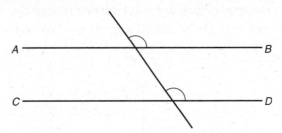

If you know that the angles marked with a ⌒ are equal to each other, then you know that line *AB* is parallel to line *CD*.

The same idea holds for other angle pairs formed by a line crossing two parallel lines. In the diagram below, you can be certain that line $\overline{AB}$ is parallel to line $\overline{CD}$ if any of the relationships shown is true (the symbol ∠ indicates an angle).

$$\angle x = \angle y \qquad \angle t = \angle u \qquad \angle r = \angle s$$

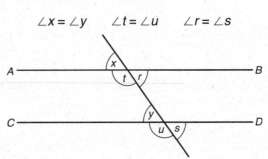

Practice

10. Which strategy illustrated below would guarantee that the spindles of a deck railing are parallel?

(a)

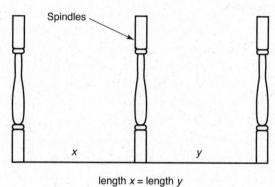

length *x* = length *y*

(b)

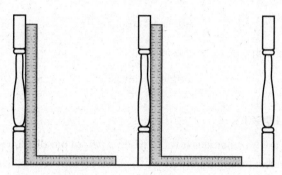

Use a carpenter square, which makes certain that the angles are 90°.

ANSWERS

10. (b); If you used choice (a), the spindles could look like this:

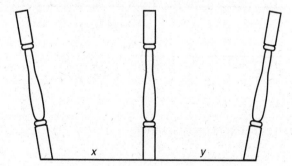

VERTICAL ANGLES

The number of degrees in angles can often be calculated by knowing about angles that are close by. Angles that lie directly across from each other are called vertical angles, and they are equal to each other. In the diagram below, angles a and c are equal to each other, and angles b and d are equal to each other.

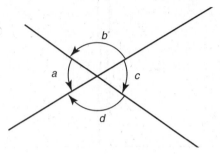

Angle b and angle d are across from each other and so they are vertical angles. Vertical angles are equal, so:

$$\text{angle } b = \text{angle } d$$

Angle a and angle c are also vertical angles, so:

$$\text{angle } a = \text{angle } c$$

CORRESPONDING ANGLES

Corresponding angles are those angles formed when a pair of parallel lines is cut by a third line, called a transversal. In the following diagram, the pairs of corresponding angles are a and b, c and d, e and f, and g and h.

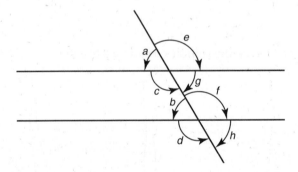

Corresponding angles are equal to each other.

Practice

Use the ideas of corresponding angles, vertical angles, square angles (90 degrees), and straight angles (180 degrees) to find the number of degrees in these angles.

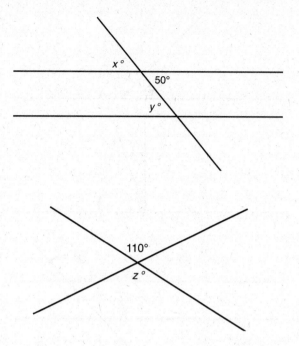

11. Angle $x =$

12. Angle $y =$

13. Angle $z =$

Recall that there are 90° in a right angle, and 180° in a straight angle. Identify the number of degrees in each of the lettered angles below.

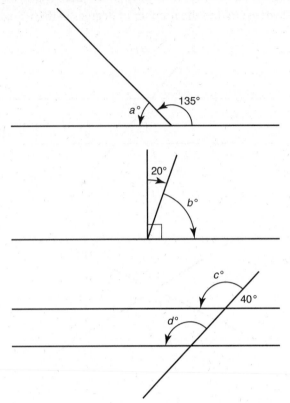

14. $a =$

15. $b =$

16. $c =$

17. $d =$

ANSWERS

11. Angle $x = 50°$ because angle x and 50° are vertical angles
12. Angle $y = 50°$ because angles y and x are equal (corresponding angles are equal)
13. Angle $z = 110°$ because it is a vertical angle with 110°
14. 45°, because 45 + 135 = 180° (straight line)
15. 70°, because 90 − 20 = 70°
16. 40°, because 180 − 140 = 40°
17. 140°, because c and d are corresponding angles

COORDINATES

In the figure below, which shows the *coordinate plane*, the horizontal line is called the *x*-axis and the vertical line is called the *y*-axis. Notice that each axis divides the other into positive and negative numbers. The positive *x*-values are to the right of the *y*-axis, and the positive *y*-values are above the *x*-axis. The negative *x*-values are to the left of *y*-axis, and the negative *y*-values are below the *x*-axis. This arrangement is standard practice and should be memorized if you do not already know it. The point where the *x*-axis and the *y*-axis meet is called the origin. The *x*- and *y*-axis values there are both zero.

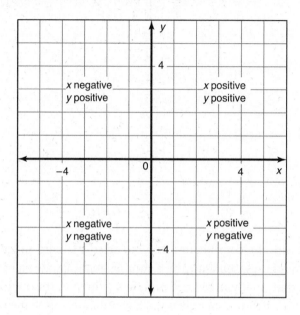

Practice

18. Sketch the *x*-axis shown below, and place each letter next to the point that it represents.

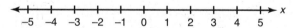

$A = -5$

$B = 3$

$C = 4$

$D = -2$

19. Sketch the *y*-axis shown below, and place each letter next to the point that it represents.

$E = -2$ $\qquad\qquad$ $F = 2$ $\qquad\qquad$ $G = 0$ $\qquad\qquad$ $H = -3$

When working with the coordinate plane, it is also standard practice to use a pair of numbers in parentheses, separated by a comma, to designate values for *x* and *y*. The *x* is always given first, so if you see two numbers written in this manner, such as (–3, 5), this means that the first number gives the *x*-coordinate, or the measurement along the *x*-axis, and the second number gives the *y*-coordinate, or the measurement along the *y*-axis. To find the location for the point with coordinates (–3, 5) travel on the *x*-axis three spaces to the left of zero (you go left because you are locating negative 3), and then travel up five spaces (you would have gone down if the five had been a negative 5). The location of (–3, 5) is shown on the coordinate plane below.

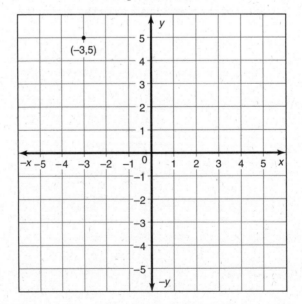

20. Give the coordinates in the form (x, y) for each of the points labeled on the coordinate plane below.

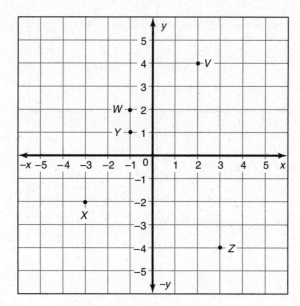

ANSWERS

18.

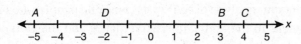

19.

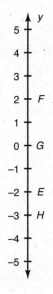

20.

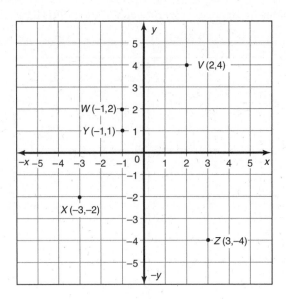

SHAPES

Some of the shapes that dominate our world are squares, rectangles, triangles, circles, cubes, rectangular solids, and cylinders. To get your mind accustomed to thinking geometrically, take a visual tour of your home to see where these shapes are. As you do this, you will be laying the foundation for your analysis of GED questions. The people who make the GED® test look for geometry ideas in the home, the marketplace, and the workplace when they write questions. Becoming more aware of the geometry all around you will help you be ready for these questions.

Squares

Squares have four sides that all have the same length. Every angle in a square is a right angle, or 90° angle.

Rectangles

Rectangles have four sides, all meeting at right angles. Each pair of opposite sides has the same length. No matter how a rectangle is turned, the longer sides are the length, and the shorter sides are the width.

Triangles

Triangles have three sides. The properties of triangles are so useful for GED topics that a detailed analysis of triangles follows.

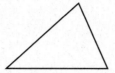

Circles

Circles are collections of all the points that are the same distance, called the radius, from a given point, called the center.

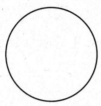

Cylinders

Perhaps the most familiar cylinder is the soft drink can. A cylinder can be thought of as a stack of circles, as the circle defines many of the mathematical properties of cylinders.

TRIANGLES

Although everyone knows what a triangle is, not everyone knows the special things about triangles that make them extremely useful in matters from home improvement projects to laying out quilting designs.

A right triangle is one that has one 90° angle in it, like the triangle shown below. You can recognize a right triangle by looking to see that one of the angles looks like the angle that the wall of a room makes with the floor or ceiling.

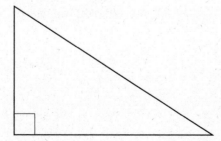

Some special right triangles that are very useful are shown below.

Notice that the total number of degrees in both the 45°, 45°, 90° triangle and the 30°, 60°, 90° triangle is 180°. It turns out that this is true not just for these triangles, but for *all* triangles. That is, the total number of degrees in the angles of a triangle is always 180.

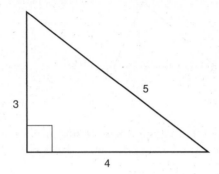

The 3, 4, 5 right triangle

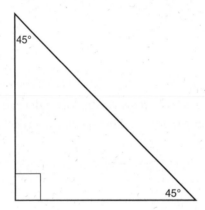

The 45°, 45°, 90° right triangle

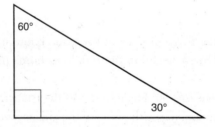

The 30°, 60°, 90° right triangle

Practice

For each triangle below, calculate the number of degrees in the angle marked *x*:

21.

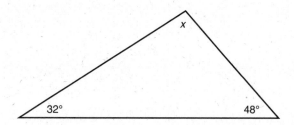

22.

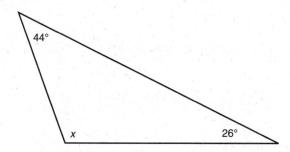

23.

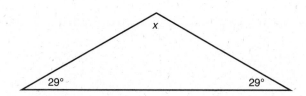

Decide whether each of the following statements is true or false:

24. If two angles of a triangle add up to 90°, the third angle will have to be 90°.

25. The bigger the triangle is, the larger the sum of its angles.

26. If you know the number of degrees in one angle, you can find the other two angles.

27. If you wanted to create a quilting piece with angles of 45°, 90°, and 90°, it could not be a triangle.

Suppose you need to make some kind of device for drawing 90° angles using a pencil, a ruler, scissors, and cardboard. Decide whether each of the following will work:

28. Make a triangle with two equal angles. The remaining angle will be a 90° angle.

29. Draw a triangle with a 3 inch side and a 4 inch side.

30. Use a corner in one room of the house as a guide.

31. Draw a triangle with a 3 inch side and a 4 inch side, and adjust the triangle until the remaining side is 5 inches.

ANSWERS

21. 100°; 180° − 32° − 48° = 100°
22. 110°; 180° − 44° − 26° = 110°
23. 122°; 180° − 29° − 29° = 122°
24. true; 180° − 90° = 90°
25. false; The sum of all angles of any triangle is 180°.
26. false; You can find the *total* of the other two angles, but not the angles separately.
27. true; These angles total 225°, which is not possible in a triangle.
28. no; For example, if the two equal angles are each 20°, then the third angle equals 180° − 40° = 140°
29. no; a 3 inch side and a 4 inch side won't assure that the other side will be a 5 inch side, creating a right triangle.
30. no; You can't count on walls and floors to be perfectly square.
31. yes; a 3, 4, 5 triangle is always a right triangle.

THE PYTHAGOREAN RELATIONSHIP

Pythagoras was an early mathematician who discovered something very useful about right triangles. He found that if you take a right triangle, such as the one below, the equation shown is always true:

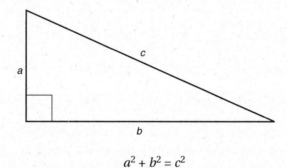

$$a^2 + b^2 = c^2$$

That is, if you square the lengths of each of the sides that form the right angle, and then add the squares, their sum equals the squares of the length of the side across from the right angle. The sides that form the 90° angle (*a* and *b*) are called the legs, and the side opposite the 90° angle (*c*) is called the hypotenuse. This special right triangle relationship is called the Pythagorean relationship.

> ## WARNING!
> Problems involving the Pythagorean relationship are the most frequently missed questions on the math section of the GED® test. You should be certain that you work hard to master this topic.

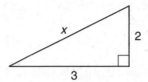

1. Calculate x using the Pythagorean relationship.

x^2	$=$	3^2	$+$	2^2
x^2	$=$	9	$+$	4
x	$=$	$\sqrt{13}$		
x	$=$	3.60		

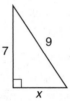

2. Calculate the length of x.

9^2	$=$	7^2	$+$	x^2
$9^2 - 7^2$	$=$	x^2		
$81 - 49$	$=$	x^2		
$\sqrt{32}$	$=$	x		
5.66	$=$	x		

Practice

32. Use the Pythagorean relationship to find the length of the hypotenuse in the triangle below.

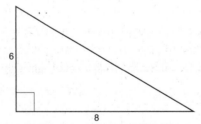

33. Solve for x.

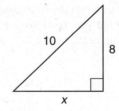

34. Solve for x.

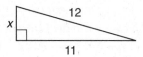

35. Solve for x.

ANSWERS

32. 10; $a^2 + b^2 = 6^2 + 8^2 = 36 + 64 = 100$, so $c^2 = 100$, which is true for $c = 10$.

33.
a^2	$+$	b^2	$=$	c^2
8^2	$+$	x^2	$=$	10^2
64	$+$	x^2	$=$	100
		x^2	$=$	$100 - 64 = 36$
		x	$=$	6

34.
a^2	$+$	b^2	$=$	c^2
11^2	$+$	x^2	$=$	12^2
		x^2	$=$	$144 - 121 = 23$
		x	$=$	4.8

35.
a^2	$+$	b^2	$=$	c^2
5^2	$+$	6^2	$=$	x^2
25	$+$	36	$=$	x^2
		61	$=$	x^2
		7.81	$=$	x

CONGRUENT TRIANGLES

Congruent is a fancy word that basically means the same size and shape. If you were trying to decide if two triangles are congruent, imagine that you cut out a pattern of one of the triangles. If you can turn that pattern to make it fit perfectly on top of the other triangle, the two triangles are congruent.

For example, the triangles below could be turned to fit each other perfectly, so they are congruent.

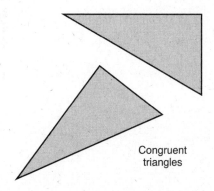

Congruent
triangles

You might ask what good it is to know that triangles are congruent. The idea is most often used as a way to find distances or angles that you cannot measure directly. For example, if you wanted to know the distance between the two sides of the canyon in the diagram below, it would certainly be nice if you did not have to measure that distance directly. You can lay out a congruent triangle over the land that is easy to measure, so you can indirectly measure the canyon width.

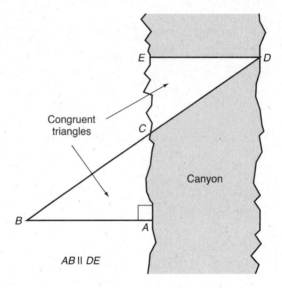

Practice

Use the preceding figure to answer questions 36 and 37.

36. Which side in triangle *ABC* corresponds to the distance across the canyon?

37. For the two triangles to be congruent, which side would have to be the same length as side $\overline{CA}$?

ANSWERS

36. side $\overline{AB}$

37. side $\overline{EC}$

SIMILAR TRIANGLES

Two triangles are similar if you could take a picture of one triangle and either enlarge or shrink the picture to fit the second triangle. The triangle on the left below could be reduced to get the triangle on the right, so they are similar.

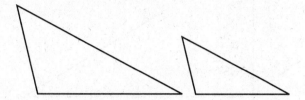

Similar triangles are useful, once again, for indirect measurement. You can set up a ratio between two similar triangles in order to solve for the distance or angle that you are looking for. The only thing you have to watch is that you really do compare similar parts.

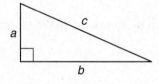 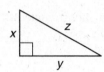

These are similar triangles, so we can say:

$$\frac{a}{c} = \frac{x}{z}$$

Suppose that $a = 4$, $b = 6$, and $y = 3$, then:

$$\frac{4}{2} = \frac{x}{3}$$
$$12 = 2x$$
$$6 = x$$

As an example, look at the following diagram. It would be no easy job to find the height of the tree directly. Similar triangles can help. Triangle ABC is just a smaller version of triangle ADE. Because they are similar, the ratio of each side of the larger triangle to the corresponding side of the smaller triangle is the same. This gives the following relationship:

$$\frac{DE}{BC} = \frac{DA}{BA} = \frac{EA}{CA}$$

Notice also that the two triangles have the same angles.

Practice

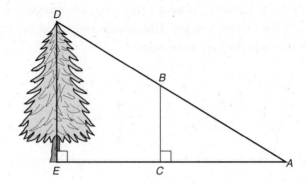

38. What three letters define the larger triangle in the diagram above?

_____, _____, and _____

39. What line in the smaller triangle *ABC* can be compared to the height of the tree in the larger triangle *ADE*? _____

40. Complete this proportion.

$$\frac{DE}{BC} = \frac{EA}{?}$$

? = _____

41. Calculate the height of the tree shown above from these measurements:

EA = 40 feet
BC = 6 feet
CA = 8 feet

ANSWERS

38. *ADE*
39. Line *BC*
40. Line *CA*
41. 30 ft; The height of the tree is *DE*, so use the proportion $\frac{DE}{BC} = \frac{EA}{CA}$, or $\frac{DE}{6} = \frac{40}{8}$.

Cross multiplying gives 8(*DE*) = 240, so *DE* = 30 feet.

Circles

From automobile tires to cake pans, circles play a large part in our everyday lives. The parts of a circle are terms that you need to memorize if you do not already know them. These parts are the *circumference*, the *radius*, and the *diameter*, as shown below. If you have difficulty remembering any of these terms, make a note card for your study.

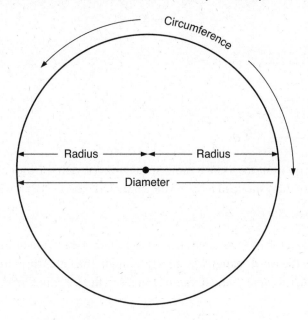

Formulas that you will need about circles:

π = 3.14

c = πd where c = circumference and d = diameter

A = πr^2 where A = area and r = radius

Practice

Use the circle in this diagram to answer Questions 42–44.

42. $r =$ _____

43. $d =$ _____

44. $c =$ _____

Use the circle in this diagram to answer Questions 45–47.

45. $d =$ _____

46. $c =$ _____

47. $r =$ _____

48. Suppose that you want to install a radio speaker in the door of your automobile. The instructions say that you need a hole with a 5 inch diameter. What will be the radius of this hole?

49. Wire is manufactured in sizes ranging from as thin as a thread to quite thick. The size is described by the word "gauge." Strangely enough, the fatter the wire, the smaller the gauge. Knowing this, match the different gauges to the letter of the wire to which it must correspond.

Gauge of Wire	Diameter of Wire
24	A: 13.1 mm
18	B: 5.2 mm
12	C: 7.0 mm

ANSWERS

42. $r = \dfrac{1}{2} d = 5$

43. $d = 10$

44. $c = 3.14 \times 10 = 31.4$

45. $d = 2r = 2 \times 3 = 6$

46. $c = \pi d = 3.14 \times 6 = 18.84$

47. $r = 3$

48. $2\dfrac{1}{2}$ in.; The radius is half of the diameter.

49. 24 corresponds to B, 18 to C, and 12 to A, since 24 gauge is the thinnest wire and 12 gauge is the thickest.

Cylinders

This is a cylinder:

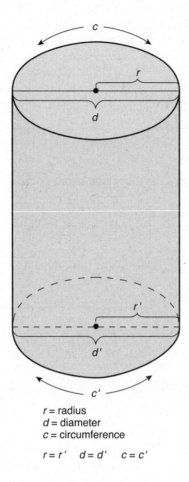

r = radius
d = diameter
c = circumference

$r = r'$ $d = d'$ $c = c'$

The top and bottom of cylinders are circles, so you can describe a cylinder using radius, diameter, and circumference. Familiar cylinders include soup cans, prescription bottles, and a roll of candy.

Since cylinders are usually containers, the volume of a cylinder is a frequent consideration. The topic of volume will be taken up later in the chapter.

USING SHAPES

Perimeter

Perimeter is the total distance around something. For example, the total length of a fence gives the perimeter of the field or lawn. So, for a straight-sided shape, you just add the lengths of each side to find the perimeter.

➡ EXAMPLES

1. To calculate the perimeter of the following diagram, add the lengths of all sides.

$$P = 5 + 8 + 5 + 15 + 10 + 23 = 66$$

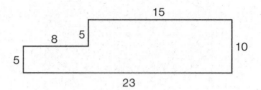

2. To find the perimeter of this diagram, you first need to know the lengths of x and y.

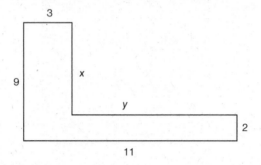

Examining the diagram shows:

x	+	2	=	9
		x	=	7
y	+	3	=	11
		y	=	8

Now the perimeter equals

$$9 + 3 + 7 + 8 + 2 + 11 = 40$$

Practice

50. Calculate the perimeter of the diagram below:

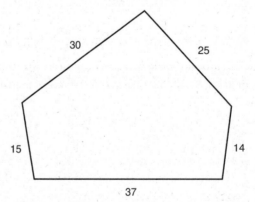

51. Wallpaper borders are decorative strips of wallpaper used to improve the appearance of a room. They are customarily pasted at the top of the wall. After studying the diagram below, how many feet of wallpaper border would you need for the room?

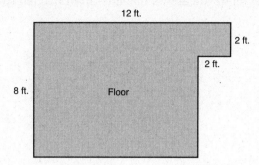

52. Calculate the perimeter of this figure.

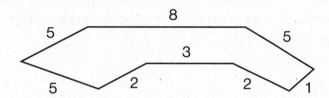

53. Calculate the perimeter of this circle. Recall that circumference is the perimeter of a circle.

ANSWERS

50. 121 ft; 15 + 30 + 25 + 14 + 37 = 121
51. On this diagram there are two unknown lengths to find, 8 – 2 = 6 and 12 – 2 = 10.

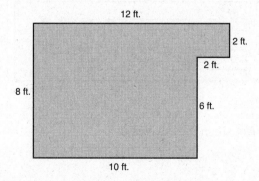

Perimeter = 40; (8 + 12 + 2 + 2 + 6 + 10)
52. $P = 5 + 8 + 5 + 1 + 2 + 3 + 2 + 5 = 31$
53. $P = c = \pi d = 3.14 \times 14 = 43.96$

Area

Area is a term frequently encountered in geometry applications. If you imagine that you are painting the floor of the room you are in, the amount of painted surface is the area of the surface.

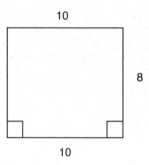

10

8

10

If the above diagram represents the floor that you are painting, to find the area of that floor, you multiply the length by the width. That makes the area 8 times 10, which equals 80.

area = length × width

$A = 10 \times 8$

$A = 80$

The units of area are square units, so the floor has an area of 80 square units. If the floor had been measured in feet, the 80 would be called "square feet." The reason for that is that if you could imagine that you were installing tile on the floor and each tile were a square one foot on each side, you could place 80 of these tiles on the floor. You would have 80 square feet of tile.

The idea of area comes up in a large variety of everyday uses, including how much paint to buy, how many bags of lawn fertilizer to spread on your lawn, how much fabric you need for drapes…the list goes on and on.

Practice

Suppose your house and yard have the dimensions and shape shown below.

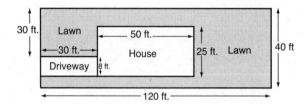

54. How many square feet are in the driveway?

55. How many square feet does the house sit on?

56. How many square feet are in the lawn?

ANSWERS

54. 240; 30 × 8 = 240
55. 1,250; 50 × 25 = 1,250
56. 3,310; The area of the lawn is the area of the entire lot minus the area of the dirveway minus the area of the house. This gives (120 × 40) – 240 – 1,250 = 4,800 – 1,490 = 3,310.

AREA OF A CIRCLE

When you want to compare sizes of pizza, you are considering the area of a circle. Finding the area of a circle is a little bit different from finding the area of a square or a rectangle. You must use a formula. The formula follows:

$$A = \pi r^2, \text{ where } A = \text{area}, \pi \approx 3.14, \text{ and } r = \text{radius}$$

You should practice using this formula until you are very comfortable using it.

➡ **EXAMPLES** _____

1. Calculate the area of the circle in this diagram.

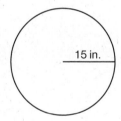

15 in.

$A = \pi r^2$
$A = 3.14\,(15)(15)$
$A = 706.5$ square inches

2. Calculate the area of this circle.

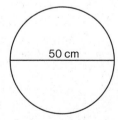

50 cm

$A = \pi r^2$
$A = 3.14\,(25)(25)$
$A = 1,962.5$ square centimeters

Practice

57. Find the area of the circle shown below. Remember that the units of area are square units.

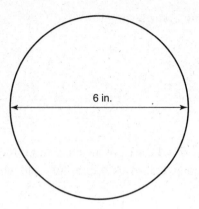

6 in.

58. Find the area of the circle shown below.

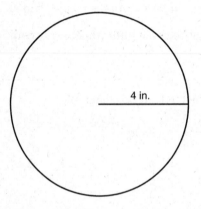

4 in.

ANSWERS

57. $A = \pi$ times radius squared
    $A = (3.14)(3)(3)$
    $A = 28.26$ square inches
58. $A = \pi$ times radius squared
    $A = (3.14)(4)(4)$
    $A = 50.24$ square inches

AREA OF A TRIANGLE

The formula for the area of a triangle is given on the formula page as:

$$A = \frac{1}{2} \times \text{base} \times \text{height}$$

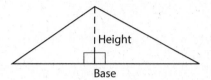

Base

Height

The base is the longest side of the triangle. The height is the distance from the base to the vertex opposite the base.

➡ **EXAMPLE**

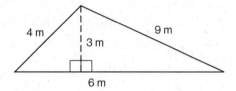

4 m   3 m   9 m

6 m

$$A = \frac{1}{2} \text{(base)(height)}$$

$$A = \frac{1}{2} \text{(6 meters)(3 meters)}$$

$$A = 9 \text{ square meters}$$

Practice

59. Calculate the area of this triangle:

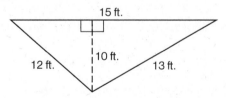

15 ft.

10 ft.

12 ft.   13 ft.

60. Calculate the area of this triangle:

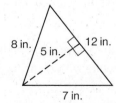

8 in.   5 in.   12 in.

7 in.

59. $A = \dfrac{1}{2}$ (15 ft.)(10 ft.)

   $A = 75$ square feet

60. $A = \dfrac{1}{2}$ (12 in.)(5 in.)

   $A = 30$ square inches

Volume

The volume of a three-dimensional shape describes how much space it takes up, or how much it could hold if it were a hollow container. For example, if you were comparing the volume of a basketball with the volume of a soccer ball, you could visualize pouring each one full of water and measuring which one held the most.

Volume measurements are given in *cubic* units. They could be cubic centimeters (as in car engine descriptions), cubic feet (as in refrigerator size), or cubic yards (used in ordering concrete), to name a few.

You can picture a cubic foot like this:

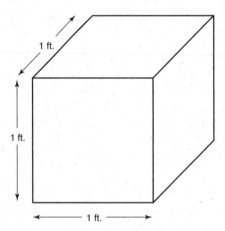

If you were to buy a 15 cubic foot refrigerator, the refrigerator would hold as much as you could put in 15 of the cubes above. Notice that the cube above has the same measurements on each of its sides.

Practice

61. Lake Baikal in Russia contains the largest volume of fresh water in the world. It does this even though it does not have nearly the surface area (the part you could see from flying over it) as the Great Lakes of the United States. Which of the following is a conclusion that you could logically draw from just this information?

   (A) Lake Baikal must be spring fed to have so much fresh water.
   (B) Lake Baikal must have a shoreline with many bays and inlets.
   (C) Lake Baikal must be extremely deep.
   (D) The Great Lakes empty into the nearby ocean.

ANSWER

61. 3; If two containers, for example, cylinders, have the same size top, then for one to hold more it must be deeper, so the depth must be greater for Lake Baikal to have a larger volume.

VOLUME OF A RECTANGULAR SOLID

Anything you can think of that is shaped like a shoe box is a rectangular solid and has a volume that can be found by using this formula:

Volume = length × width × height

or

$$V = l \times w \times h$$

If you measure the three different dimensions and multiply them together, you have found the volume. It really does not matter what you call these three sides, as long as you measure three different dimensions. These dimensions are customarily called length, width, and height.

To find the volume of the rectangular solid shown below, substitute $l = 20$, $w = 8$, and $h = 5$ into the formula to obtain $V = (20)(8)(5) = 800$ cubic units.

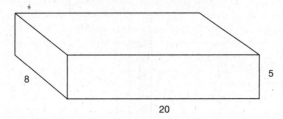

➡ **EXAMPLE** _____

Calculate the volume of this object.

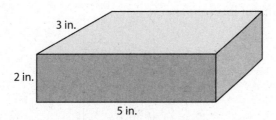

V = length × width × height
V = (5 in.)(3 in.)(2 in.)
V = 30 cubic inches

Practice

62. Concrete is sold by the cubic yard, usually referred to simply as "yards." It is the amount of concrete that would fill a box that is 1 yard long on each of its sides. Suppose you wanted to pour a concrete driveway and parking area as shown below, to a depth of 3 inches ($\frac{1}{12}$ of a yard). How many yards of concrete would you need to order?

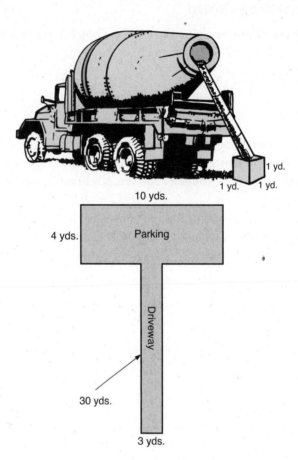

63. Calculate the volume of this container.

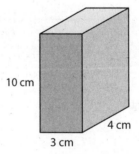

64. Calculate the volume of this container.

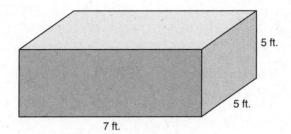

ANSWER

62. 10.8; Split the figure into two rectangles as shown below.

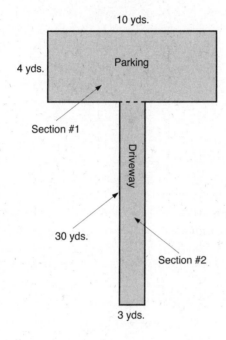

Section # 1

$V = $ (length)(width)(height)

$V = (10)(4)(\frac{1}{12})$

$V = 3.33$

Section # 2

$V = $ (length)(width)(height)

$V = (30)(3)(\frac{1}{12})$

$V = 7.5$

The total of the two sections is about 10.8 cubic yards.

63. $V = (4 \text{ cm})(3 \text{ cm})(10 \text{ cm})$

    $V = 120$ cubic centimeters

64. $V = (7 \text{ feet})(5 \text{ feet})(5 \text{ feet})$

    $V = 175$ cubic feet

Remember that you will have a sheet of formulas for your use. On that sheet is this formula for the volume of a cylinder.

$$V = \pi(r^2)(h)$$

➡ **EXAMPLE** _____

Calculate the volume of this cylinder.

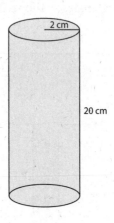

$V = \pi(2 \text{ cm})(2 \text{ cm})(20 \text{ cm})$

$V = 251.2$ cubic centimeters

Practice

65. Calculate the volume of this cylinder.

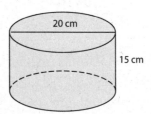

66. Calculate the volume of this cylinder.

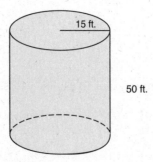

ANSWERS

65. $V = \pi(r^2)(h)$

    $V = 3.14\ (10\ \text{cm})(10\ \text{cm})(15\ \text{cm})$

    $V = 4{,}710$ cubic centimeters

66. $V = \pi(r^2)(h)$

    $V = 3.14\ (15\ \text{feet})(15\ \text{feet})(50\ \text{feet})$

    $V = 35{,}325$ cubic feet

END OF CHAPTER PRACTICE

This practice set is in the same format that you will see on the GED® test. The questions are meant to help you practice the skills that you have worked on in this chapter. Try to answer the questions without looking back in the chapter. Mark the ones for which you have to look back for help. This will help you know where to concentrate your studying.

1. After studying the figure below, decide which of the statements is true.

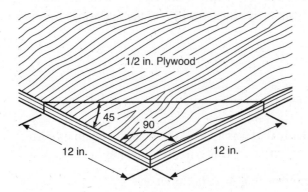

(A) The one angle with no degrees listed will be a 45° angle.

(B) A triangle with two sides equally long will always have two 45° angles.

(C) Two equally long triangle sides will guarantee that the angle between them is a 90° angle.

(D) The two equally long sides must be parallel.

2. Cereal boxes frequently have a statement that says, "This product is sold by weight, not by volume. Contents may have settled during shipment." Which of the following choices reflects the meaning of that cereal statement?

(A) When the cereal gets wet, its volume gets smaller.

(B) The volume can get smaller without affecting the quantity of cereal.

(C) Volume and weight measure the same things.

(D) The density of the cereal would get smaller as the volume shrinks.

Use the information in this passage to answer questions 3 and 4.

The following is a diagram of an automobile tire. On the sidewall of the tire there is information printed. All tires follow the same general organization of this information.

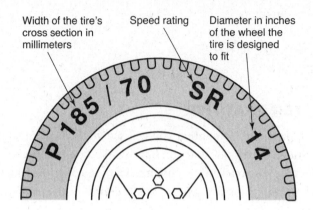

3. When the tire has rolled through one full rotation, the distance it has traveled on the ground is approximately equal to which of the following?

   (A) area
   (B) radius
   (C) diameter
   (D) circumference

4. If you bought a tire that was a size P 195/70 SR 14 when its correct size should have been a size P 185/70 SR 13, which of the following would happen?

   (A) The tire would be too big to fit the wheel.
   (B) The tire would be too small to fit the wheel.
   (C) There would be less contact with the road surface.
   (D) The circumference of the incorrect size would be too small.

5. Which of the following choices is *not* about perimeter?

   (A) The border of a state.
   (B) The double line in the center of the highway.
   (C) The circumference of a circle.
   (D) The shoreline of a lake.

6. On the back of a box of cake mix, the directions include what size pan to use. Suppose the box suggests an 8 inch by 8 inch pan. You try that and your cake turns out well and is $2\frac{1}{2}$ inches high. Approximately how high will the cake be in a 9 inch by 9 inch pan?

   (A) 1 inch
   (B) $1\frac{1}{2}$ inches
   (C) 2 inches
   (D) $2\frac{1}{2}$ inches

7. A ship leaves port and sails 6 miles west. It then sails 6 miles south, and then 6 miles west again. Approximately how many miles is it from port?

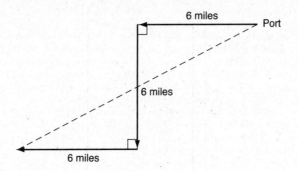

   (A) 9
   (B) 11
   (C) 13
   (D) 15

Use the following diagram as you answer questions 8 and 9.

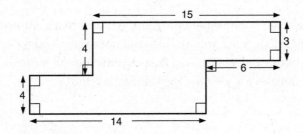

8. What is the perimeter shown in the diagram?

   (A) 46
   (B) 51
   (C) 55
   (D) 56

9. What is the area (in square units) shown in the diagram?

   (A) 106
   (B) 110
   (C) 116
   (D) 160

10. If you had a cylinder with the dimensions shown in the diagram, what would be the volume?

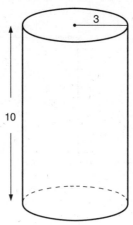

(A) $V = (3.14)(3)(2)(10)$
(B) $V = (3.14)(9)(10)$
(C) $V = (3.14)(3)(100)$
(D) $V = (3.14)(4)(10)$

11. In listening to a home improvement program, you hear that a correctly installed roof has a certain angle to it. Since you would prefer not to climb on the roof, you take a picture of your house and label it as in the diagram. You can measure angle y. Which of the following strategies will give you the value for angle x?

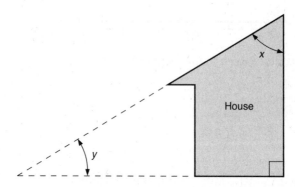

(A) $x = y$
(B) $x = 90 - y$
(C) $x = 180 - y$
(D) $x = \dfrac{1}{2} y$

12. What are the coordinates of point P?

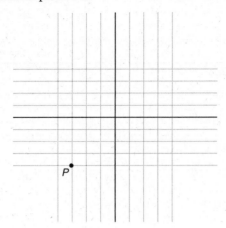

(A) –3,–4

(B) 3, 4

(C) –4, –3

(D) 4, 3

13. Calculate the value of x in the following diagram. Note that a calculator will be allowed for problems like this.

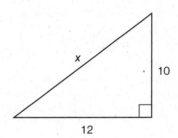

(A) 15.62

(B) 15.00

(C) 14.00

(D) 10.95

14. Calculate the circumference of this circle.

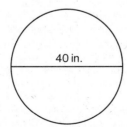

(A) 20 inches

(B) 62.8 inches

(C) 125.6 inches

(D) 1256 inches

15. How many degrees are in angle *g*?

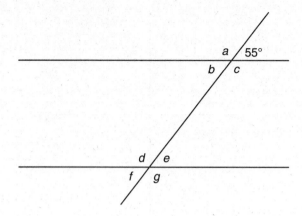

(A) 90 degrees
(B) 125 degrees
(C) 135 degrees
(D) 180 degrees

16. Calculate the area of this triangle.

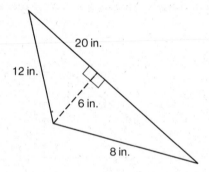

(A) (12)(8)(20)

(B) $\left(\frac{1}{2}\right)(8)(12)$

(C) $\left(\frac{1}{2}\right)(20)(8)$

(D) $\left(\frac{1}{2}\right)(20)(6)$

Answers

1. **A** The sum of the angles of a triangle is 180°, so 180 – 45 – 90 = 45.

2. **B** The cereal manufacturer is saying that the weight will not be changed, even if the amount of cereal looks smaller.

3. **D** The tire rolls on its outer border, which is its circumference, because the tire is circular.

4. **A** Since the 14 is the diameter of the tire, the tire would be too big to fit a wheel that is only 13" in diameter.

5. **B** This is the only choice that doesn't measure the distance around the border of something.

6. **C** The volume of cake batter in the 9" pan will be the same as in the 8" pan. You can then equate the two volumes; letting x represent the height in the 9" pan:

    Volume in 8" pan = Volume in 9" pan

    $$(8)(8)(2\tfrac{1}{2}) = (9)(9)(x)$$
    $$160 = 81x$$
    $$1.975 = x$$

    Since the answers are listed as approximate values, the 2 inches would be closest.

7. **C** The dotted line is found by applying the Pythagorean relationship. Half of the dotted line would be the square root of $6^2 + 3^2$, or about 6.7. Doubling this gives about 13.

8. **D** The missing horizontal segment has length 5 because the total length across the upper horizontal segments must equal the total length along the lower horizontal segments, and 5 + 15 = 14 + 6. Likewise, the missing vertical segment has length 5 because 5 + 3 = 4 + 4.
    Starting in the bottom left corner and traveling clockwise gives Perimeter = 4 + 5 + 4 + 15 + 3 + 6 + 5 + 14 = 56.

9. **B** Look at the diagram below:

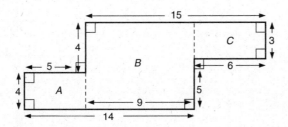

    Total area = area of section "A" + area of section "B" + area of section "C"

    Area = (5)(4) + (9)(8) + (6)(3)

    So, Area = 20 + 72 + 18 = 110 sq. units.

10. **B** The formula for the volume of a cylinder will be given on the GED® test. It is $V = \pi r^2 h$, where r is the radius and h the height.
    So, $V = (3.14)(3)(3)(10)$, since $(3)(3) = 9$.

11. **B** Remember that the total of the angles in a triangle is 180°. So, x will be $180 - 90 - y$ (the 90 came from the little box in the bottom right-hand corner that stands for 90°). Subtract the 90 from 180, giving the final answer $90 - y$.

12. **A** The x-coordinate is –3, because P lies 3 spaces to the left of the y-axis. The y-coordinate is –4 because P lies 4 units below the x-axis.

13. **A** The is a Pythagorean problem because it is a right triangle and you are looking for the hypotenuse. From the formula page:

$$
\begin{array}{rcl}
a^2 \quad + \quad b^2 & = & c^2 \\
10^2 \quad + \quad 12^2 & = & c^2 \\
100 \quad + \quad 144 & = & c^2 \\
244 & = & c^2 \\
15.62 & = & c
\end{array}
$$

14. **C** The circumference is found by:

$$C = \pi d$$
$$C = 3.14 \times 40 \text{ in.}$$
$$C = 125.6 \text{ in.}$$

15. **B** There are several ways to go about this question. For example, angle $e = 55$ degrees because angle e is a corresponding angle. Then angle g would be $180 - 55 = 125$, because angles e and g make up a straight line, which is 180 degrees.

16. **D** The base is the longest side, so $b = 20$ inches. The height is the distance from the base to the opposite vertex, so $h = 6$ inches. Then substituting in the triangle area formula:

$$A = \frac{1}{2}(\text{base})(\text{height})$$

$$A = \frac{1}{2}(20 \text{ inches})(6 \text{ inches})$$

Data Analysis, Statistics, and Probability

7

Data analysis combines common sense and math skills. One of the most common forms of data analysis that you do every day is evaluating advertisements. Whenever you first see an ad for something that interests you, you analyze the content of the ad. For example, suppose that a store is having a "buy one . . . get one free" deal on a product that you like. The analysis that you do is to find out the price of the one you have to buy. If the price is twice the normal price, then the deal is not a deal at all, but just a come-on. So you can see that data analysis is an everyday event and one with which you have practice. In this chapter you will learn how to analyze data in graphs, tables, and statistics.

GRAPHS

Graphs are found in the daily newspaper, on TV—even in the booklet that you get from the IRS for filing your tax return. You have heard that a picture is worth a thousand words—this is very true for the picture that is a graph. It is a way of telling the reader a lot of information in a picture format. There are three basic kinds of graphs that you will work with here: the line graph, the bar graph, and the pie graph.

AXES

Line graphs and bar graphs have two axes, which are the horizontal and vertical lines that tell you how to read the graph and give you its scale. The axis that runs up and down is called the y-axis. The axis that runs across is called the x-axis. These axes are always labeled so that the reader will know what they represent.

Line Graphs

Line graphs are generally used to show a change in measurement. When you examine a line graph—for example, the jagged line that shows the ups and downs of the stock market—it helps to follow the mental steps detailed below. Try this as you examine the line graph that follows these steps.

Step One: Read the words written along the x- and the y-axes.
Step Two: Study the numbers, or scales, along the two axes.
Step Three: Form an idea in your mind of what the graph is showing.

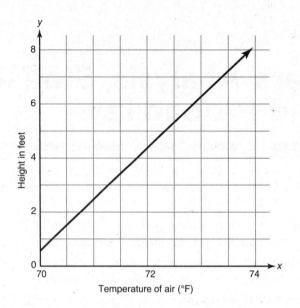

Temperature of air (°F)

Applying these steps to the preceding graph, the words along the *x*-axis explain that we are measuring the temperature of the air. The words along the *y*-axis explain that we are also measuring the height above the floor. The numbers on the *x*-axis let us know that the temperature range is from 70° to 74°. The numbers on the *y*-axis let us know that the heights range from 0 feet to 8 feet.

Now, to decide what the graph is showing, notice that the line is tilted in a certain way. To see what this means, pick two points on the line, as shown below. Any two points will do. Look at point *A* and ask yourself what is happening both to temperature and to height as you move along the graph to point *B*. The answer is that temperature is increasing and height is increasing. From this observation you can decide what the graph is about. You might say that it shows that hot air rises. You might say that the temperature of the air increases as you go up.

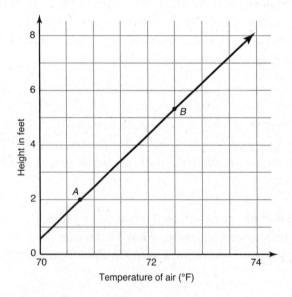

Temperature of air (°F)

Practice

For each graph below, write a statement describing what the graph shows.

1.

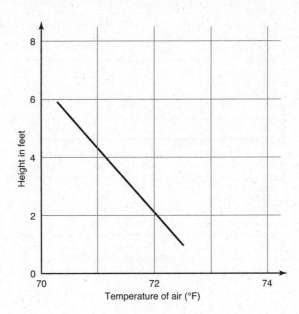

2.

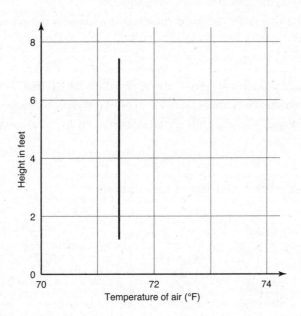

3.

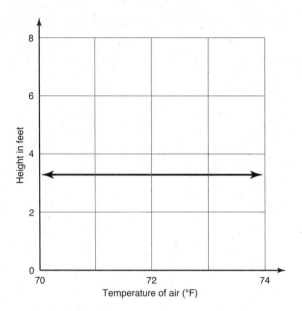

ANSWERS

1. As the height decreases, the temperature increases, so it is warmest near the floor.
2. The temperature is the same for all heights shown.
3. This graph shows that at the same height, there is a range of temperatures.

Bar Graphs

Bar graphs are very similar to line graphs. The only real difference is that instead of a line joining all the data (very much like the "connect the dot" type of puzzle), there will be a bar drawn from each data point to the axis. These graphs are an effective way to *compare* measurements.

Practice

Evaluate the bar graphs below and answer these questions:

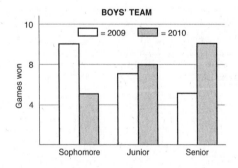
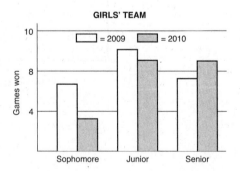

4. Which boys' team won the most games in 2009?

5. Which junior team was the best in 2010, the boys or the girls?

6. If the 2009 senior boys played the 2010 junior boys, who would probably win?

7. Looking at all six teams, which team improved the most from 2009 to 2010?

ANSWERS

4. sophomore
5. girls
6. junior boys; They had the better record.
7. senior boys

Circle or Pie Graphs

The graph shown below is called a *circle* or a *pie* graph. With this style of graph, it is possible to visualize how the parts of a whole relate to each other. Sometimes the numbers are given in percents, and so their total will be 100%. At other times the numbers are given in fraction form, and so their total will be l.

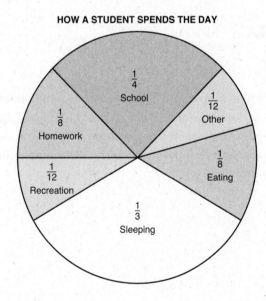

HOW A STUDENT SPENDS THE DAY

Practice

Use the pie graph above to answer questions 8–11.

8. How does a student spend the largest part of the day?

9. How many hours are spent in school each day?

10. The time spent in recreation is one-fourth the time spent doing what?

11. How many hours are spent eating and sleeping?

ANSWERS

8. sleeping; This is the largest section of the pie.

9. 6 hours; $\frac{1}{4}$ (24 hours) = 6 hours

10. sleeping; $\frac{1}{4}\left(\frac{1}{2}\right) = \frac{1}{12}$

11. 11 hours; $\frac{1}{8}$ (24) + $\frac{1}{3}$ (24) = 3 + 8 = 11

ANALYZING DATA

Tables

A table organizes information in rows and columns. This lets you present a lot of information in a relatively small space, and in a format that allows you to find relationships more easily than if the information were in paragraph or other form. When you examine a table, do not be overwhelmed by its appearance. Take your time, and remember that all the answers you are looking for are right there.

Practice

Use the portion of the income tax table shown below to answer Questions 12–14.

If line 39 (taxable income) is—		And you are—			
At least	But less than	Single	Married filing jointly	Married filing sepa-rately	Head of a house-hold
			Your tax is—		
44,000					
44,000	44,050	8,726	6,604	9,282	7,576
44,050	44,100	8,739	6,611	9,296	7,589
44,100	44,150	8,753	6,619	9,309	7,603
44,150	44,200	8,767	6,626	9,323	7,617
44,200	44,250	8,781	6,634	9,337	7,631
44,250	44,300	8,794	6,641	9,351	7,644
44,300	44,350	8,808	6,649	9,364	7,658
44,350	44,400	8,822	6,656	9,378	7,672
44,400	44,450	8,836	6,664	9,392	7,686
44,450	44,500	8,849	6,671	9,406	7,699
44,500	44,550	8,863	6,679	9,419	7,713
44,550	44,600	8,877	6,686	9,433	7,727
44,600	44,650	8,891	6,694	9,447	7,741
44,650	44,700	8,904	6,701	9,461	7,754
44,700	44,750	8,918	6,709	9,474	7,768
44,750	44,800	8,932	6,716	9,488	7,782
44,800	44,850	8,946	6,724	9,502	7,796
44,850	44,900	8,959	6,731	9,516	7,809
44,900	44,950	8,973	6,739	9,529	7,823
44,950	45,000	8,987	6,746	9,543	7,837

12. If your taxable income is $44,748, what would be the tax if you were married filing jointly?

13. If you file as the head of a household and your tax is $7,713, between what two figures is your taxable income?

14. How much tax would a single person pay on a taxable income of $44,732?

ANSWERS

12. $6,709
13. between $44,500 and $44,550
14. $8,918

Probability

We have been using both the terms "data" and "information" in this chapter, but in mathematics, they are practically the same. The word data means a collection of pieces of information. The baseball information below is data organized in a table. We can use this baseball data to look at the idea of probability.

Times at Bat	What Happened (H = hit and O = out)
1	O
2	H
3	O
4	H
5	O
6	O
7	O
8	H
9	O
10	H

When you flip a coin, you expect it to come up heads one out of every two times, on average. That is, the *probability* of heads is $\frac{1}{2}$. The probability of something happening is the number of times you expect it to occur out of the total number of times, or:

$$P = \frac{\text{Number of favorable outcomes}}{\text{Total number of outcomes}}$$

In looking at the baseball data, there are 10 total outcomes (at-bats), while the number of favorable outcomes (hits) is 4. So, the probability of getting a hit is 4 out of 10. This probability can be expressed as the fraction $\frac{4}{10}$, or as the decimal 0.4. Baseball players call this a batting average of 400. The actual decimal (0.4) is always multiplied by 1,000 in baseball.

Practice

15. Sam is designing a board game for children. It has 40 squares that you can "land on."

> Hot pink = 8 squares
> Lemon yellow = 2 squares
> Wild blue = 20 squares
> Neon green = 10 squares

(a) What is the probability of landing on a neon green square using the phrase "out of"?

(b) Use a fraction to describe the probability of landing on a hot pink square (remember to reduce).

(c) Use a decimal to describe the probability of landing on a wild blue square.

ANSWERS

15a. 10 out of 40, or reduce it to 1 out of 4; There are 10 favorable squares (neon green) out of the 40 total squares.

15b. $\frac{8}{40} = \frac{1}{5}$; There are 8 hot pink squares; divide this by 40, the total number of squares.

15c. $\frac{20}{40} = 0.5$; There are 20 wild blue squares; divide this by 40, the total number of squares.

Statistics

Statistics are different measurements that you make of data. For example, the gross national product is a statistic about our economy. Three of the statistics that you will see frequently are the mean, or average, the median, and the mode.

THE MEAN

The idea of an average is a familiar one. You have heard of a batting average, and your grades in school were averages. Even credit card balances are calculated as an average balance. The word *mean* is a synonym for average, though you may not see it as often. The average yearly amount of rain in a particular area is called the mean annual rainfall.

To calculate the average, add together all of the values and then divide by the number of these values. A formula page will be provided with your GED® math test. There is also one in this book right before the first test.

For example, the yearly snowfall in a location is shown in the table below.

Year	Snowfall in Inches
1995	96.1
1994	78.5
1993	70.9
1992	81.0

To calculate the average snowfall, add the yearly snowfalls and divide by the number of years:

$$\text{average (mean)} = \frac{96.1+78.5+70.9+81.0}{4}$$

$$= 81.625$$

Practice

16. Calculate Joe's average lawn mowing income for May through August from the following data.

Month	Income
May	$550.00
June	$725.00
July	$650.00
August	$675.00

17. What is the skier's average time for the downhill based on these times:

> 9 minutes and 3 seconds
>
> 8 minutes and 30 seconds
>
> 9 minutes and 54 seconds

ANSWERS

16. The months' incomes added together = $2,600. Then divide by 4 months to get $650.
17. The addition of the times gives 26 minutes and 87 seconds. The 87 seconds is 1 minute and 27 seconds, so the total time is 27 minutes and 27 seconds. Dividing this total by 3 gives an average of 9 minutes and 9 seconds.

THE MEDIAN

You may also encounter the statistic called the *median* while taking the GED® test. The median is the middle item in an ordered set of data. To find the median of a set of data, arrange the data from lowest number to highest number. After doing that, if there is an odd number of values, then the median is the middle number. If there is an even number of values, then the median is the average of the two middle numbers.

Practice

18. Find the median weight for this group of puppies. All weights are in pounds.

> 10.5, 9.5, 10.2, 9.4, 10.0, 9.7,
>
> 9.8, 10.1, 9.9, 10.7

ANSWER

18. Step one is to arrange the values from smallest to largest. Since there is an even number of values, the median will be the average of the two middle weights, or the fifth and sixth weights. They weigh 9.9 and 10.0 pounds, so the average is 9.95.

THE MODE

Mode is another aspect of a set of data. Mode refers to the value that occurs most often. For example, suppose that the weights of persons in the room were 200, 150, 205, 135, 150, 185, 165, 200, 150, and 120. The weight of 150 pounds appears the most at three times, and so 150 is said to be the mode for this set of numbers.

Manufacturers would like to know the most frequently selected product so that they can produce according to the customer's preference. For example, a t-shirt manufacturer needs to know the most popular sized shirt, and the output of a bakery is dictated by the purchaser's choices. There are times when there are two modes, because there could be two sizes, flavors, or numbers that are present equally. It could also be that there is no mode. It would be most likely, however, that for the GED® test there will always be just one mode for a mode question.

Practice

19. Find the mode for this set of color preferences for automobiles: blue, black, white, silver, red, red, green, tan, white, red, black, white, silver, green, and white.

20. What is the mode of this set of shoe sizes? 6½, 8, 5, 7, 8½, 9, 5, 5½, 7, 8, 7.

ANSWERS

19. white
20. size 7

Uses of Statistical Data

Statistical information is an influential component in advertising. For example, you might see an advertisement like this one:

> "8 out of 10 doctors prescribe the
> ingredient found in Prestige Pills!"

The advertiser is hoping that you will think that 8 out of 10 doctors favor Prestige Pills. If you think about what the ad really says, you will realize that it could be that no doctors actually favor Prestige Pills, but rather they favor other brands that have the same ingredient as that found in Prestige Pills. So, whenever you come across some statistic, read it carefully to see what it is really saying.

Practice

21. Regular coffee is 97% caffeine free. What percent caffeine does it contain?

ANSWER

21. 3%; If 100% represents the whole amount of coffee, then 3% must be caffeine if the other 97% is not.

END OF CHAPTER PRACTICE

1. Jean, age 22, has a job that gives her a take-home paycheck of $2,500 each month. According to the pie graph shown below, which of these statements is true?

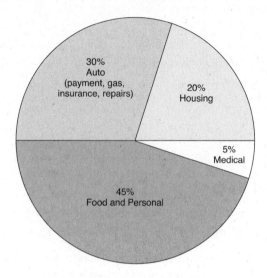

(A) Jean can afford a $540 car payment.
(B) There is no money in Jean's budget for clothes.
(C) Charitable contributions would have to come out of Jean's medical budget.
(D) Jean's rent, including utilities, should not exceed $500 a month.

2. From the x-axis shown below, what is the correct x-value for A?

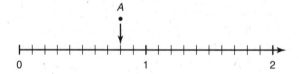

(A) 0.8

(B) $\frac{3}{4}$

(C) 7.5

(D) 8

3. From the *y*-axis shown below, what is the correct *y*-value for *B*?

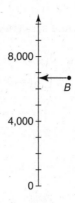

(A) 4,250

(B) 4,480

(C) 6,800

(D) 7,500

4. From the race car test drive graph below, which of the following is true?

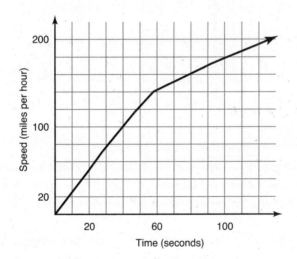

(A) When the car's speed reached 100 miles per hour, 30 seconds had elapsed.

(B) After 10 minutes, the car's speed will be nearly 500 miles per hour.

(C) The car can go from 0 to 140 miles per hour in 60 seconds.

(D) The car accelerated at the same rate throughout the test.

5. From the snowfall data graph below, which of these statements is true?

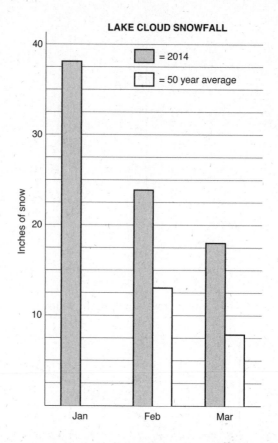

LAKE CLOUD SNOWFALL

■ = 2014
□ = 50 year average

Inches of snow

Jan   Feb   Mar

(A) January is normally the snowiest month in Lake Cloud.
(B) In 2014 the February snowfall was more than the 50 year average.
(C) Future years will likely be colder than average.
(D) In February of 2014, 28 inches of snow fell in Lake Cloud.

6. Many retirement plans base their benefit package on the average salary for the last five years worked. What would be Sam's average salary if he had earned these amounts the last five years?

$60,000 $60,000 $50,000

$50,000 $40,000

(A) $45,000
(B) $50,000
(C) $52,000
(D) $55,000

7. Calculate the median height of the basketball team with these heights:
   6' 10", 6' 9", 6' 7", 6' 5", 6' 3", 6' 2", 6' 1", 6' 0".

   (A) 6' 3"
   (B) 6' 4"
   (C) 6' 4.6"
   (D) 6' 5"

8. The Chamber of Commerce is sponsoring a game at the town carnival. The game box contains the following:

   Blue balls: 30
   Red balls: 15
   Yellow balls: 20
   Green balls: 35

   What is the probability of getting a yellow ball with one draw?

   (A) 0.02
   (B) 0.2
   (C) 0.5
   (D) 2

9. Use the chart of caloric requirements for dogs below to choose the correct response.

Caloric Requirements of Dogs

Weight of Dog in Pounds	Calories in Summer	Calories in Winter*	Calories for Growing Puppies**
2	120	180	200
5	250	375	400
10	420	630	700
20	700	1,050	1,200
30	930	1,400	1,400
50	1,350	2,000	2,000
70	1,680	2,500	2,500
100	2,400	3,600	3,600

*Only for dogs living outdoors more than 50% of the time.

**Puppies are considered to be growing until they reach adulthood, or at about 9 to 18 months, depending on breed.

   (A) Dogs weighing more than 100 pounds still require 2,400 calories in summer.
   (B) A 15 pound dog requires 500 calories a day in summer.
   (C) When the weight of the dog doubles, the calorie requirement also doubles.
   (D) Calorie requirement is always higher in winter than in summer for outside dogs.

Answers

1. **D** Twenty percent of $2,500 is $500. Utilities certainly fit in the category of housing.

2. **A** The 0.8 value can be checked by counting back to 0 and forward to 1.0.

3. **C** Each of the tic marks is equal to 1,000, so point *B* lies between 6,000 and 7,000. There is only one choice in this range.

4. **C** As you test each of the other responses, you will notice that there is a problem with each of them.

5. **B** Even when you discover the correct answer before having read all of the choices, it is a good idea to read the rest of the choices as a way to check yourself.

6. **C** When you add the salaries, you get $260,000. Dividing by 5 produces $52,000.

7. **B** The heights are arranged from tallest to shortest. Since there is an even number of values, the median will be the average of the middle two. This will equal 6' 4".

8. **B** There are 100 balls in all. Out of these, the number of favorable possibilities (drawing yellow) is 20, and $\frac{20}{100} = 0.2$.

9. **D** As you read each of the other choices, you will find there to be some inaccuracy in each.

Practice Tests

8

As you take these practice tests, try to see how they relate to the skills and ideas you have learned and practiced throughout this book. At the end of the practice test there is a chart that lets you relate the questions you missed to the topic in the book that deals with that idea. This way you can travel back for a review of the idea without spending a long time trying to find it. Remember that in order for you to pass the math section of the GED® test, you do not need to be able to answer every question. The number of questions you have to get right depends on the state where you take the test, but in every case there is a generous allowance for errors.

Take this test as though you were taking the real GED® exam. Provide your own scratch paper and several pencils. You will be allowed 115 minutes for the math section of the GED® test, so choose a time for taking this test when you will have an uninterrupted 115 minutes. This strategy will give you a better idea of how ready you are for the test.

The mathematics part of the GED® test is allocated 115 minutes. The first five questions (Part 1) are to be answered without the use of a calculator. For the remaining questions on the test (Part 2) a calculator will be available as an online feature of the computer you will be using for the test, or you may use your own TI-30XS. The answers to each of these tests are provided after the test questions. After you have finished the test and checked your answers, review the self-analysis chart to see where your strengths and weaknesses are. Review the topics pertaining to the questions you did not answer correctly.

Mathematical Reasoning

Part 1

1. Ⓐ Ⓑ Ⓒ Ⓓ
2. Ⓐ Ⓑ Ⓒ Ⓓ
3. Ⓐ Ⓑ Ⓒ Ⓓ
4. Ⓐ Ⓑ Ⓒ Ⓓ
5. Ⓐ Ⓑ Ⓒ Ⓓ

Part 2

6. Ⓐ Ⓑ Ⓒ Ⓓ
7. Ⓐ Ⓑ Ⓒ Ⓓ
8. Ⓐ Ⓑ Ⓒ Ⓓ
9. Ⓐ Ⓑ Ⓒ Ⓓ
10. Ⓐ Ⓑ Ⓒ Ⓓ
11. Ⓐ Ⓑ Ⓒ Ⓓ
12. Ⓐ Ⓑ Ⓒ Ⓓ
13. Ⓐ Ⓑ Ⓒ Ⓓ
14. Ⓐ Ⓑ Ⓒ Ⓓ
15. Ⓐ Ⓑ Ⓒ Ⓓ
16. [   ]

17. Ⓐ Ⓑ Ⓒ Ⓓ
18. Ⓐ Ⓑ Ⓒ Ⓓ
19. Ⓐ Ⓑ Ⓒ Ⓓ
20. Ⓐ Ⓑ Ⓒ Ⓓ
21. Ⓐ Ⓑ Ⓒ Ⓓ
22. Ⓐ Ⓑ Ⓒ Ⓓ
23. [   ]
24. Ⓐ Ⓑ Ⓒ Ⓓ
25. [   ]
26. Ⓐ Ⓑ Ⓒ Ⓓ
27. Ⓐ Ⓑ Ⓒ Ⓓ
28. Ⓐ Ⓑ Ⓒ Ⓓ
29. Ⓐ Ⓑ Ⓒ Ⓓ
30. Ⓐ Ⓑ Ⓒ Ⓓ
31. Ⓐ Ⓑ Ⓒ Ⓓ
32. Ⓐ Ⓑ Ⓒ Ⓓ
33. Ⓐ Ⓑ Ⓒ Ⓓ
34. Ⓐ Ⓑ Ⓒ Ⓓ

35. Ⓐ Ⓑ Ⓒ Ⓓ
36. Ⓐ Ⓑ Ⓒ Ⓓ
37. Ⓐ Ⓑ Ⓒ Ⓓ
38. Ⓐ Ⓑ Ⓒ Ⓓ
39. Ⓐ Ⓑ Ⓒ Ⓓ
40. Ⓐ Ⓑ Ⓒ Ⓓ
41. Ⓐ Ⓑ Ⓒ Ⓓ
42. Ⓐ Ⓑ Ⓒ Ⓓ
43. Ⓐ Ⓑ Ⓒ Ⓓ
44. Ⓐ Ⓑ Ⓒ Ⓓ
45. Ⓐ Ⓑ Ⓒ Ⓓ
46. Ⓐ Ⓑ Ⓒ Ⓓ
47. Ⓐ Ⓑ Ⓒ Ⓓ
48. [   ]
49. Ⓐ Ⓑ Ⓒ Ⓓ
50. Ⓐ Ⓑ Ⓒ Ⓓ

Mathematics Formula Sheet & Explanation

The 2014 GED® Mathematical Reasoning test contains a formula sheet, which displays formulas relating to geometric measurement and certain algebra concepts. Formulas are provided to test-takers so that they may focus on *application*, rather than the *memorization*, of formulas.

Area of a:

square	$A = s^2$
rectangle	$A = lw$
parallelogram	$A = bh$
triangle	$A = \frac{1}{2}bh$
trapezoid	$A = \frac{1}{2}h(b_1 + b_2)$
circle	$A = \pi r^2$

Perimeter of a:

square	$P = 4s$
rectangle	$P = 2l + 2w$
triangle	$P = s_1 + s_2 + s_3$
Circumference of a circle	$C = 2\pi r$ OR $C = \pi d$; $\pi \approx 3.14$

Surface area and volume of a:

rectangular/right prism	$SA = ph + 2B$	$V = Bh$
cylinder	$SA = 2\pi rh + 2\pi r^2$	$V = \pi r^2 h$
pyramid	$SA = \frac{1}{2}ps + B$	$V = \frac{1}{3}Bh$
cone	$SA = \pi rs + \pi r^2$	$V = \frac{1}{3}\pi r^2 h$
sphere	$SA = 4\pi r^2$	$V = \frac{4}{3}\pi r^3$

(p = perimeter of base with area B; $\pi \approx 3.14$)

Data

mean	mean is equal to the total of the values of a data set, divided by the number of elements in the data set
median	median is the middle value in an odd number of ordered values of a data set, or the mean of the two middle values in an even number of ordered values in a data set

Algebra

slope of a line	$m = \dfrac{y_2 - y_1}{x_2 - x_1}$
slope-intercept form of the equation of a line	$y = mx + b$
point-slope form of the equation of a line	$y - y_1 = m(x - x_1)$
standard form of a quadratic equation	$y = ax^2 + bx + c$
quadratic formula	$x = \dfrac{-b \pm \sqrt{b^2 - 4ac}}{2a}$
Pythagorean theorem	$a^2 + b^2 = c^2$
simple interest	$I = Prt$ (I = interest, P = principal, r = rate, t = time)
distance formula	$d = rt$
total cost	total cost = (number of units) × (price per unit)

© Copyright 2014 GED Testing Service. All rights reserved. GED® and GED Testing Service® are registered trademarks of the American Council on Education (ACE). They may not be used or reproduced without the express written permission of ACE or GED Testing Service. The GED® and GED Testing Service® brands are administered by GED Testing Service LLC under license from the American Council on Education.

Part 1

> **Directions:** You will have 115 minutes to complete this test. For the first five questions (Part 1), you will NOT be allowed to use a calculator. For the remainder of the test (Part 2), you may use either your own TI-30XB calculator or the calculator that is in the computer.

1. If there are 12,000 cubic feet of water in the pool in this diagram, how many cubic feet of empty space are there?

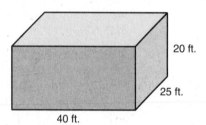

(A) 80
(B) 1,000
(C) 8,000
(D) 10,000

2. Solve this problem:

$$\frac{2(60-10)+15}{5}$$

(A) 14.6
(B) 23
(C) 29
(D) 50

3. How many $3\frac{1}{2}$ -inch pieces of wood could be cut from a 5-foot strip?

(A) 17.1
(B) 7.0
(C) 8.4
(D) 17

4. In order to find the area of the shaded portion of the diagram below, which of the processes listed would provide the correct answer?

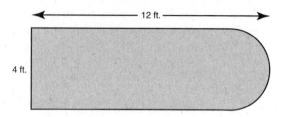

(A) $48 + \dfrac{4\pi}{2}$

(B) $48 + 4\pi$

(C) $48 + \dfrac{16\pi}{2}$

(D) $48 + 16\pi$

5. For a line whose equation is $y = 2x + 1$, the y-coordinate of a point on this line is -1. What is the value of the corresponding x-coordinate?

(A) $x = 0$
(B) $x = 1$
(C) $x = -1$
(D) $x = -2$

GO ON TO THE NEXT PAGE

Part 2

6. In creating a scale drawing of an automobile, using a scale of $\frac{1}{4}$ inch for every foot, how long would the drawing be, if the car is 10 feet long?

(A) $\frac{1}{2}$ inch

(B) 2 inches

(C) $2\frac{1}{4}$ inches

(D) $2\frac{1}{2}$ inches

7. English chemist Robert Boyle discovered a relationship between the volume of a gas and the pressure exerted by it. The table below lists some volumes and pressures for a gas. Determine the pressure when the volume is 10 units.

Volume	Pressure
1 unit	60 units
2 units	30 units
3 units	20 units
4 units	15 units

(A) 4

(B) 6

(C) 8

(D) 10

8. How many 50-foot rolls of fencing should be purchased for fencing the field shown in the diagram below? Choose the correct calculation plan.

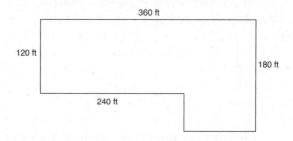

(A) 15

(B) 20

(C) 21

(D) 22

9. What number does point *P* represent on the number line?

(A) –8

(B) –4

(C) –0.4

(D) 4

10. For how many hours will Zack be paid if he came to work at 7:30, went to lunch at 11:45, returned at 12:15, and worked until 3:45?

(A) 7 hours 15 minutes

(B) 7 hours 30 minutes

(C) 7 hours 45 minutes

(D) 8 hours

GO ON TO THE NEXT PAGE

11. The school's chess coach has the funds to take three players to an event. She will definitely take Stan, but there are four other players. They are Jean, Emma, Carol, and Fred. How many combinations of players could the coach choose to take?

(A) 5
(B) 6
(C) 8
(D) 10

12. In prescribing medications for dogs, the pet's weight determines the dosage. If a 10-pound dog requires 120 mg of a medicine, how many milligrams would be appropriate for a 45-pound dog?

(A) 420
(B) 450
(C) 480
(D) 540

13. David subscribed to four magazines costing $20.00, $19.00, $24.00, and $28.00 per year. He paid one half of the total and paid the remainder in three equal payments. How much were each of these payments?

(A) $15.00
(B) $15.17
(C) $22.75
(D) $30.00

14. A survey in the town of Spring Valley showed that there was an average of 2.8 television sets per household. If the town has 18,000 households, how many television sets would that be?

(A) 504
(B) 643
(C) 5,040
(D) 50,400

15. Stanley's paycheck stub is shown in the table below. What percent of his income is deducted for state income tax?

gross pay	$2,573
federal income tax	$295
social security	$206
retirement	$68
state income tax	$54

(A) 0.021
(B) 0.24
(C) 0.48
(D) 2.10

16. Tom's new boss explains that he will get a 10% commission for the first five cars that he sells, and 15% for each car after that. What is Tom's commission if he sells eight cars at $20,000 each?

[Fill in the box on your answer sheet]

17. On the ruler segment in the diagram below, which letter corresponds to $6\frac{5}{8}$ inches?

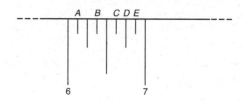

(A) A
(B) B
(C) C
(D) D

TIP

On the computerized test, a question like this would have you drag a marker to the correct location on the line.

GO ON TO THE NEXT PAGE

18. As a back-to-school assistance program, many states eliminate sales tax on school items for a few days. If the tax rate is 6%, how much would a family save if they bought one shirt at $19.88, two pairs of jeans at $38.00 each, and one pair of shoes at $75.00?

    (A) $1.02
    (B) $7.97
    (C) $10.25
    (D) $102.58

19. Calculate the value of $\frac{(x^2+3)}{2y} - 2$ if $x = 5$ and $y = 2$.

    (A) 0
    (B) 2
    (C) 5
    (D) 6.5

20. Solve the quadratic equation $x^2 - x - 2 = 0$. What are the possible values for x?

    (A) –2 and 1
    (B) 2 and –1
    (C) 0 and –2
    (D) –4 and 2

21. The lifetime of automobile tires can be increased by 8% if the tires are rotated regularly and kept at the recommended inflation pressure. Jane ignored these guidelines and got 50,000 miles from her tires. How many miles could she have gotten by following the guidelines?

    (A) 50,400
    (B) 50,800
    (C) 54,000
    (D) 58,000

22. Calculate the area of the diagram below.

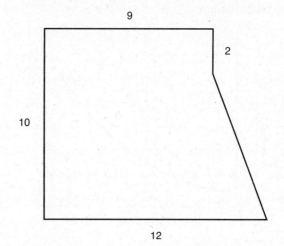

    (A) 102
    (B) 114
    (C) 132
    (D) 144

23. Calculate the distance from the bridge to the river from the information provided in the diagram below.

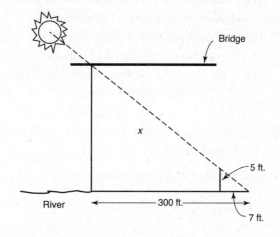

[Fill in the box on your answer sheet]

GO ON TO THE NEXT PAGE

PRACTICE TEST ONE

Questions 24 and 25 refer to the following graph and information.

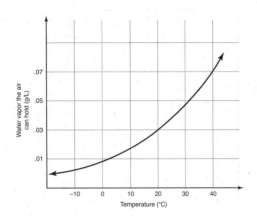

24. The graph shows the relationship between the amount of water vapor that the air can hold and the temperature of the air.

    Which of the following conclusions can be drawn from the graph?

    (A) As air temperature increases, the amount of water vapor it can hold increases.
    (B) As air temperature increases, the amount of water vapor it can hold decreases.
    (C) As the temperature of the water vapor increases, the probability of rain increases.
    (D) As the weight of the water vapor increases, the probability of snow increases.

25. How much water vapor, in grams per liter, can air at 35°F hold?

    [Fill in the box on your answer sheet]

26. Each of the wood piles in the diagram contains a cord of wood. Inspect the diagram to determine which of the following defines a cord of wood.

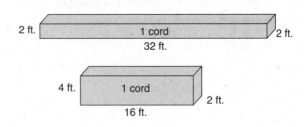

    (A) 2 feet wide
    (B) 4 feet high
    (C) 96 cubic feet of wood
    (D) 128 cubic feet of wood

27. Flood stage at Shady Springs is 19 feet. At 6 P.M. the river is at $14\frac{1}{2}$ feet. At 8 P.M., the river is at 16 feet. If the river is rising at a steady rate, when will it be at flood stage?

    (A) 9 P.M.
    (B) 10 P.M.
    (C) midnight
    (D) 3 A.M.

28. Solve the proportion below for x.

    $$\frac{3}{5} = \frac{24}{x}$$

    (A) $x = 9$
    (B) $x = 24$
    (C) $x = 40$
    (D) $x = 360$

GO ON TO THE NEXT PAGE

29. Which of the following points lies within the shaded area?

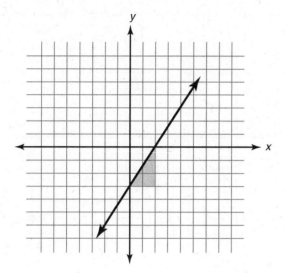

(A) 3, –2

(B) 2, 3

(C) 2, –3

(D) –2, –3

30. Write the inequality for the solution set graphed below.

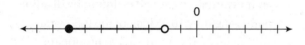

(A) $-8 \leq x < -2$

(B) $-8 < x \leq -2$

(C) $8 < x \leq 2$

(D) $8 \leq x < 2$

31. In which of the following are the numbers in order from least to greatest?

(A) –0.2, –0.08, 0.9, 1.15

(B) –0.08, –0.2, 0.9, 1.15

(C) –0.2, 0.08, 1.15, 0.9

(D) 1.15, 0.9, –0.2, –0.08

32. Use the slope-intercept form, $y = mx + b$, to find the equation of the line that passes through the point (–2, –4) and has a slope of 4.

(A) $y = -2x + 4$

(B) $y = 4x + 4$

(C) $y = x + 12$

(D) $y = 4x + 8$

33. Given $x = m^7$ $y = m^{-2}$ $z = m^3$

What would be the value of $\frac{xy}{z}$?

(A) m^2

(B) m^3

(C) m^{-2}

(D) m^{-1}

34. Andy starts filling the swimming pool at 7:30 A.M. By 11:30 A.M., the pool is $\frac{2}{3}$ full. At what time will the pool be full?

(A) 12:30 P.M.

(B) 1:00 P.M.

(C) 1:30 P.M.

(D) 2:00 P.M.

GO ON TO THE NEXT PAGE

35. Rob needs to know the height of the tree in the diagram. Which of the following set-ups will provide him with that information?

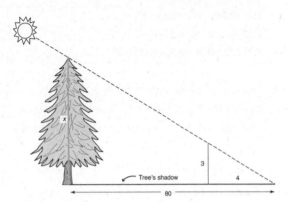

(A) $\dfrac{3}{4} = \dfrac{80}{x}$

(B) $\dfrac{3}{4} = \dfrac{x}{80}$

(C) $\dfrac{3}{80} = \dfrac{4}{x}$

(D) $\dfrac{3}{80} = \dfrac{x}{4}$

36. In a soccer game the Rovers beat the Bowsers. The losing team had one more than half the winning goals. What would be an appropriate equation to determine how many goals the Bowsers got?

(A) Bowsers $= \dfrac{x+1}{2}$

(B) Bowsers $= x + 1\dfrac{1}{2}$

(C) Bowsers $= 1\dfrac{1}{2} x$

(D) Bowsers $= \dfrac{x}{2} + 1$

37. Determine the equation for line AB in the following graph.

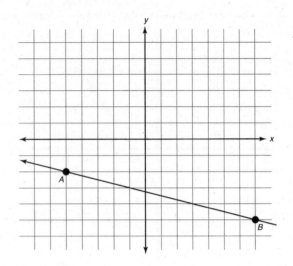

(A) $y = 4x - 3$

(B) $y = -\dfrac{1}{4} x + 8$

(C) $y = \dfrac{1}{4} x - 3$

(D) $y = -\dfrac{1}{4} x - 3$

38. The approximate number of pints of blood in an individual's body can be found by dividing body weight by 16. Which of the following will calculate the approximate number of quarts of blood in Ray's body if he weighs 180 pounds. There are 2 pints in 1 quart.

(A) $\dfrac{180}{16}$

(B) $\dfrac{180}{(16)(2)}$

(C) $\dfrac{180(2)}{16}$

(D) $180 - (16)(2)$

GO ON TO THE NEXT PAGE

39. Which of the following equations contains all points less than *G* and greater than or equal to *B*?

(A) $-10 > x < 15$

(B) $-10 \leq x \leq 15$

(C) $-10 \leq x < 15$

(D) $-10 < x < 15$

40. What is the value of the expression:

$$\left(\frac{x^3}{x}\right) - 3\left(\frac{x^2}{x^5}\right) \text{ when } x = -2$$

(A) $-3\frac{5}{8}$

(B) $3\frac{5}{8}$

(C) $4\frac{3}{8}$

(D) 20

41. How many buckets of driveway sealer will be needed to cover the driveway in the following diagram, if one bucket will cover 600 square feet?

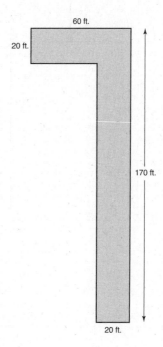

(A) 6.0

(B) 7.0

(C) 7.7

(D) 8.0

42. Peggy's doctor prescribed an antibiotic to be taken every 8 hours. There are eight tablets, and she starts taking them at 6 P.M. on Tuesday. When will she take the last tablet?

(A) 2 A.M. Friday

(B) 10 A.M. Friday

(C) 6 A.M. Saturday

(D) 6 P.M. Saturday

GO ON TO THE NEXT PAGE

43. Calculate the surface area of the window shown in the diagram.

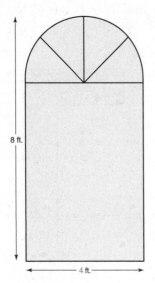

(A) 22.28

(B) 30.28

(C) 36.56

(D) 38.28

44. Round 121.445 to the tens place.

(A) 121.45

(B) 121.4

(C) 121.5

(D) 120

45. A king size bed measures 76 inches wide and 80 inches long. If the square bedroom in the diagram below is 16 feet on each side, how much room in inches on each side of the bed would there be for nightstands?

(A) 30

(B) 44

(C) 56

(D) 58

GO ON TO THE NEXT PAGE

Questions 46 and 47 refer to the following graph and information.

Sam left his office at noon and walked to the bank, which was 1 mile away. He then walked back to his office, making one stop at the office supply store. He arrived back at the office at 1:45.

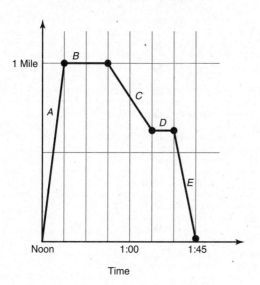

46. Which segment of the graph shows the length of time that Sam spent in the bank?

    (A) A
    (B) B
    (C) C
    (D) D

47. What fraction of Sam's time away from the office was spent walking?

    (A) $\frac{2}{7}$

    (B) $\frac{3}{7}$

    (C) $\frac{4}{7}$

    (D) $\frac{5}{7}$

48. The gift wrapping department at the new department store has 8 colors of wrapping paper, 2 ribbon colors, and 10 card styles. How many different combinations of paper, ribbon, and card will be available to the shopper?

    [Fill in the blank box on your answer sheet.]

49. Temperatures in the United States are most often reported in degrees Fahrenheit (°F). In many other countries, temperatures are reported in degrees Celsius (°C). If you were in one of these countries and wondered what the weather report meant in more familiar terms, you could use an approximation that says you could double the Celsius degrees and add thirty. Which of these equations should be used to make that calculation?

    (A) $(2)(°C)(30) = °F$
    (B) $(2)(°C + 30) = °F$
    (C) $°C + (2)(30) = °F$
    (D) $(2)(°C) + 30 = °F$

50. The following chart offers a comparison of the varieties of ground beef that are available to the consumer.

Ground Beef Type	Calories	Total Fat (grams)	Saturated Fat (grams)
90% lean, 10% fat	169	9	3.7
85% lean, 15% fat	204	12	4.8
80% lean, 20% fat	228	15	6.0
73% lean, 27% fat	248	18	7.0

Which of these conclusions can accurately be drawn from the information?

    (A) Saturated fat content increases as does the calorie amount.
    (B) Saturated fat makes up half of the total fat.
    (C) The 10% fat beef is the best buy.
    (D) As the fat doubles, the calories double.

END OF EXAMINATION

ANSWER KEY
Practice Test One

Part 1

1. **C**
2. **B**
3. **D**
4. **A**
5. **C**

Part 2

6. **D**
7. **B**
8. **D**
9. **B**
10. **C**
11. **B**
12. **D**
13. **B**
14. **D**
15. **D**
16. **$19,000**
17. **C**
18. **C**

19. **C**
20. **B**
21. **C**
22. **A**
23. **214.3**
24. **A**
25. **0.06**
26. **D**
27. **C**
28. **C**
29. **C**
30. **A**
31. **A**
32. **B**
33. **A**
34. **C**
35. **B**
36. **D**
37. **D**
38. **B**
39. **C**

40. **C**
41. **B**
42. **A**
43. **B**
44. **D**
45. **D**
46. **B**
47. **C**
48. **160**
49. **D**
50. **A**

SELF-ANALYSIS

Did you get at least 35 correct answers? If not, you need more practice for the Mathematical Reasoning Test. You can improve your performance to Good or Excellent by analyzing your errors. To determine the areas in which you need further study, review the chart below. The question numbers from Practice Test One appear in the column to the left. Circle the questions you answered incorrectly. (Unsolved problems are counted as incorrect.) Refer to the Chapter and Chapter Section indicated for each question for additional review.

WHAT'S YOUR SCORE?

Your rating	Number of correct answers	Equivalent GED® score
Outstanding	45–50	180–200
Excellent	40–44	160–179
Good	35–39	140–159
Fair	30–34	120–139
Passing (min.)*	25–29	100–119

*The acceptable passing score varies with each state. Your state GED® test sites can provide this information. If your score is low on this practice test, the explanation of the correct answers that follows will help you. You may obtain additional help by reviewing the self-analysis chart below.

SELF-ANALYSIS CHART

Question	Chapter	Topic
Part I		
1.	6	Volume
2.	4	Order of operations
3.	3	Long division
4.	6	Area
5.	4	Equations
Part II		
6.	4	Proportion
7.	4	Proportion
8.	6	Perimeter
9.	4	Signed numbers
10.	5	Time
11.	7	Combinations
12.	4	Proportion
13.	5	Money
14.	7	Statistical data
15.	4	Percent
16.	4	Percent
17.	5	Measurement
18.	4	Percent
19.	4	Percent

Question	Chapter	Topic
20.	4	Quadratic equation
21.	4	Substitution
22.	6	Area
23.	6	Similar triangles
24.	7	Line graph
25.	7	Line graph
26.	6	Volume
27.	4	Proportion
28.	4	Equations
29.	6	Coordinate plane
30.	4	Inequalities
31.	3	Sequencing
32.	6	Point slope
33.	4	Exponents
34.	4	Proportion
35.	6	Similar triangles
36.	4	Formulas
37.	5	Measurement
38.	3	Long division
39.	4	Inequality
40.	4	Substitution
41.	6	Area
42.	5	Time
43.	6	Area
44.	3	Rounding
45.	6	Perimeter
46.	7	Line graphs
47.	7	Line graphs
48.	7	Statistics
49.	4	Modeling
50.	7	Charts

ANSWERS EXPLAINED

Part 1

1. **C** The volume of the whole pool is found by using the volume formula from the formula page. Volume = length × width × height. This would be 40 × 20 × 25 = 20,000 cubic feet. Since the problem asks for empty space, you would subtract the water (12,000) from the whole amount (20,000) to give 8,000 cubic feet.

2. **B** This is an order of operations problem (PEMDAS). Using PEMDAS, the subtraction is done first because it is inside the parentheses. The division and addition follow as in the usual order of an operations problem.

3. **D** The first step is to change 5 feet into inches by multiplying by 12 (the number of inches in one foot). Then divide 60 inches into $3\frac{1}{2}$ inch pieces, by dividing 60 by $3.5 \left(\text{or } 3\frac{1}{2} \right)$. This produces an answer of 17.1. However, the question asked how many $3\frac{1}{2}$ -inch pieces could be cut. The answer is 17. Discard the leftover.

4. **A** You can think of the area as a combination of a rectangle with dimensions of 12 feet by 4 feet. This part would have an area of 12 × 4 = 48 square feet. Then the rest of the diagram is a half circle. The formula for the area of a circle is pi times the radius squared. The radius of this circle would be 2 (the distance from its outer edge to its center), so the calculation would be 3.14 (the value of pi) times 2^2. The area of the circle should be divided by 2, as there is just half a circle in the diagram. The answer is reflected in choice A.

5. **C** Substitute –1 for y in $y = 2x + 1$. Then solve for x.

Part 2

6. **D** If one foot equals $\frac{1}{4}$ inch, then 10 feet would be $10 \times \frac{1}{4} = 2\frac{1}{2}$.

7. **B** Examine the chart until you can see a pattern. In this case, the pattern is that whatever you multiply the volume by to get a new volume, you divide the pressure by to get a new pressure. Therefore, if you multiply 1 unit of volume by 10 to get a volume of 10, you would divide the pressure of 60 units by 10 to get a pressure of 6.

8. **D** Perimeter means the distance around. You can think of it as putting a fence around something. The unlabeled parts are 60 feet and 120 feet. When added together and divided by 50 = 21.6. Round to 22 rolls.

9. **B** Notice that point P is 4 units to the left of the zero, and left is the negative direction on the number line.

10. **C** From 7:30 to 11:45 is a time length of 4 hours and 15 minutes. The afternoon time from 12:15 to 3:45 is 3 hours and 30 minutes. The total of these times would be 7 hours and 45 minutes.

11. **B** There are 4 students and there are 6 possible pairs to add to Stan.

12. **D** If a 10-pound dog requires 120 mg, you could say that is 12 mg for each pound. Then you could multiply that 12 mg per pound by 45 pounds to get 540 mg.

13. **B** The first step would be to add all the dollar amounts ($91), then divide that by 2 ($45.50). Divide this into 3 equal payments to get $15.17.

14. **D** If there are 2.8 televisions per household, multiply that number by the number of households to get 50,400.

15. **D** Remember that percent is "part over the whole times 100." The part is the $54 state income tax and the whole is the $2,573 gross pay. The resulting 2.0987 is rounded to 2.10 to give choice 4.

16. **$19,000** First, 10% times $20,000 times 5 cars = $10,000. Then 15% times $20,000 times 3 cars = $9,000. This gives a total of $19,000.

17. **C** Examine the ruler to find where $6\frac{1}{2}$ would be. Then go halfway back to the 6 and this will be $6\frac{1}{4}$. If you split the distance back to the 6 from here in two, you will see how big one eighth is. Now that you know which lines are the $\frac{1}{8}$ lines, count five of them to get to $\frac{5}{8}$. This is position C.

18. **C** First, calculate the total of all the items. This would be $170.88. Then, to take 6%, multiply by 0.06 to get $10.25.

19. **C** Following the order of operations, the exponent is taken care of first to give 28 within the parenthesis. The next step is a division by 4 to give 7. Finally, the 2 is subtracted to give 5.

20. **B** $x^2 - x - 2$ factors into $(x - 2)(x + 1)$. Setting each factor equal to 0 gives $x - 2 = 0$ and $x + 1 = 0$. Solving for each x gives 2 and −1.

21. **C** Change to a decimal, so 8% = .08. Then $0.08 \times 50,000 = 4,000$. This is the increased number of miles and so is added to the 50,000 to give 54,000.

22. **A** From the formula page, the area of a triangle is found by multiplying the base by $\frac{1}{2}$ of the height. Multiplying 3 times $\frac{1}{2}$ of 8 = 12. Add to the 9×10 rectangle beside the triangle.

23. **214.3** This is a similar triangle problem in which you can say that x is to 5 as 300 is to 7. Cross multiplying and then dividing produces 214.3.

24. **A** When you look at the two axes, you can see that increasing on the x-axis goes along with increasing on the y-axis. This causes choice (A) to be correct.

25. **0.06** As with all situations involving reading graphs, find the given value on its axis, in this case 35 degrees. Make an imaginary line up to the graph line and then across to the y-axis. It is at this point that you encounter the 0.06.

26. **D** The key to this question is that both piles of wood represent a cord of wood. The first two responses are not true, so it falls to the last two to be possibilities. Since they are both in cubic feet, this means that the volume has been calculated. When you multiply

length times width times height for both, you find that 128 is the answer for both cords, and therefore the correct answer.

27. **C** To figure the rate at which the river is rising, notice that in 2 hours the river went up $1\frac{1}{2}$ feet. To get from 16 feet to flood stage of 19 feet is 3 feet. If it took 2 hours to go $1\frac{1}{2}$ feet, it will take 4 hours to go 3 feet. Four hours from 8 P.M. puts the time at midnight.

28. **C** $\dfrac{3}{5} = \dfrac{24}{x}$

     $3x = 120$

       $x = 40$

29. **C** Notice that the shaded area is where the x-value is positive and the y-value is negative. Only choices (A) and (C) qualify, but the shaded area does not go as far as $x = 3$. The correct answer is (C).

30. **A** The closed circle means include x. The open circle does not include x.

31. **A** Negative numbers are the smallest, so you have to begin with one of the first three choices. –0.2 is the smallest possibility.

32. **B** Use $y = mx + b$
     $-4 = 4(-2) + b$
     $+4 = b$
      $y = 4x + 4$

33. **A** $\dfrac{xy}{z} = \dfrac{(m^7)(m^{-2})}{m^3} = m^{7-3-2} = m^2$

34. **C** If the pool is $\frac{2}{3}$ full after being filled for 4 hours, it would have been $\frac{1}{3}$ full after 2 hours. So, to fill the pool completely $\left(\frac{3}{3}\right)$ would take 3 times 2 hours, or 6 hours. From 7:30 A.M. to 6 hours later would be 1:30 P.M.

35. **B** This is a similar triangle problem, in which you can say that 3 is to 4 as the tree (x) is to 80.

36. **D** Let x = winners (Rovers), so losers (Bowsers) = $\frac{1}{2}$ of winners goals, or $\frac{x}{2}$, plus 1, or $\frac{x}{2} + 1$.

37. **D** Set up $y = mx + b$. Use $\dfrac{\text{rise}}{\text{run}}$ to get $\dfrac{1}{-4}$ or $\dfrac{-1}{4}$. Look at the graph to see that the y-intercept is –3. So, $y = -\dfrac{1}{4}x - 3$.

38. **B** Notice that pints and quarts both appear in the problem. The question asks for quarts, so when you get the pint answer by using the formula, then you have to change to quarts by dividing by 2. Response 2 is the only one that divides body weight both by 2 and by the 16 spoken of in the formula.

39. **C** Recall that the open circle means not including. The closed circle means including.

40. **C** Substitute –2 for each x.

41. **B** Calculate the area of the driveway by dividing the driveway into two rectangles (in your mind), and then using the area formula of length times width. One rectangle is 170 feet $\times$ 20 feet = 3,400 square feet. The other rectangle is 20 feet $\times$ 40 feet = 800 square feet. The total square footage is 4,200. Dividing 4,200 by 600 gives 7 buckets.

42. **A** It is likely to be easier and more error free to just count.

43. **B** The surface area of the window is the addition of two surfaces: the area of the rectangle ($6 \times 4 = 24$), and the area of half a circle ($3.14 \times 2^2 \times \frac{1}{2} = 6.28$). Adding the surfaces together gives 30.28.

44. **D** The tens place is the place that is 2 spaces to the left of the decimal, so in this case there is a 2 there. There can be no nonzero digits to the right of that place, so the answer is 120. You have to preserve the approximate value of the number you began with.

45. **D** Since the room is square, the wall where the bed is measures 16 feet, or 192 inches. The bed takes up 76 inches, leaving 116 inches for the nightstands. Divide by 2 for the space for one nightstand.

46. **B** Sam's first stop after leaving his office was a stop at the bank. The line marked with an A shows his walk to the bank. Line B is flat, showing that there is no change in distance; therefore, Sam is staying at the bank.

47. **C** Notice on the x-axis that there are 7 time units (15 minutes each). The parts of the graph that show walking are A, C, and E, for a total of 4 out of the 7 units.

48. **160** The number of combinations is found by multiplying the variety of choices together. $8 \times 2 \times 10 = 160$.

49. **D** Response D is the only one in which the degrees C are first doubled and then 30 is added to that.

50. **A** The correct response is the first one, but it is always a good idea to check the truth of the other responses to make certain that you have not made an error.

Mathematical Reasoning

Part 1

1. Ⓐ Ⓑ Ⓒ Ⓓ
2. [   ]
3. Ⓐ Ⓑ Ⓒ Ⓓ
4. Ⓐ Ⓑ Ⓒ Ⓓ
5. Ⓐ Ⓑ Ⓒ Ⓓ

Part 2

6. Ⓐ Ⓑ Ⓒ Ⓓ
7. Ⓐ Ⓑ Ⓒ Ⓓ
8. Ⓐ Ⓑ Ⓒ Ⓓ
9. Ⓐ Ⓑ Ⓒ Ⓓ
10. [   ]
11. Ⓐ Ⓑ Ⓒ Ⓓ
12. Ⓐ Ⓑ Ⓒ Ⓓ
13. Ⓐ Ⓑ Ⓒ Ⓓ
14. [   ]
15. Ⓐ Ⓑ Ⓒ Ⓓ
16. Ⓐ Ⓑ Ⓒ Ⓓ

17. Ⓐ Ⓑ Ⓒ Ⓓ
18. Ⓐ Ⓑ Ⓒ Ⓓ
19. Ⓐ Ⓑ Ⓒ Ⓓ
20. Ⓐ Ⓑ Ⓒ Ⓓ
21. [   ]
22. Ⓐ Ⓑ Ⓒ Ⓓ
23. Ⓐ Ⓑ Ⓒ Ⓓ
24. Ⓐ Ⓑ Ⓒ Ⓓ
25. Ⓐ Ⓑ Ⓒ Ⓓ
26. Ⓐ Ⓑ Ⓒ Ⓓ
27. Ⓐ Ⓑ Ⓒ Ⓓ
28. Ⓐ Ⓑ Ⓒ Ⓓ
29. [   ]
30. Ⓐ Ⓑ Ⓒ Ⓓ
31. Ⓐ Ⓑ Ⓒ Ⓓ
32. Ⓐ Ⓑ Ⓒ Ⓓ
33. Ⓐ Ⓑ Ⓒ Ⓓ
34. Ⓐ Ⓑ Ⓒ Ⓓ

35. Ⓐ Ⓑ Ⓒ Ⓓ
36. Ⓐ Ⓑ Ⓒ Ⓓ
37. Ⓐ Ⓑ Ⓒ Ⓓ
38. [   ]
39. Ⓐ Ⓑ Ⓒ Ⓓ
40. Ⓐ Ⓑ Ⓒ Ⓓ
41. Ⓐ Ⓑ Ⓒ Ⓓ
42. Ⓐ Ⓑ Ⓒ Ⓓ
43. Ⓐ Ⓑ Ⓒ Ⓓ
44. Ⓐ Ⓑ Ⓒ Ⓓ
45. Ⓐ Ⓑ Ⓒ Ⓓ
46. Ⓐ Ⓑ Ⓒ Ⓓ
47. Ⓐ Ⓑ Ⓒ Ⓓ
48. Ⓐ Ⓑ Ⓒ Ⓓ
49. [   ]
50. Ⓐ Ⓑ Ⓒ Ⓓ

Mathematics Formula Sheet & Explanation

The 2014 GED® Mathematical Reasoning test contains a formula sheet, which displays formulas relating to geometric measurement and certain algebra concepts. Formulas are provided to test-takers so that they may focus on *application*, rather than the *memorization*, of formulas.

Area of a:

square	$A = s^2$
rectangle	$A = lw$
parallelogram	$A = bh$
triangle	$A = \frac{1}{2} bh$
trapezoid	$A = \frac{1}{2} h(b_1 + b_2)$
circle	$A = \pi r^2$

Perimeter of a:

square	$P = 4s$
rectangle	$P = 2l + 2w$
triangle	$P = s_1 + s_2 + s_3$
Circumference of a circle	$C = 2\pi r$ OR $C = \pi d$; $\pi \approx 3.14$

Surface area and volume of a:

rectangular/right prism	$SA = ph + 2B$	$V = Bh$
cylinder	$SA = 2\pi rh + 2\pi r^2$	$V = \pi r^2 h$
pyramid	$SA = \frac{1}{2} ps + B$	$V = \frac{1}{3} Bh$
cone	$SA = \pi rs + \pi r^2$	$V = \frac{1}{3} \pi r^2 h$
sphere	$SA = 4\pi r^2$	$V = \frac{4}{3} \pi r^3$

(p = perimeter of base with area B; $\pi \approx 3.14$)

Data

mean	mean is equal to the total of the values of a data set, divided by the number of elements in the data set
median	median is the middle value in an odd number of ordered values of a data set, or the mean of the two middle values in an even number of ordered values in a data set

Algebra

slope of a line	$m = \dfrac{y_2 - y_1}{x_2 - x_1}$
slope-intercept form of the equation of a line	$y = mx + b$
point-slope form of the equation of a line	$y - y_1 = m(x - x_1)$
standard form of a quadratic equation	$y = ax^2 + bx + c$
quadratic formula	$x = \dfrac{-b \pm \sqrt{b^2 - 4ac}}{2a}$
Pythagorean theorem	$a^2 + b^2 = c^2$
simple interest	$I = Prt$ (I = interest, P = principal, r = rate, t = time)
distance formula	$d = rt$
total cost	total cost = (number of units) × (price per unit)

© Copyright 2014 GED Testing Service. All rights reserved. GED® and GED Testing Service® are registered trademarks of the American Council on Education (ACE). They may not be used or reproduced without the express written permission of ACE or GED Testing Service. The GED® and GED Testing Service® brands are administered by GED Testing Service LLC under license from the American Council on Education.

Part 1

> **Directions:** You will have 115 minutes to complete this test. For the first five questions (Part 1), you will NOT be allowed to use a calculator. For the remainder of the test (Part 2), you may use either your own TI-30XB calculator or the calculator that is in the computer.

1. Given that: $x = 2p$, $y = p^3$, $z = p^2$, what would be the value of $\dfrac{2x^2}{yz}$?

    (A) $4p^{-3}$
    (B) $8p^3$
    (C) $8p^{-3}$
    (D) $8p^{-4}$

2. Joe's house has 2,000 square feet. The room he uses for his office is 10 feet by 12 feet. What percent of his house is his office?

    [Fill in the blank box on your answer sheet.]

3. Solve the following equation for x.
    $$8x - 3 = 3x + 4$$

    (A) $x = \dfrac{7}{5}$

    (B) $x = -\dfrac{7}{5}$

    (C) $x = \dfrac{5}{7}$

    (D) $x = -\dfrac{5}{7}$

4. Calculate the value of $4x - 2y - xy$ if $x = -3$ and $y = 2$.

    (A) -2
    (B) -10
    (C) -14
    (D) -22

5. In the diagram below, what is the number to which the arrow points?

    (A) 22.5
    (B) 25.0
    (C) 30.2
    (D) 32.0

GO ON TO THE NEXT PAGE

Part 2

6. What is the value of $(a - 2b)(b^2 + 3c)$ when $a = 4$, $b = 3$, and $c = -2$?

   (A) –6
   (B) 1
   (C) 6
   (D) 13

7. From the following equation for a straight line

   $$y = \frac{1}{2}x + 6$$

   if the y-coordinate for a point on the line was 5, what would the x-coordinate be for that point?

   (A) $x = \frac{1}{2}$

   (B) $x = -\frac{1}{2}$

   (C) $x = 2$
   (D) $x = -2$

8. Using the lengths in the diagram to the right, solve for the length of x.

   (A) 5.66
   (B) 25.96
   (C) 32.00
   (D) 87.50

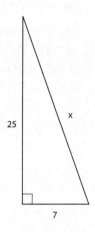

9. Determine the slope of line AB using any method you choose.

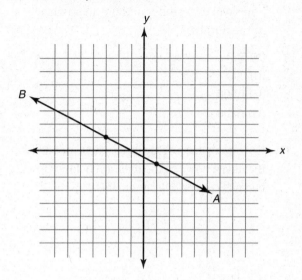

   (A) $-\frac{1}{2}$

   (B) $\frac{1}{2}$

   (C) –2
   (D) 2

10. Solve for x: $3[6(12 - 3)] - 17 = x$

    [Fill in the blank box on your answer sheet.]

11. Calculate the area in the diagram below.

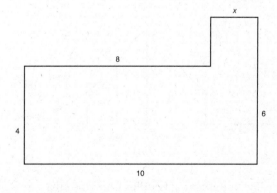

    (A) 40
    (B) 44
    (C) 48
    (D) 60

GO ON TO THE NEXT PAGE

12. A spinner has a three in five chance of landing on a prime number. In 2,000 spins, how many times will the spinner probably land on a prime number?

    (A) 500
    (B) 800
    (C) 1,000
    (D) 1,200

13. How many bags of fertilizer will be needed for the lawn shown in the diagram below. One bag will cover 2,500 square feet.

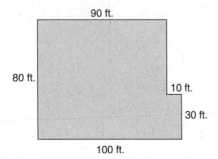

    90 ft.

    80 ft.

    10 ft.

    30 ft.

    100 ft.

    (A) 1
    (B) 2
    (C) 3
    (D) 4

14. For a certain part of the United States, the annual income per family is shown in the graph below.

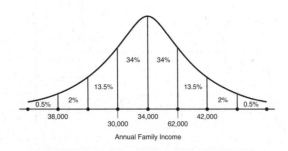

    34%   34%

    13.5%   13.5%

    0.5%   2%   2%   0.5%

    38,000   34,000   42,000
         30,000   62,000

    Annual Family Income

    What percent of families from this area will have an annual income greater than $62,000?

    [Fill in the blank box on your answer sheet.]

15. Mark will form a two-letter prefix for his bank identification number, using two different letters from his name in any order. Assume that MA and AM are different prefixes. How many different two-letter prefixes can be formed using the letters M-A-R-K without repeating a letter?

    (A) 4
    (B) 6
    (C) 8
    (D) 12

16. What is the scientific notation equivalent of 0.00315?

    (A) 3.15×10^3
    (B) 3.15×10^{-3}
    (C) 31.5×10^{-4}
    (D) 0.00315×10^0

17. Which of the following is the correct set of factors for $6x^2 + 5x - 6$?

    (A) $(2x + 3)(3x + 2)$
    (B) $(2x + 3)(3x - 2)$
    (C) $(2x - 3)(3x - 2)$
    (D) $(2x - 3)(3x + 2)$

18. Solve the following inequality for x.

    $$6x + 1 \le 3x - 6$$

    (A) $x \le -3$
    (B) $x \le -\dfrac{5}{3}$
    (C) $x \ge -\dfrac{7}{3}$
    (D) $x \le -\dfrac{7}{3}$

GO ON TO THE NEXT PAGE

19. The road from Ocean Park to Coastal Dunes is 22 miles long. In order to make a scale drawing, the map maker chooses to use a scale in which l mile will be represented by $\frac{1}{4}$ inch. How many inches long will the road be on the map?

(A) $2\frac{1}{2}$

(B) $3\frac{1}{2}$

(C) $4\frac{1}{2}$

(D) $5\frac{1}{2}$

20. The doctor told Frank that 2,000 calories a day would keep him at his ideal weight. Today Frank had a lunch of one grilled chicken sandwich (570 calories), small fries (340 calories), and a medium coke (190 calories). What percent of his daily calorie allotment is this meal?

(A) 5.5%

(B) 18.8%

(C) 51.8%

(D) 55.0%

21. If the refrigerator in the diagram below contains 12 cubic feet of food, how much space is empty?

[Fill in the blank box on your answer sheet.]

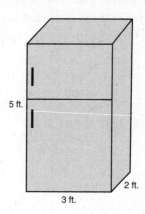

22. Which of the following expresses this inequality?

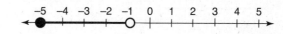

(A) $-5 \geq x > -1$

(B) $-5 < x \leq -1$

(C) $-5 \leq x < 1$

(D) $-5 \leq x < -1$

23. Calculate the length of x in this diagram.

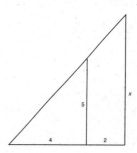

(A) $2\frac{1}{2}$

(B) $3\frac{1}{3}$

(C) $6\frac{1}{2}$

(D) $7\frac{1}{2}$

GO ON TO THE NEXT PAGE

24. The Financial Fitness Club was begun to help its members become their own financial planners. The club had 10 members to start with, 20 by the end of the first year, 40 by the end of the second year, and 80 at the end of the third year. Which of the following graphs best represents the history of the club?

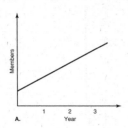

A.

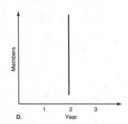

D.

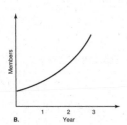

B.

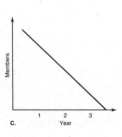

C.

(A) A
(B) B
(C) C
(D) D

25. Homer measured the angle between his line of sight and the moon, as shown in the following diagram. These measurements are recorded in the table below.

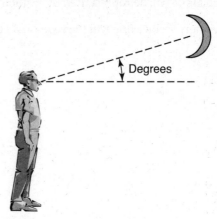

8:00 P.M.	8:20 P.M.	8:40 P.M.	9:00 P.M.
35 degrees	40 degrees	45 degrees	50 degrees

If this pattern continues, at what time will the moon be directly over Homer's head?

(A) 11:00 P.M.
(B) 11:40 P.M.
(C) midnight
(D) 12:20 A.M.

26. Which of the following choices is the correct solution for the quadratic equation $x^2 + 2x - 15 = 0$.

(A) 5, –3
(B) –5, 3
(C) –5, –3
(D) 0, 0

27. Simplify $\dfrac{(x^2)(3x^3)}{x^4} + 2x$.

(A) $5x$
(B) $3x^2 + 2x$
(C) $5x^3$
(D) $3x^9 + 2x$

GO ON TO THE NEXT PAGE

PRACTICE TEST TWO

28. What is the equation for line *AC* in the graph below?

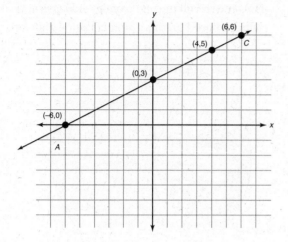

(A) $y = \frac{1}{2}x + 1$

(B) $y = \frac{1}{2}x + 2$

(C) $y = -\frac{1}{2}x + 2$

(D) $y = -\frac{1}{2}x + 1$

29. In one week at Mercy Hospital, twice as many girl babies were born as boy babies. If 60 babies were born, how many were girls?

[Fill in the blank box on your answer sheet.]

30. Inspect the diagrams below with respect to the cubic feet of space they contain. Which of the following statements is true?

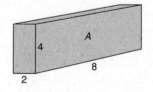 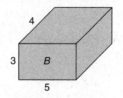

(A) *A* has 4 more cubic feet than *B*.
(B) *A* has 2 more cubic feet than *B*.
(C) *B* has 4 more cubic feet than *A*.
(D) *B* has 2 more cubic feet than *A*.

31. On the number line below, which lettered point most closely represents the number $-\frac{5}{3}$?

(A) *A*
(B) *B*
(C) *C*
(D) *D*

32. How many rpm (revolutions per minute) is the car's engine turning according to the tachometer shown in the diagram?

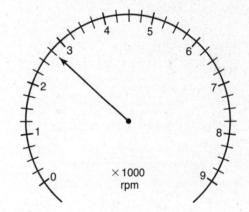

(A) 2.60
(B) 2.75
(C) 2,300
(D) 2,750

GO ON TO THE NEXT PAGE

PRACTICE TEST TWO

33. What is the equation for line *AB*?

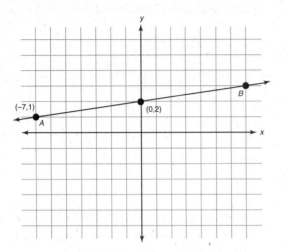

(A) $y = \frac{1}{7}x + 2$

(B) $y = -\frac{1}{7}x + 2$

(C) $y = 7x + 2$

(D) $y = -7x + 2$

34. Calculate the area in the diagram below:

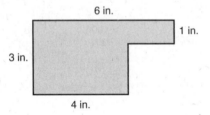

(A) 14 square inches
(B) 16 square inches
(C) 18 square inches
(D) 26 square inches

35. The new company in town estimates that its monthly operating costs will be $100,000. How much will they be paying for wages and salaries based on this graph of their expenses?

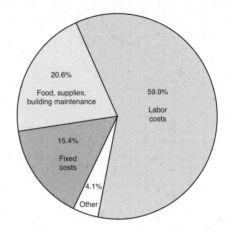

(1) $59,900
(B) $5,990
(C) $499
(D) $1,788.91

36. The solution set of the following quadratic equation has two possible values for *x*. What are they?

$$x^2 - 5x + 6 = 0$$

(A) $x = 1, -1$
(B) $x = 3, 2$
(C) $x = -3, -2$
(D) $x = -5, 6$

37. Rachel's $10,000 investment in the stock market grew 110% over a 15-year period. How much did it increase in value?

(A) $10,011
(B) $10,100
(C) $11,000
(D) $110,000

GO ON TO THE NEXT PAGE

PRACTICE TEST TWO

38. From the calorie values given in the chart, calculate the total number of calories in 1 popcorn, 2 Cokes, and 2 boxes of Junior Mints.

Item	Calories
Coke	205
Popcorn	1,221
Junior Mints	360

[Fill in the blank box on your answer sheet.]

39. Which of the following is the correct choice for writing the number 28,495 in scientific notation?

(A) 28.495×10^3
(B) 2.8495×10^4
(C) 2.8495
(D) 2.8495×10^{-4}

40. Written in ordinary number format, the number 8.95×10^{-1} is

(A) 0.0895
(B) 0.895
(C) 8.95
(D) 89.5

41. A rectangular design for a banner is shown in the diagram. What is the area of the shaded portion?

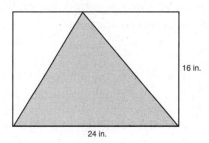

16 in.

24 in.

(A) 128 square inches
(B) 192 square inches
(C) 256 square inches
(D) 288 square inches

42. How far will the tire in the diagram travel if it goes completely around 100 times?

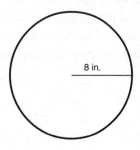

8 in.

(A) 3.14(16)(100)
(B) 3.14(8)(100)
(C) $3.14(8^2)(100)$
(D) 3.14(16)

43. The number of live births recorded in the states that lie along the Pacific Ocean is given in the table below, rounded to the nearest 1,000 for each.

Alaska	12,000
California	618,000
Hawaii	20,000
Oregon	46,000
Washington	77,000

What was the median number of live births in those Pacific states?

(A) 20,000
(B) 46,000
(C) 96,000
(D) 155,000

44. Given that $x = 2$ and $y = -4$, find the value of the expression $3x - 2y + xy$.

(A) −4
(B) −10
(C) 6
(D) 12

GO ON TO THE NEXT PAGE

45. The diagram below is that of the fuel gauge on the dashboard of a car. If the driver also has the information that the tank holds 11 gallons, and the car gets 25 miles to the gallon of gasoline, which of these processes will tell how far the car can go without more gasoline?

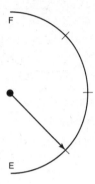

(A) $(11)(25)\left(\dfrac{1}{4}\right)$

(B) $\dfrac{(11)\left(\dfrac{1}{4}\right)}{25}$

(C) $\dfrac{(25)\left(\dfrac{1}{4}\right)}{11}$

(D) $(4)(11)(25)$

46. Tom had some hospital tests that resulted in a bill of $2,000. He has not yet met his deductible of $500, so he will have to pay that. His medical insurance will then pay 80% of the balance. How much totally will Tom pay for these tests?

(A) $300
(B) $800
(C) $900
(D) $1,100

47. When Ms. Thomas meets a client, the probability that she will make a sale is 1 in 4. How many sales can she expect if she meets with 144 clients?

(A) 145
(B) 48
(C) 36
(D) 24

48. A leading bookseller is selling a book normally priced at p dollars at a sale price of 20% off. Which equation represents c, the cost of the book after the discount?

(A) $c = p - 0.2p$
(B) $c = p - 0.2$
(C) $c = 0.2p + p$
(D) $c = p - 20$

49. Rene's daily earnings can be found by the equation:

$$\$160 + \$30x$$
where x is the number of
overtime hours worked that day

How much does Rene earn on a day when she worked three hours of overtime?

[Fill in the blank box on your answer sheet.]

50. Suppose that you walk 2 miles due east and then 2 miles due south. How many miles are you from your starting point?

(A) 2
(B) 2.8
(C) 4
(D) 4.8

END OF EXAMINATION

ANSWER KEY
Practice Test Two

Part 1

1. **C**
2. **6%**
3. **A**
4. **B**
5. **D**

Part 2

6. **A**
7. **D**
8. **B**
9. **A**
10. **145**
11. **B**
12. **D**
13. **C**
14. **16**
15. **D**
16. **B**
17. **B**
18. **D**

19. **D**
20. **D**
21. **18**
22. **D**
23. **D**
24. **B**
25. **B**
26. **B**
27. **A**
28. **B**
29. **40**
30. **A**
31. **C**
32. **D**
33. **A**
34. **A**
35. **A**
36. **B**
37. **C**
38. **2,351**
39. **B**

40. **B**
41. **B**
42. **A**
43. **B**
44. **C**
45. **A**
46. **B**
47. **C**
48. **A**
49. **250**
50. **B**

SELF-ANALYSIS

Did you get at least 35 correct answers? If not, you need more practice for the Mathematical Reasoning Test. You can improve your performance to Good or Excellent by analyzing your errors. To determine the areas in which you need further study, review the chart below. The question numbers from Practice Test Two appear in the column to the left. Circle the questions you answered incorrectly. (Unsolved problems are counted as incorrect.) Refer to the Chapter and Chapter Section indicated for each question for additional review.

WHAT'S YOUR SCORE?

Your rating	Number of correct answers	Equivalent GED® score
Outstanding	45–50	180–200
Excellent	40–44	160–179
Good	35–39	140–159
Fair	30–34	120–139
Passing (min.)*	25–29	100–119

*The acceptable passing score varies with each state. Your state GED® test sites can provide this information. If your score is low on this practice test, the explanation of the correct answers that follows will help you. You may obtain additional help by reviewing the self-analysis chart below.

SELF-ANALYSIS CHART

Question	Chapter	Topic
Part I		
1.	4	Exponents
2.	6/4	Area/percent
3.	4	Solve for *x*
4.	4	Algebra
5.	4	Substitution
Part II		
6.	4	Polynomials
7.	3	Fractions
8.	6	Pythagorean relationship
9.	4	Slope
10.	4	Order of operations
11.	6	Area
12.	7	Probability
13.	6/3	Area/long division
14.	7	Probability
15.	7	Combinations
16.	4	Scientific notation
17.	4	Factoring
18.	4	Inequalities
19.	5	Measurement

Question	Chapter	Topic
20.	4	Percent
21.	6	Volume
22.	4	Inequalities
23.	3	Similar triangle
24.	7	Line graph
25.	4	Proportions
26.	4	Quadratic equations
27.	4	Simplify
28.	4	Slope
29.	4	Proportions
30.	6	Volume
31.	4	Signed numbers
32.	5	Measurement
33.	4	Equation from line
34.	6	Area
35.	7	Circle graph
36.	4	Quadratic equations
37.	4	Percent
38.	3	Addition/multiplication
39.	4	Scientific notation
40.	4	Scientific notation
41.	6	Area
42.	6	Circle
43.	7	Median
44.	4	Substitution
45.	5	Measurement
46.	4	Percent
47.	7	Probability
48.	4	Equations
49.	4	Substitution
50.	6	Pythagorean relationship

ANSWERS EXPLAINED

Part 1

1. **C** Use the $\dfrac{2x^2}{yz}$ and substitute the given values. This produces $\dfrac{2(2)^2}{p^3 p^2} = \dfrac{2(4p^2)}{p^5} = \dfrac{8p^2}{p^5}$

   $= 2p^{2-5} = 2p^{-3}$.

2. **6%** The office has $10 \times 12 = 120$ square feet. Its percent of the whole house is

   $\dfrac{120}{2,000}$ times 100 for percent. This equals 6%.

3. **A** Solve for x in the usual way. First add 3 to both sides of the equation to get $8x = 3x + 7$. Then subtract $3x$ from both sides to get $5x = 7$. Finally, divide both sides by 5 to get

   $x = \dfrac{7}{5}$.

4. **B** Substituting in the equation gives $-12 - 4 + 6 = -12 + 2 = -10$.

5. **D** Look at the scale to decide how much each line is worth. Each line is 5. The arrow lies between 30 and 35. There is only one choice in this area, and it is choice (D).

Part 2

6. **A** Substitute given values to get $(4 - 2 \times 3)(9 + -6) = (4 - 6)(9 - 6) = (-2)(3) = -6$.

7. **D** Substitute given values into the slope equation $(y = mx + b)$ to get $5 = \dfrac{1}{2}x + 6$.

   Solve for x to get -2.

8. **B** $c^2 = a^2 + b^2$
   $c^2 = 25^2 + 7^2$
   $c^2 = 625 + 49$
   $c^2 = 674$
   $c = 25.96$

9. **A** Use the equation slope $= \dfrac{\text{rise}}{\text{run}}$ to get $\dfrac{2}{-4} = -\dfrac{1}{2}$.

10. **145** The first step is to subtract 3 from 12 within the parentheses to get 9. Then multiply that by 6 to get 54. The next step is to multiply by 3 to get the product 162. Finally subtracting 17 from 162 produces 145.

11. **B** The line marked x added to 8 must equal the bottom line of 10. This means that x must be 2.

12. **D** Divide 2,000 by 5 to get 400. Then multiply $400 \times 3 = 1,200$.

13. **C** The first step is to calculate the number of square feet in the lawn. The lawn can be thought of as two rectangles. One of them is 90 feet $\times$ 80 feet = 7,200 square feet. The other rectangle is 10 feet $\times$ 30 feet = 300 square feet. The total square footage of the lawn is $300 + 7,200 = 7,500$. If one bag will cover 2,500 square feet, divide 2,500 into 7,500 to get 3 bags.

14. **16** Locate $62,000 on the x-axis. Since the question asks for everything over $62,000, add all the percents to the right of that point. $13.5 + 2 + 0.5 = 16$.

15. **D** To start thinking about this, start with M and see that MA, MR, and MK are the possibilities. For each of the four letters in his name, there are three possibilities. $4 \times 3 = 12$.

16. **B** 3.15×10^{-3} is the answer because the decimal must be between the first two digits and the exponent must be negative to move the decimal to the left.

17. **B** Using FOIL, multiply to get the beginning equation.

18. **D** Solve the equation just as if it were a usual equation without thinking about the inequality sign. Then, when you are finished, ask yourself if you divided by a negative. You did not, and so you can leave the direction of the sign the same as it was in the beginning.

19. **D** Multiplying 22 times $\frac{1}{4}$ equals $5\frac{1}{2}$.

20. **D** Two cookies times the amount of saturated fat in one cookie (1 gram) = 2 grams.

21. **18** To find the empty space, find the volume of the whole refrigerator and subtract the food in it. The whole volume is length $\times$ width $\times$ height = $5 \times 3 \times 2 = 30$ cubic feet. Subtract 12 and get 18 cubic feet of empty space.

22. **D** The solid circle means that the –5 is included, while the open circle means that the line goes up to but does not include the –1.

23. **D** This is a similar triangle problem, so you set up a proportion using those similar parts. One possibility is $\frac{x}{5} = \frac{6}{4}$. Cross multiplying and solving produces $x = 7\frac{1}{2}$. Any other correct proportion will produce the same answer.

24. **B** Since the membership goes up each year, the only possibilities are graphs A and B. Looking more critically at these, notice that the increase in membership was not steady, but grew at a greater rate each year. Graph A is the steady growth, while graph B is the bigger rate, so choice (B) is correct.

25. **B** Examine the chart to see that every 20 minutes the number of degrees increases by 5. Directly overhead will be 90 degrees, so that is 40 degrees past the 9:00 P.M. point. Divide 5 degrees into 40 degrees to get 8. Then multiply 8 by 20 minutes to get 160 minutes. 160 minutes = 2 hours and 40 minutes. Adding this to 9:00 P.M. gives 11:40 P.M.

26. **B** Factoring the equation gives $(x + 5)(x - 3) = 0$. Solving for x in both results in $x = -5$ and $x = 3$.

27. **A** The answer is $5x$. The $2x$ cannot be included because unknowns with different exponents cannot be added to each other.

28. **B** Use the slope formula, $y = mx + b$, and substitute the values you can figure from the question. You can tell that the slope is $\frac{1}{2}$ and that the y-intercept is +3, so $y = \frac{1}{2}x + 3$.

29. **40** $3x$ (total babies) = 60, so $x = 20$. Since there were twice as many girl babies, $2x = 40$.

30. **A** Calculate the volume of $A = 2 \times 4 \times 8 = 64$. The volume of B = $3 \times 4 \times 5 = 60$. Knowing these volumes allows you to compare them and choose (A).

31. **C** Looking at the improper fraction $-\frac{5}{3}$, make it into a mixed number of $-1\frac{2}{3}$. Now you know that it is located between negative 1 and negative 2 at point C.

32. **D** As you examine the tachometer, notice the $\times 1000$. This means that the numbers shown are to be multiplied by 1,000. Then look at the region of the arrow, which is between 2 and 3. The arrow is pointing to 2.75, as each of the smaller marks is 0.25 in size. Multiplying $2.75 \times 1,000 = 2,750$.

33. **A** Look at the graph to calculate the slope, using the idea of $\frac{\text{rise}}{\text{run}}$. $\frac{\text{Rise}}{\text{Run}} = \frac{2}{14}$, so slope $(m) = \frac{1}{7}$. The graph intersects the y-axis at 2, so $b = 2$. Put these together to get $y = \frac{1}{7}x + 2$.

34. **A** The diagram can be thought of as two rectangles. One is $3 \times 4 = 12$, while the other is $1 \times 2 = 2$. Adding these two areas equals 14.

35. **A** Wages and salaries is the same as the 59.9% labor cost part of the graph. To find the dollar amount, multiply the $100,000 by 0.599 to get $59,900.

36. **B** Factor the given equation to get $(x-3)(x-2) = 0$. Then, set each factor equal to zero and solve each for x. These two solutions, $x = 3$ and $x = 2$, are the answers.

37. **C** Multiply 1.10 by $10,000. The answer is $11,000.

38. **2,351** Adding for the various foods gives a total of 2,351 calories.

39. **B** Since the decimal must be directly after the first digit, choice (A) can be eliminated immediately. Choice (B) is correct because moving the decimal four spaces in the positive (right) direction will produce the original number.

40. **B** Choice (B) is correct, because moving the decimal one place to the left (-1) produces the original number.

41. **B** The shaded portion is a triangle. The area of a triangle, as found on the formula page, is area $= \frac{1}{2} \times$ base $\times$ height. $A = \frac{1}{2} \times 16 \times 24 = 192$.

42. **A** This is a problem about the circumference of a circle. The formula for circumference is $C =$ pi times diameter. $C = 3.14 \times 16$ (the diameter is twice the radius). Then it is necessary to multiply by 100 to find the distance for 100 turns.

43. **B** Median is the middle value when the values are arranged from low to high. This shows that the third value in line is 46,000.

44. **C** Substituting 2 for x and -4 for y, gives $6 + 8 - 8 = 6$.

45. **A** The fuel gauge diagram is marked so that each mark is one quarter of a tank of gasoline. If the tank holds 11 gallons, it has $\frac{11}{4}$ gallons left. If it gets 25 miles for each of these gallons, it can go $25 \times \frac{11}{4}$.

46. **B** The patient will have to pay the deductible of $500. The patient will then pay 20% of the remaining $1,500, or another $300. The total owed by the patient will be $800.

47. **C** Divide 144 into 4 parts, so that each part is 36.

48. **A** Choice 1 correctly shows that the new price will be the old price minus the discount of 0.20 times the old price of p.

49. **250** Rene's earnings will be

$160 + \$30x$ =

$160 + \$30\ (3)$ =

$160 + \$90$ = $250

50. **B** If you were to make a diagram of this hike, it would look like this:

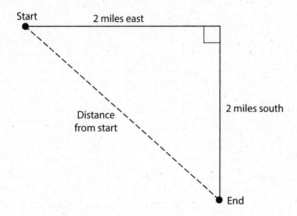

Then, using the Pythagorean theorem:

$c^2 = a^2 + b^2$

$c^2 = 2^2 + 2^2$

$c^2 = 4 + 4$

$c^2 = 8$

$c = 2.828$

ANSWER SHEET
Practice Test Three

Mathematical Reasoning

Part 1

1. [_____]

2. Ⓐ Ⓑ Ⓒ Ⓓ

3. Ⓐ Ⓑ Ⓒ Ⓓ

4. Ⓐ Ⓑ Ⓒ Ⓓ

5. Ⓐ Ⓑ Ⓒ Ⓓ

Part 2

6.

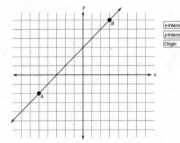

Slope = [_____]

7. Ⓐ Ⓑ Ⓒ Ⓓ

8. Ⓐ Ⓑ Ⓒ Ⓓ

9. Ⓐ Ⓑ Ⓒ Ⓓ

10. Ⓐ Ⓑ Ⓒ Ⓓ

11. Ⓐ Ⓑ Ⓒ Ⓓ

12. Ⓐ Ⓑ Ⓒ Ⓓ

13. Ⓐ Ⓑ Ⓒ Ⓓ

14. Ⓐ Ⓑ Ⓒ Ⓓ

15. Ⓐ Ⓑ Ⓒ Ⓓ

16. Ⓐ Ⓑ Ⓒ Ⓓ

17. Ⓐ Ⓑ Ⓒ Ⓓ

18. Ⓐ Ⓑ Ⓒ Ⓓ

19. Ⓐ Ⓑ Ⓒ Ⓓ

20. Ⓐ Ⓑ Ⓒ Ⓓ

21. Ⓐ Ⓑ Ⓒ Ⓓ

22. Ⓐ Ⓑ Ⓒ Ⓓ

23. [_____]

24. [_____]

25. [_____]

26. Ⓐ Ⓑ Ⓒ Ⓓ

27. Ⓐ Ⓑ Ⓒ Ⓓ

28. Ⓐ Ⓑ Ⓒ Ⓓ

29. [_____]

30. Ⓐ Ⓑ Ⓒ Ⓓ

31. Ⓐ Ⓑ Ⓒ Ⓓ

32. Ⓐ Ⓑ Ⓒ Ⓓ

33. [_____]

34. Ⓐ Ⓑ Ⓒ Ⓓ

35. [_____]

36. Ⓐ Ⓑ Ⓒ Ⓓ

37. Ⓐ Ⓑ Ⓒ Ⓓ

38. Ⓐ Ⓑ Ⓒ Ⓓ

39. [_____]

40. Ⓐ Ⓑ Ⓒ Ⓓ

41. Ⓐ Ⓑ Ⓒ Ⓓ

42. Ⓐ Ⓑ Ⓒ Ⓓ

43. [_____]

44. Ⓐ Ⓑ Ⓒ Ⓓ

45. Ⓐ Ⓑ Ⓒ Ⓓ

46. Ⓐ Ⓑ Ⓒ Ⓓ

47. Ⓐ Ⓑ Ⓒ Ⓓ

48. Ⓐ Ⓑ Ⓒ Ⓓ

49. Ⓐ Ⓑ Ⓒ Ⓓ

50. Ⓐ Ⓑ Ⓒ Ⓓ

Mathematics Formula Sheet & Explanation

The 2014 GED® Mathematical Reasoning test contains a formula sheet, which displays formulas relating to geometric measurement and certain algebra concepts. Formulas are provided to test-takers so that they may focus on *application*, rather than the *memorization*, of formulas.

Area of a:

square	$A = s^2$
rectangle	$A = lw$
parallelogram	$A = bh$
triangle	$A = \frac{1}{2} bh$
trapezoid	$A = \frac{1}{2} h(b_1 + b_2)$
circle	$A = \pi r^2$

Perimeter of a:

square	$P = 4s$
rectangle	$P = 2l + 2w$
triangle	$P = s_1 + s_2 + s_3$
Circumference of a circle	$C = 2\pi r$ OR $C = \pi d$; $\pi \approx 3.14$

Surface area and volume of a:

rectangular/right prism	$SA = ph + 2B$	$V = Bh$
cylinder	$SA = 2\pi rh + 2\pi r^2$	$V = \pi r^2 h$
pyramid	$SA = \frac{1}{2} ps + B$	$V = \frac{1}{3} Bh$
cone	$SA = \pi rs + \pi r^2$	$V = \frac{1}{3} \pi r^2 h$
sphere	$SA = 4\pi r^2$	$V = \frac{4}{3} \pi r^3$

(p = perimeter of base with area B; $\pi \approx 3.14$)

Data

mean	mean is equal to the total of the values of a data set, divided by the number of elements in the data set
median	median is the middle value in an odd number of ordered values of a data set, or the mean of the two middle values in an even number of ordered values in a data set

Algebra

slope of a line	$m = \dfrac{y_2 - y_1}{x_2 - x_1}$
slope-intercept form of the equation of a line	$y = mx + b$
point-slope form of the equation of a line	$y - y_1 = m(x - x_1)$
standard form of a quadratic equation	$y = ax^2 + bx + c$
quadratic formula	$x = \dfrac{-b \pm \sqrt{b^2 - 4ac}}{2a}$
Pythagorean theorem	$a^2 + b^2 = c^2$
simple interest	$I = Prt$ (I = interest, P = principal, r = rate, t = time)
distance formula	$d = rt$
total cost	total cost = (number of units) × (price per unit)

© Copyright 2014 GED Testing Service. All rights reserved. GED® and GED Testing Service® are registered trademarks of the American Council on Education (ACE). They may not be used or reproduced without the express written permission of ACE or GED Testing Service. The GED® and GED Testing Service® brands are administered by GED Testing Service LLC under license from the American Council on Education.

Part 1

> **Directions:** You will have 115 minutes to complete this test. For the first five questions (Part 1), you will NOT be allowed to use a calculator. For the remainder of the test (Part 2), you may use either your own TI-30XB calculator or the calculator that is in the computer.

1. A rectangle is 6 inches wide and 10 inches long. What is the length of its diagonal? (Making a sketch will help.)

   [Fill in the blank box on your answer sheet.]

2. Evaluate the following expression if $x = -2$.

$$\frac{x^2 - 5x + 6}{x^2 - 9}$$

   (A) $\frac{0}{-5}$

   (B) $\frac{-4}{13}$

   (C) 4

   (D) -4

3. Portions of employment tests are designed to measure the ability of the applicant to read measuring devices. Look at the diagram below.

   Which of the following provides a measure of the value between the two arrows?

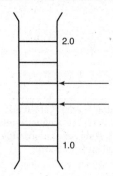

   (A) 1.2 to 1.3
   (B) 1.4 to 1.6
   (C) 2.2 to 2.3
   (D) 2.4 to 2.6

4. The diagram below is of a Norman window. Calculate the perimeter of this window.

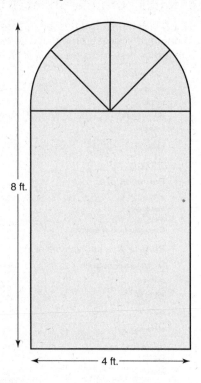

   (A) 18.28
   (B) 22.28
   (C) 26.56
   (D) 28.56

5. The owner's manual for a chain saw states that the fuel used must be a mixture that is a 16:1 ratio of unleaded gasoline to 2-cycle oil. Which of these is the correct number of gallons of gasoline to use with an 8 ounce container of 2-cycle oil? Remember: 1 gallon = 128 ounces.

   (A) $\frac{1}{2}$

   (B) 1
   (C) 4
   (D) 8

GO ON TO THE NEXT PAGE

Part 2

6. Draw an arrow from the boxed items in the diagram on your answer sheet to their correct locations on the graph.

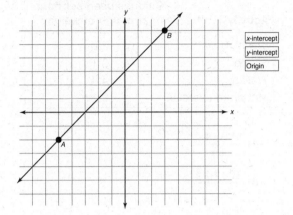

Use the graph to calculate the slope of line *AB*.

> **TIP**
>
> **On the computerized form of the GED® exam you would be asked to drag these boxes and drop them on the appropriate location.**

7. In order to purchase full-length draperies (84 inches long) for a window that is 68 inches wide, which of the following should be selected? Be certain to follow the advice explained in the drapery description.

Pole-top draperies include tiebacks. Unlined. Order 1½ to 2 times rod width.	
width × length	Catalog number
82 × 63	24B 27H
82 × 84	25B 28H

(A) 1 pair of the 82 × 63
(B) 1 pair of the 82 × 84
(C) 2 pairs of the 82 × 63
(D) 2 pairs of the 82 × 84

8. Solve the inequality $3x - 4 < 11$.

(A) $x < -5$
(B) $x > -5$
(C) $x < 5$
(D) $x > 5$

9. The electric company has announced a 13% rate increase. If you pay $90.30 per month, which of the following strategies will calculate the bill after the rate increase?

(A) ($90.30)(0.13)
(B) $90.30 + 13
(C) ($90.30)(0.13) + $90.30
(D) ($90.30)(0.013) + $90.30

10. Solve the following equation for *x*.

$$x + 5 = \frac{1}{3}(5x - 5)$$

(A) $x = \frac{3}{5}$

(B) $x = \frac{5}{3}$

(C) $x = 5$
(D) $x = 10$

GO ON TO THE NEXT PAGE

11. Calculate the slope of line *AB*.

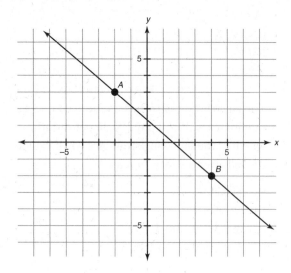

(A) $\dfrac{5}{6}$

(B) $-\dfrac{5}{6}$

(C) $\dfrac{6}{5}$

(D) $-\dfrac{6}{5}$

12. When traveling in Europe, dollars need to be exchanged for European money, called euros. If the exchange rate is $1.495 for one euro, how would you calculate the number of euros you would get for $200?

(A) 1/1.495

(B) 200(1.495)

(C) 1.495/200

(D) 200 – 1.495

13. Calculate the number of calories a 130-pound woman would use by walking for 20 minutes. Use the data in the chart, and then select the strategy for solving the problem.

Activity	Calories used per hour per pound of weight
Sleeping	2.0
Sitting	3.1
Walking	4.4
Moderate exercise	9.1

(A) $\dfrac{130 \times 4.4}{20}$

(B) $\dfrac{130 \times 4.4}{3}$

(C) $\dfrac{130 \times 3}{4.4}$

(D) $\dfrac{130 \times 3}{20}$

14. Determine the equation of line *AB*.

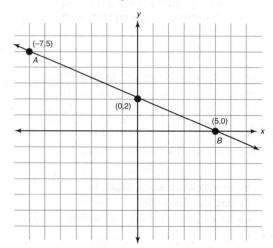

(A) $y = -\dfrac{5}{12}x + 5$

(B) $y = \dfrac{5}{12}x + 5$

(C) $y = -\dfrac{5}{12}x + 2$

(D) $y = -\dfrac{12}{5}x + 2$

GO ON TO THE NEXT PAGE

15. In the figure below, what must be the lengths of the sides of the square in order for the square to have an area equal to the area of the rectangle?

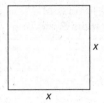 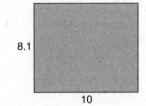

(A) 3
(B) 4.25
(C) 8
(D) 9

16. The two sailboats in the diagram have sails that form similar triangles. Which proportion could be used to determine the length of x?

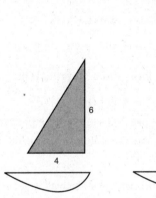 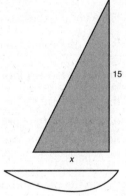

(A) $6:4 = 15:x$
(B) $6:4 = x:15$
(C) $6:15 = x:4$
(D) $6:x = 4:15$

17. Solve the following inequality.

$$3x + 9 \leq 2x + 2$$

(A) $-7 \geq x$
(B) $-7 \leq x$
(C) $7 \geq x$
(D) $7 \leq x$

18. The Delgado family spends $\frac{1}{3}$ of their monthly income for rent and $\frac{1}{4}$ for food. What fraction of their income remains for other expenses each month?

(A) $\frac{11}{12}$
(B) $\frac{7}{12}$
(C) $\frac{5}{12}$
(D) $\frac{2}{7}$

19. Sterling silver is not pure silver. It is a combination that is 92.5% silver and the remainder copper. Which of the following should be used to calculate the number of grams of copper in a 125 gram sterling silver bracelet?

(A) 125×7.5
(B) 125×0.075
(C) $125 - 7.5$
(D) $125 - 0.075$

GO ON TO THE NEXT PAGE

PRACTICE TEST THREE

20. What would be the value of the x-coordinate at the point where the y-coordinate is –3 for the straight line whose equation is $y = 4x - 7$?

    (A) $x = -1$
    (B) $x = 1$
    (C) $x = 4$
    (D) $x = 16$

21. A random sampling of outgoing business letters at a large company produced the results shown in the graph.

    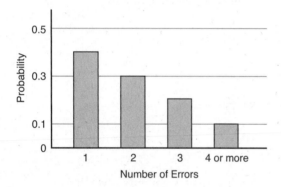

    What is the probability that an outgoing business letter from this company will have more than two errors?

    (A) $\dfrac{3}{10}$

    (B) $\dfrac{1}{3}$

    (C) $\dfrac{1}{2}$

    (D) $\dfrac{7}{10}$

22. An automobile dealer asked 40 potential customers their preference if buying a new vehicle. The results are shown in the following table.

Type of Vehicle	Number of Customers Preferring
Sedan	15
Pickup	8
SUV	5
Hybrid	12

Based on the data in the table, what is the probability that a person coming in to buy a new vehicle will buy a pickup?

    (A) 1 in 2
    (B) 1 in 3
    (C) 1 in 4
    (D) 1 in 5

23. For a certain packet of flower seeds, there is a $\dfrac{3}{4}$ probability that each seed will grow into a flowering plant, and a $\dfrac{1}{3}$ probability that a flowering plant will produce red blossoms. If there are 200 seeds in the packet, how many plants with red blossoms should be expected?

    [Fill in the blank box on your answer sheet.]

24. How many cubic yards of concrete would be necessary to fill the space for a patio that is 9 feet wide by 15 feet long and 3 inches deep?

    [Fill in the blank box on your answer sheet.]

25. The equation for the maximum safe weight of a person entering a crowded elevator is $\dfrac{(2,800 + w)}{10} = 302$. Rearrange this formula so that w is on one side of the equation by itself.

    [Fill in the blank box on your answer sheet.]

GO ON TO THE NEXT PAGE

26. A piece of rope x yards long is cut into six pieces. One piece of rope is 3 yards long, and the other five pieces are equal in length. What is the length, in yards, of one of those pieces?

    (A) $\dfrac{x-3}{5}$

    (B) $\dfrac{x}{5} - 3$

    (C) $\dfrac{3-x}{5}$

    (D) $5(x-3)$

27. Some prescription drugs are dispensed with a syringe. How many ccs (cubic centimeters) are shown by the arrow in the diagram below?

    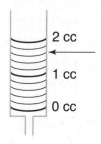

    (A) 0.6

    (B) 1.3

    (C) 1.6

    (D) 2.4

28. In scientific notation, what would the number 0.0405 be?

    (A) 40.5×10^{-3}

    (B) 4.05×10^{-2}

    (C) 40.5×10^{3}

    (D) 4.05×10^{2}

29. Janet's paycheck is shown below. How much is her take-home pay? Round to the nearest dollar.

Gross pay	$7,540.00
Federal income tax	$1,658.80
State income tax	$452.40
FICA	$1,102.14
Life insurance	$57.10

    [Fill in the blank box on your answer sheet.]

30. Woodlawn Nursery planted some seeds and recorded the heights of the plants as they grew. The following graph shows the data for one of those plants.

    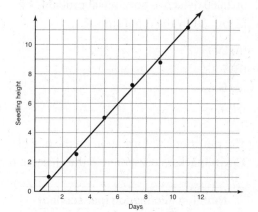

    Which conclusion is best supported by the graph?

    (A) The plant's height is the same as the number of days it has grown.
    (B) Growth slows as the plant ages.
    (C) Growth speeds up as the plant ages.
    (D) Growth remains constant as the plant ages.

GO ON TO THE NEXT PAGE

PRACTICE TEST THREE

31. The chart below shows the results of a sampling done by a bottling company to determine when defective products are identified.

When identified	Number of defective bottles
During processing	26 bottles
At final inspection	16 bottles
By retail stores	5 bottles
By consumers	3 bottles
Total	50 bottles

Based on the results of the sample, how many of 2,000 defective bottles will probably be identified by the retail stores?

(A) 200
(B) 150
(C) 5
(D) 3

32. The nutritional information on the bag of Flavo-Snacks is presented in the chart below.

Nutrition information (per serving)	
Serving size	1 ounce
Servings per container	2½
Calories	150
Protein	1 gram

Which of the following strategies would allow for the calculation of the number of calories in the whole bag?

(A) 150 calories × 1 bag
(B) 150 calories × 1 ounce serving
(C) 150 calories × $2\frac{1}{2}$ servings
(D) 150 calories + $2\frac{1}{2}$ servings

33. Recipes sometimes specify the temperature at which a food should be fried. After consulting the chart below, how many seconds should it take to fry a 1-inch cube of bread to a golden brown if the desired pan temperature is 370 degrees?

Gauge oil temperature by noting how long it takes to fry a 1-inch cube of white bread until golden brown.

20 seconds	385 to 395 degrees
40 seconds	375 to 385 degrees
50 seconds	365 to 375 degrees
60 seconds	355 to 365 degrees

[Fill in the blank box on your answer sheet.]

34. Sam has $3.00 in dimes and nickels. He has twice as many dimes as nickels. How many dimes and how many nickels does he have?

(A) 20 dimes and 10 nickels
(B) 24 dimes and 12 nickels
(C) 10 dimes and 20 nickels
(D) 12 dimes and 24 nickels

35. Solve the following quadratic equation to determine the two values for x.

$$2x^2 + 9x - 18 = 0$$

[Fill in the blank box on your answer sheet.]

36. Which of the inequalities listed below is the true description of the line in the diagram?

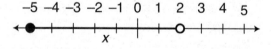

(A) $-5 < x \leq 2$
(B) $-5 < x < 2$
(C) $-5 \leq x \leq 2$
(D) $-5 \leq x < 2$

GO ON TO THE NEXT PAGE

37. The graph shown below states the relationship that exists between the outside temperature and the stopping distance of a landing
airplane.

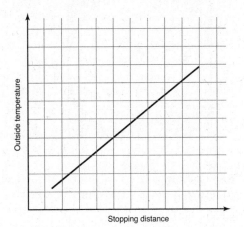

Which of the following statements is true?

(A) Larger aircraft can tolerate more heat.
(B) The cooler the temperature, the longer the
stopping distance.
(C) The hotter the temperature, the longer the
stopping distance.
(D) Cooler temperatures cause the density of
air to be less.

38. The children's heights in the fifth grade group
are 4 ft. 1 in., 4 ft. 2 in., 4 ft. 2 in., 4 ft. 4 in.,
4 ft. 4 in., and 4 ft. 4 in. What is the median
height of this group?

(A) 4 ft. 2 in.
(B) 4 ft. 2$\frac{1}{2}$ in.
(C) 4 ft. 3 in.
(D) 4 ft. 3$\frac{1}{2}$ in.

39. Carla's test scores for the semester were 87,
92, 75, 81, and 77. Calculate her test average.

[Fill in the blank box on your answer sheet.]

40. Nurses sometimes make line graphs of
patients' temperatures, taking readings at
regular intervals. The following graph covers
a day and a half of a patient's temperature.

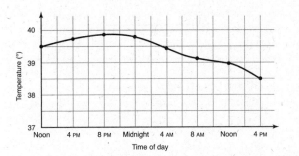

Which of the following is a true statement of
the data in the graph?

(A) The patient's temperature is falling at a
constant rate.
(B) The graph covers a 2-day period.
(C) Each mark on the x-axis is 4 hours.
(D) Each mark on the y-axis is 0.5 degrees.

GO ON TO THE NEXT PAGE

41. Look at the diagram below. Find the value of the line marked x.

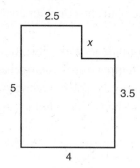

(A) 1.0
(B) 1.5
(C) 2.0
(D) 2.5

42. Which of the following algebraic expressions is the correct one for finding the total price of Joe's shirt purchased for n dollars and taxed at a rate of 6%?

(A) $n + 0.06$
(B) $n + 0.60$
(C) $n + 0.06n$
(D) $n + 0.6n$

43. Use FOIL to multiply these binomials.

$$(x - 6)(2x + 5) =$$

[Fill in the blank box on your answer sheet.]

44. Examine the shaded area of the diagram below to determine the way to go about finding how big that area is.

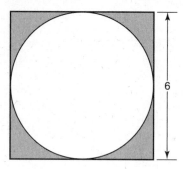

(A) $36 + 9(\pi)$
(B) $36 - 3(\pi)$
(C) $36 - 6(\pi)$
(D) $36 - 9(\pi)$

45. There are small boxes whose dimensions are $2 \times 3 \times 4$. How many of these will fit into a large box whose size is $12 \times 12 \times 4$?

(A) 6
(B) 12
(C) 18
(D) 24

46. Find the value of the following:

$$18 - (7 - 9)^2(5) - 3(4 - 1)$$

(A) −11
(B) 29
(C) 67
(D) 101

GO ON TO THE NEXT PAGE

47. Dice are frequently used in board games. Each die has six sides with a different number from 1 through 6 on each side. What is the probability of rolling a 3 on one die?

    (A) 0.50
    (B) 0.33
    (C) 0.25
    (D) 0.17

48. The label on a box of dog biscuits has the following information:

    > **Dandy Dog Biscuits**
    > Medium—for dogs 20–35 pounds
    > 4 biscuits in morning and 3 biscuits
    >   at night
    > Decrease other dog food by 25%

    Which of the following conclusions can you draw from this label?

    (A) 7 biscuits = 20 to 35 pounds
    (B) 4 morning biscuits = 3 evening biscuits
    (C) 7 biscuits = $\frac{3}{4}$ of the dog's calorie needs
    (D) 7 biscuits = $\frac{1}{4}$ of the dog's calorie needs

49. Given that $x = f^4$, $y = f^{-2}$, $z = f^2$, what would be the equivalent of $\frac{5x^2y}{z}$?

    (A) $5f^3$
    (B) $5f^4$
    (C) $5f^8$
    (D) $25f^4$

50. Rainfall is reported in inches. One cubic inch of water weighs 0.036 pounds. Which of these set-ups will tell the number of pounds of water that would be in your yard after a 1 inch rain, if your yard is 100 feet by 75 feet.

    (A) $100 \times 75 \times 0.036$
    (B) $\frac{100 \times 75}{0.036}$
    (C) $100 \times 12 \times 75 \times 12 \times 0.036$
    (D) $\frac{100 \times 12 \times 75 \times 12}{0.036}$

END OF EXAMINATION

ANSWER KEY
Practice Test Three

Part 1

1. **11.66**
2. **D**
3. **B**
4. **B**
5. **B**

Part 2

6. **See Answers Explained**
7. **D**
8. **C**
9. **C**
10. **D**
11. **B**
12. **B**
13. **B**
14. **C**
15. **D**

16. **A**
17. **A**
18. **C**
19. **B**
20. **B**
21. **A**
22. **D**
23. **50**
24. **1.25**
25. **220**
26. **A**
27. **D**
28. **B**
29. **4,270**
30. **D**
31. **A**
32. **C**
33. **50**

34. **B**
35. $\frac{3}{2}$, **–6 or** $1\frac{1}{2}$, **–6**
36. **D**
37. **C**
38. **C**
39. **82.4**
40. **C**
41. **B**
42. **C**
43. $2x^2 - 7x - 30$
44. **D**
45. **D**
46. **A**
47. **D**
48. **D**
49. **C**
50. **C**

SELF-ANALYSIS

Did you get at least 35 correct answers? If not, you need more practice for the Mathematical Reasoning Test. You can improve your performance to Good or Excellent by analyzing your errors. To determine the areas in which you need further study, review the chart below. The question numbers from Practice Test Three appear in the column to the left. Circle the questions you answered incorrectly. (Unsolved problems are counted as incorrect.) Refer to the Chapter and Chapter Section indicated for each question for additional review.

WHAT'S YOUR SCORE?

Your rating	Number of correct answers	Equivalent GED® score
Outstanding	45–50	180–200
Excellent	40–44	160–179
Good	35–39	140–159
Fair	30–34	120–139
Passing (min.)*	25–29	100–119

*The acceptable passing score varies with each state. Your state GED® test sites can provide this information. If your score is low on this practice test, the explanation of the correct answers that follows will help you. You may obtain additional help by reviewing the self-analysis chart below.

SELF-ANALYSIS CHART

Question	Chapter	Topic
Part I		
1.	6	Pythagorean relationship
2.	4	Substitution
3.	5	Measurement
4.	6	Perimeter
5.	4	Proportion
Part II		
6.	4	Graph of line
7.	5	Measurement
8.	4	Inequalities
9.	4	Percent
10.	4	Solve equations
11.	6	Slope
12.	3	Set-up style
13.	3	Multiplication/addition
14.	4	Equation of line
15.	6	Area
16.	6	Similar triangles
17.	4	Inequalities
18.	3	Fractions
19.	4	Percent

Question	Chapter	Topic
20.	6	Slope
21.	7	Line graph
22.	7	Probability
23.	3	Fractions
24.	6	Volume
25.	4	Rearrangement
26.	3	Set-up style
27.	5	Measurement
28.	4	Scientific notation
29.	3	Decimal subtraction
30.	7	Line graph
31.	7	Charts
32.	3	Fractions/set-up style
33.	7	Charts
34.	3	Multiplication
35.	4	Quadratic equations
36.	4	Inequalities
37.	7	Line graph
38.	7	Median
39.	7	Mean
40.	7	Line graph
41.	6	Perimeter
42.	4	Equations
43.	4	Binomial multiplication
44.	6	Area
45.	6	Volume
46.	4	PEMDA
47.	7	Probability
48.	3	Fractions
49.	4	Exponents
50.	3	Set-up style

ANSWERS EXPLAINED

Part 1

1. **11.66** Draw a diagonal in a rectangle and you have two right triangles. The diagonal is the hypotenuse, so you can use the Pythagorean theorem (see formula page). The square root of the diagonal is the square root of the sum of the squares of the two sides. $10^2 + 6^2 = 100 + 36 = 136$. The square root of 136 = 11.66.

2. **D** Substitute –2 for each x in the expression. The numerator will become 4 + 10 + 6, while the denominator will be –5. Dividing –5 into 20 gives –4.

3. **B** The key to the problem is to figure out the value of each mark. Each one is worth 0.2, which is easiest found out by trial and error. Counting up from 1.0, shows that the arrows are between 1.4 and 1.6.

4. **B** The perimeter is the distance around a figure. The top of the window is a half of a circle. The distance around a circle is the circumference, which is pi (3.14) times the diameter. In this case it will be $3.14 \times 4 = 12.56$. Divide this by 2 (for one half of a circle) and get 6.28. Now, examine the rectangular part of the diagram. The distance around it is 6 + 4 + 6 = 16. Adding 16 to 6.28 gives 22.28 for the perimeter.

5. **B** You can say that 16 is to 1 as x is to 8. Solving for x gives 128, which is 1 gallon.

Part 2

6.

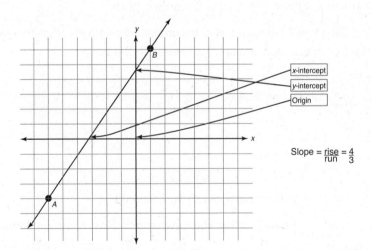

7. **D** The fact that the length is to be full length (84 inches long) immediately eliminates choices (A) and (C), as their length is too short. Then look at the width. Take the width of 68 inches and multiply that by 1.5 to get 102 inches minimum width required. Two pairs would give that and more, so choice (D) would work.

8. **C** $x < 5$. The inequality remains the same since you do not multiply or divide by a negative.

9. **C** To find the new amount:

    (old amount)(%)   = increase
    old amount + increase   = new amount
    $90.30 + ($90.30)(0.13)   = new amount

10. **D** $3(x + 5) = 3[\frac{1}{3}(5x - 5]$

$$3x + 15 = 5x - 5$$
$$15 = 2x - 5$$
$$20 = 2x$$
$$10 = x$$

11. **B** Slope = $\dfrac{\text{rise}}{\text{run}}$

$$\frac{-5}{6} = -\frac{5}{6}$$

12. **B** Because one euro is worth 1.495 dollars, you know that two euros would be worth (2)1.495, three euros would be worth (3)1.495, and so on. Therefore, 200 euros would be worth (200)1.495.

13. **B** To calculate the number of calories used, there are two things to consider. First, notice that walking uses 4.4 calories per pound, so 4.4 calories times 130 pounds would give the number of calories used in one hour. Second, the question is about twenty minutes only, which is one third of an hour. The correct strategy would be $144 \times \dfrac{0.44}{3}$.

14. **C** Use $y = mx + b$. The slope (m) is $\dfrac{5}{-12}$. The y-intercept is 2. Therefore, $y = -\dfrac{5}{12}x + 2$.

15. **D** The area of the rectangle will be 81 (from 10×8.1), so the area of the square is the same. Ask yourself, what times itself is 81 and you get 9.

16. **A** In similar triangle problems remember to compare similar parts of the triangles. Choice (A) does this by comparing vertical to horizontal for both.

17. **A** $3x + 9 \le 2x + 2$

$$\underline{\quad -2 \qquad -2 \quad}$$
$$3x + 7 \le 2x$$
$$\underline{-3x \qquad -3x \quad}$$
$$7 \le -x$$
$$-7 \ge x$$

Recall that dividing by a negative reverses the inequality.

18. **C** To add $\dfrac{1}{3}$ and $\dfrac{1}{4}$, remember that you have to get a least common denominator (12). This will cause you to add $\dfrac{4}{12}$ and $\dfrac{3}{12}$ to get $\dfrac{7}{12}$. The question asks for what is left after this $\dfrac{7}{12}$ is spent, so you would subtract from $\dfrac{12}{12}$ and get $\dfrac{5}{12}$.

19. **B** If sterling silver is 92.5% silver and the rest copper, then the copper amount would be 7.5%. The copper in 125 grams of sterling would be 125×0.075. Remember that to multiply by a percent, you must move the decimal two places to the left.

20. **B** Use $y = mx + b$.

$$-3 = 4x - 7$$
$$4 = 4x$$
$$1 = x$$

21. **A** The chances are 2 in 10 (0.2) that there could be 3 errors. This is added to the 1 in 10 chance that there could be 4 errors, so the total is a 3 in 10 chance.

22. **D** Add all the customers in the survey to get a total of 40. Of these 40, 8 would choose a pickup. $\frac{8}{40}$ reduces to $\frac{1}{5}$.

23. **50** Take this problem in stages. Three fourths of 200 = 150. These would be the ones that flowered. Then a third of these would be red, so $\frac{1}{3} \times 150 = 50$.

24. **1.25** First, change everything into yards: 9 feet = 3 yards, 15 feet = 5 yards, and 3 inches = $\frac{3}{36} = \frac{1}{12}$ yards. This is a volume problem, so $3 \times 5 \div 12 = 1.25$.

25. **220**
$$\frac{2,800 + w}{10} = 302$$
$$2,800 + w = 302(10)$$
$$w = 3,020 - 2,800$$
$$w = 220$$

26. **A** Subtract the 3 yard piece from the x first, and then split what is left into 5 equal pieces by dividing by five.

27. **D** The arrow is between 1 and 2, so the answer is 1. "something." Then the distance from 1 to 2 has five spaces, so each space is worth $\frac{1}{5}$ or 0.2. The arrow is three spaces up from the 1, and 3×0.2 is 0.6, so the arrow is pointing to 1.6.

28. **B** Recall that the decimal must be just to the right of the first digit. This immediately eliminates choices (A) and (C). Choice (B) is correct because the negative 2 exponent means to go two spaces to the left, and this produces the original number of 0.0405.

29. **4,270** Take-home pay is the amount of money that remains after all the deductions are subtracted from the gross pay.

30. **D** The fact that the graph is a straight line is saying that the growth is constant. If it were not constant, the graph would not be a straight line.

31. **A** Inspection of the data shows that out of 50 bottles examined, 5 were found to be defective at retail stores. A proportion in which you say that $\frac{5}{50} = \frac{x}{2,000}$ gives $x = 200$.

32. **C** The 150 calories is for one serving. There are $2\frac{1}{2}$ servings in the package, so multiply 150 by $2\frac{1}{2}$.

33. **50** 370 degrees falls into the range that corresponds to 50 seconds.

34. **B** The requirement of twice as many dimes as nickels reduces the choices to (A) and (B). Checking them out reveals that choice (B) is correct.

35. $\frac{3}{2}$, –6 or $1\frac{1}{2}$, –6

$$2x^2 + 9x - 18 = 0$$
$$(2x - 3)(x + 6) = 0$$
$$2x - 3 \quad\quad = 0$$
$$\quad\quad x + 6 = 0$$
$$2x = 3 \quad\quad x = -6$$
$$x = \frac{3}{2}$$

36. **D** All of the possible answers must lie between –5 and 2. The presence of the filled-in circle means that x includes the –5, so the "less than or equal to" sign is used. The open circle at the 2 means that the 2 itself is not included.

37. **C** As the temperature increases, the stopping distance increases. The reason for this is that hot air is less dense and, therefore, does not provide enough resistance to plane movement.

38. **C** Median is the middle value. In order to find the middle, it is necessary to line up the values from small to large in order to find the middle one. Since there are six values here, there will be two middle ones, and so the average of those two will be the median. The average of 4 ft. 2 in. and 4 ft. 4 in. is 4 ft. 3 in.

39. **82.4** Averages are calculated by adding all the values and dividing by the number of values. This produces an average of 82.4.

40. **C** Choice (C) is correct. A reading of the other choices will show they are incorrect.

41. **B** The left side of the diagram is a 5, so the right side must also be a 5. Since we know part of the right side is 3.5, the rest of it must be 1.5 in order to total 5.

42. **C** The shirt price is composed of two parts, the shirt itself and the tax. The tax would be 0.06 times n, while the shirt is just n.

43. **$2x^2 - 7x - 30$**
FOIL
$(x - 6)(2x + 5) = 2x^2 - 12x + 5x - 30 = 2x^2 - 7x - 30$

44. **D** The shaded area is the whole square minus the circle. Finding the whole square would be $6 \times 6 = 36$. The area of the circle is pi times radius squared, so it would be pi $\times$ 3 $\times$ 3, or pi $\times$ 9. The 3 comes from seeing that the circle has a diameter of 6, so the radius is half that.

45. **D** The volume of each of the small boxes is $2 \times 3 \times 4 = 24$ cubic inches. The big box has a volume of $12 \times 12 \times 4 = 576$. Dividing 24 into 576 equals 24.

46. **A** $18 - (-2)^2(5) - 3(3) =$
$$18 - 4(5) - 9 =$$
$$18 - 20 - 9 = -11$$

47. **D** The probability of rolling a 3 is 1 in 6.
$\frac{1}{6} = 0.17$.

48. **D** Reducing the dog's food by 25% means that the dog gets $\frac{1}{4}$ less food, so he won't get fat from too many biscuits.

49. **C**
$$\frac{5x^2 y}{z} = \frac{5(f^4)^2(f^{-2})}{f^2}$$
$$= \frac{5(f^8)(f^{-2})}{f^2}$$
$$= \frac{5f^6}{f^2}$$
$$= 5f^4$$

50. **C** The first step would be to find the cubic inches of water in the yard after an inch of rain. Since volume = length $\times$ width $\times$ height, and all values must be in inches, the set-up would be $100 \times 12 \times 75 \times 12 \times 1$. The final step would be to multiply by the weight of each cubic inch of water, which is 0.036.

Mathematical Reasoning

Part 1

1. Ⓐ Ⓑ Ⓒ Ⓓ

2. Ⓐ Ⓑ Ⓒ Ⓓ

3. Ⓐ Ⓑ Ⓒ Ⓓ

4.

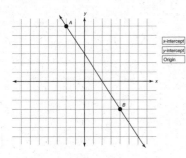

| x-intercept |
| y-intercept |
| Origin |

Slope = _____

5. Ⓐ Ⓑ Ⓒ Ⓓ

Part 2

6. Ⓐ Ⓑ Ⓒ Ⓓ

7. Ⓐ Ⓑ Ⓒ Ⓓ

8. _____

9. Ⓐ Ⓑ Ⓒ Ⓓ

10. Ⓐ Ⓑ Ⓒ Ⓓ

11. Ⓐ Ⓑ Ⓒ Ⓓ

12. Ⓐ Ⓑ Ⓒ Ⓓ

13. Ⓐ Ⓑ Ⓒ Ⓓ

14. Ⓐ Ⓑ Ⓒ Ⓓ

15. Ⓐ Ⓑ Ⓒ Ⓓ

16. Ⓐ Ⓑ Ⓒ Ⓓ

17. Ⓐ Ⓑ Ⓒ Ⓓ

18. Ⓐ Ⓑ Ⓒ Ⓓ

19. Ⓐ Ⓑ Ⓒ Ⓓ

20. Ⓐ Ⓑ Ⓒ Ⓓ

21. _____

22. Ⓐ Ⓑ Ⓒ Ⓓ

23. Ⓐ Ⓑ Ⓒ Ⓓ

24. Ⓐ Ⓑ Ⓒ Ⓓ

25. Ⓐ Ⓑ Ⓒ Ⓓ

26. Ⓐ Ⓑ Ⓒ Ⓓ

27. _____

28. _____

29. Ⓐ Ⓑ Ⓒ Ⓓ

30. Ⓐ Ⓑ Ⓒ Ⓓ

31. Ⓐ Ⓑ Ⓒ Ⓓ

32. Ⓐ Ⓑ Ⓒ Ⓓ

33. Ⓐ Ⓑ Ⓒ Ⓓ

34. Ⓐ Ⓑ Ⓒ Ⓓ

35. Ⓐ Ⓑ Ⓒ Ⓓ

36. Ⓐ Ⓑ Ⓒ Ⓓ

37. Ⓐ Ⓑ Ⓒ Ⓓ

38. Ⓐ Ⓑ Ⓒ Ⓓ

39. Ⓐ Ⓑ Ⓒ Ⓓ

40. Ⓐ Ⓑ Ⓒ Ⓓ

41. Ⓐ Ⓑ Ⓒ Ⓓ

42. Ⓐ Ⓑ Ⓒ Ⓓ

43. Ⓐ Ⓑ Ⓒ Ⓓ

44. Ⓐ Ⓑ Ⓒ Ⓓ

45. Ⓐ Ⓑ Ⓒ Ⓓ

46. Ⓐ Ⓑ Ⓒ Ⓓ

47. Ⓐ Ⓑ Ⓒ Ⓓ

48. Ⓐ Ⓑ Ⓒ Ⓓ

49. Ⓐ Ⓑ Ⓒ Ⓓ

50. Ⓐ Ⓑ Ⓒ Ⓓ

Mathematics Formula Sheet & Explanation

The 2014 GED® Mathematical Reasoning test contains a formula sheet, which displays formulas relating to geometric measurement and certain algebra concepts. Formulas are provided to test-takers so that they may focus on *application*, rather than the *memorization*, of formulas.

Area of a:

square	$A = s^2$
rectangle	$A = lw$
parallelogram	$A = bh$
triangle	$A = \frac{1}{2}bh$
trapezoid	$A = \frac{1}{2}h(b_1 + b_2)$
circle	$A = \pi r^2$

Perimeter of a:

square	$P = 4s$
rectangle	$P = 2l + 2w$
triangle	$P = s_1 + s_2 + s_3$
Circumference of a circle	$C = 2\pi r$ OR $C = \pi d$; $\pi \approx 3.14$

Surface area and volume of a:

rectangular/right prism	$SA = ph + 2B$	$V = Bh$
cylinder	$SA = 2\pi rh + 2\pi r^2$	$V = \pi r^2 h$
pyramid	$SA = \frac{1}{2}ps + B$	$V = \frac{1}{3}Bh$
cone	$SA = \pi rs + \pi r^2$	$V = \frac{1}{3}\pi r^2 h$
sphere	$SA = 4\pi r^2$	$V = \frac{4}{3}\pi r^3$

(p = perimeter of base with area B; $\pi \approx 3.14$)

Data

mean	mean is equal to the total of the values of a data set, divided by the number of elements in the data set
median	median is the middle value in an odd number of ordered values of a data set, or the mean of the two middle values in an even number of ordered values in a data set

Algebra

slope of a line	$m = \dfrac{y_2 - y_1}{x_2 - x_1}$
slope-intercept form of the equation of a line	$y = mx + b$
point-slope form of the equation of a line	$y - y_1 = m(x - x_1)$
standard form of a quadratic equation	$y = ax^2 + bx + c$
quadratic formula	$x = \dfrac{-b \pm \sqrt{b^2 - 4ac}}{2a}$
Pythagorean theorem	$a^2 + b^2 = c^2$
simple interest	$I = Prt$ (I = interest, P = principal, r = rate, t = time)
distance formula	$d = rt$
total cost	total cost = (number of units) × (price per unit)

© Copyright 2014 GED Testing Service. All rights reserved. GED® and GED Testing Service® are registered trademarks of the American Council on Education (ACE). They may not be used or reproduced without the express written permission of ACE or GED Testing Service. The GED® and GED Testing Service® brands are administered by GED Testing Service LLC under license from the American Council on Education.

Part 1

> **Directions:** You will have 115 minutes to complete this test. For the first five questions (Part 1), you will NOT be allowed to use a calculator. For the remainder of the test (Part 2), you may use either your own TI-30XB calculator or the calculator that is in the computer.

Questions 1 and 2 refer to the following chart and information.

SCRABBLE GAME

Number of Tiles of Each Letter	Letters
1	J, K, Q, X, Z
2	B, C, F, H, M, P, V, W, Y, blank
3	G
4	D, L, S, U
6	N, R, T
8	O
9	A, I
12	E

When playing Scrabble, each player begins with seven letter tiles. The number and kind of all the tiles in the game box are shown in the chart above.

1. What is the probability of choosing a K if no tiles have been selected yet?

   (A) 1 in 26
   (B) 1 in 5
   (C) 5 in 26
   (D) 1 in 100

2. What is the probability of choosing a B if 28 tiles have already been selected, and one of them was a B?

   (A) 2 in 26
   (B) 1 in 26
   (C) 1 in 28
   (D) 1 in 72

3. The diagram below is from an automobile owner's manual. It shows the relationship between outside temperature and the recommended oil for the car. Which of these statements is the best conclusion about the diagram?

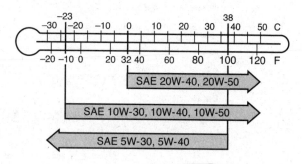

   (A) 5W-30 would be the best oil for a hot climate.
   (B) 20W-40 would be ideal for winter driving.
   (C) Motor oil gets thicker as it gets hotter.
   (D) 10W-30 oil is the best choice for temperatures between 10°F and 110°F.

GO ON TO THE NEXT PAGE

PRACTICE TEST FOUR

4. Draw an arrow from each of the circled terms to their correct locations on the graph, on your answer sheet. Calculate the slope of line *AB*.

[Fill in the blank box on your answer sheet.]

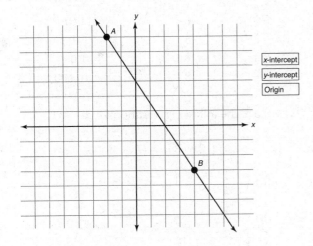

x-intercept

y-intercept

Origin

5. What is the relationship between what the two containers shown below will hold?

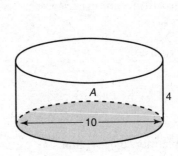
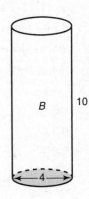

(A) $A > B$

(B) $A < B$

(C) $A = B$

(D) $2A = B$

TIP

If this were the computerized form of the GED® exam, you would be directed to place the cursor on each boxed item and drag it to its correct location and drop it there. This is called a drag-and-drop question format.

GO ON TO THE NEXT PAGE

PRACTICE TEST FOUR

Part 2

6. The temperature at 12:00 noon is –12°F. At 2:00 P.M. the temperature is 6°F. If the temperature rises at a constant rate, what will be the temperature reading in degrees Fahrenheit at 4 P.M.?

   (A) 14
   (B) 16
   (C) 24
   (D) 30

7. Sara's financial planner suggests that she save 12% of her salary for retirement. This year she is making $64,000. She will get a 4% raise next year. At the end of that year, how much will be in her retirement account?

   (A) $15,360
   (B) $15,667
   (C) $15,840
   (D) $15,915

8. Sandra makes an item to sell in craft shows. She can make 2 in an hour. Each item has 3 pieces, costing $.50, $.25, and $1.00. If she sells the items for $20.00 each, how much profit is Sandra making per hour?

   [Fill in the blank box on your answer sheet.]

9. A pain killer capsule weighs 1.5 grams and contains 325 milligrams of the pain killing substance. How many milligrams is the rest of the pill?

   (A) 1.175
   (B) 117.50
   (C) 175
   (D) 1,175

10. Many states have a law that states that a person is legally intoxicated with a blood alcohol content of 0.08%. Which of the following is true of that blood alcohol content?

	Parts of Alcohol	Parts of Blood
(A)	8	10
(B)	8	100
(C)	8	1,000
(D)	8	10,000

11. Solve the following equation for x.

$$2x - 3 = \frac{1}{4}(7x - 4)$$

   (A) $x = \frac{1}{3}$
   (B) $x = \frac{2}{7}$
   (C) $x = 8$
   (D) $x = 16$

12. What is the correct equation for line AB?

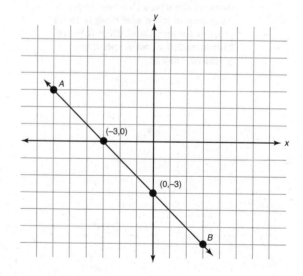

   (A) $y = x + 3$
   (B) $y = x - 3$
   (C) $y = -x + 3$
   (D) $y = -x - 3$

GO ON TO THE NEXT PAGE

13. If you worked two long days as recorded below, how many total hours did you work?

    Day 1: 13 hours, 43 minutes
    Day 2: 8 hours, 24 minutes

    (A) 21 hours, 7 minutes
    (B) 21 hours, 17 minutes
    (C) 22 hours, 7 minutes
    (D) 22 hours, 17 minutes

14. If you were going to put a door in the wall under the stairs as shown below, which of the following choices would be the set-up for finding the length of x?

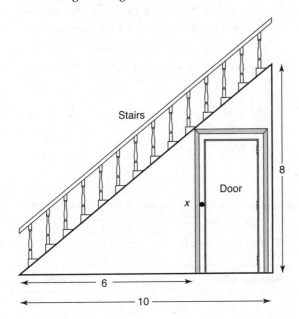

    (A) $\dfrac{4}{10} = \dfrac{x}{8}$

    (B) $\dfrac{6}{4} = \dfrac{x}{8}$

    (C) $\dfrac{6}{x} = \dfrac{8}{10}$

    (D) $\dfrac{6}{10} = \dfrac{x}{8}$

15. The meteorologist at Moose Bay measures the outside temperature at 6 A.M. every day, getting the following data:

Day	Temperature (degrees F)
Monday	–18
Tuesday	–2
Wednesday	4
Thursday	10
Friday	18

    What is the mean temperature for the time shown?

    (A) –2.4
    (B) 0
    (C) 2.4
    (D) 4.0

16. In 2013 the interest payment on the national debt was 5.5×10^{10} dollars. If this interest were cut in half, how many dollars would it be?

    (A) 2.75×10^{10}
    (B) 2.75×10^{5}
    (C) 5.50×10^{5}
    (D) 5.50×10^{-5}

GO ON TO THE NEXT PAGE

17. Highways in hilly country have signs that give the percent of the road's slope. The percent slope is the rise times 100 divided by the run (see the figure below). Which of these diagrams shows a 5% slope?

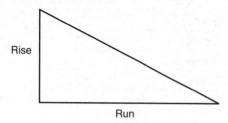

Rise

Run

Note: Drawings are not to scale.

(A)
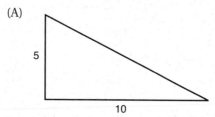
5

10

(B)
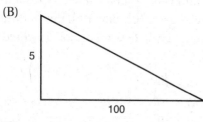
5

100

(C)
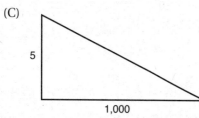
5

1,000

(D)
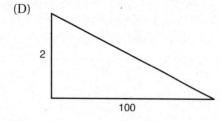
2

100

18. The phrase "time and a half" for overtime means that the worker receives $1\frac{1}{2}$ times the normal hourly wage for each overtime hour worked. What would the pay be for the week shown below?

    40 hours at $10 per hour
    12 hours at time and a half

(A) $418
(B) $520
(C) $580
(D) $600

19. The average Alaskan night is only 4 hours long during the month of May, because of the position of the sun in the sky. What is the probability of darkness for a randomly selected time in May?

(A) 0.33
(B) 0.25
(C) 0.20
(D) 0.17

20. After evaluating the nutrition labels on the milk labels shown below, which of these is true for 2% milk?

Regular Milk		2% Milk
8 oz.	Serving Size	8 oz.
150	Calories	120
8 grams	Fat	4 grams

(A) It has 2% of the fat of regular milk.
(B) It has one-half the fat of regular milk.
(C) It has 2% of the nutritional value of regular milk.
(D) It has 2% of the calories of regular milk.

GO ON TO THE NEXT PAGE

21. Rachel makes an annual salary of $45,000. The cost of living is expected to go up $6\frac{1}{2}$ % in the next year. How much would Rachel need to make in order to just stay even?

    [Fill in the blank box on your answer sheet.]

22. Choose the correct set-up for the calculation of the volume of a pyramid if it is 40 feet high and its base is a square whose area is 3,025 square feet. The formula for the volume of a pyramid is Volume = $\frac{1}{3}$ (base edge)2(height)

    (A) $\frac{1}{3}$ (55)^2(40)

    (B) $\frac{1}{3}$ (55 × 4)^2(40)

    (C) $\frac{1}{3}\left(\frac{3,025}{4}\right)$ (40)

    (D) 3(55)^2(40)

23. Solve the following inequality:
    $$-4 > \frac{x}{3}$$

    (A) $-12 > x$
    (B) $-12 < x$
    (C) $-\frac{3}{4} < x$
    (D) $\frac{3}{4} > x$

24. What is 926 rounded to the nearest hundred?

    (A) 900
    (B) 925
    (C) 930
    (D) 1,000

25. What is the solution of the following quadratic equation?
    $$x^2 - 7x + 12 = 0$$

    (A) $x = -4$ or $x = -3$
    (B) $x = -4$ or $x = 3$
    (C) $x = 4$ or $x = -3$
    (D) $x = 4$ or $x = 3$

26. How many square inches of wood would be scrap (see striped area in the drawing below) when cutting out the design?

    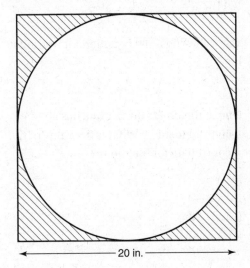

    ← 20 in. →

    (A) 20
    (B) 63
    (C) 86
    (D) 100

27. Phil's retirement benefit package is based on the formula that says that his retirement pay will be 2% of the average annual salary of the last five years times his years of experience. What will be his retirement income if he worked 34 years and the average of his last five years' salary is $60,000?

    [Fill in the blank box on your answer sheet.]

GO ON TO THE NEXT PAGE

PRACTICE TEST FOUR

28. The other test takers in your group scored 75, 88, 67, 95, 84, 91, and 75. What is the mode of this group?

    [Fill in the blank box on your answer sheet.]

29. If your insurance premium has been increased from $350 a month to $500 a month, what percent increase is this?

    (A) 30%
    (B) 43%
    (C) 70%
    (D) 167%

30. The following is the equation for a straight line.

    $$y = -\frac{2}{7}x - 3$$

    One of the points on this line has a y-coordinate of –1. What is the value of the x-coordinate for that point?

    (A) $x = 7$
    (B) $x = -7$
    (C) $x = 14$
    (D) $x = -14$

31. Which of the following is equivalent to $\frac{2xy}{z}$ if

    $$x = k^{-2}, \quad y = k^3, \quad z = k^{-1}?$$

    (A) $2k$
    (B) $2k^2$
    (C) $2k^3$
    (D) $25k^5$

32. Suppose you were applying for a job with a landscape firm. They want to know if you can handle drawing to scale. If you were to draw the lot shown below, with a scale of $\frac{1}{2}$ inch to equal 10 feet, what would be the dimensions of the lot in inches for your drawing?

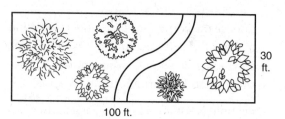

100 ft.

    (A) 1.0×0.3
    (B) 10×3
    (C) 3×1.5
    (D) 5×1.5

33. Choose the correct factorization of $2x^2 - x - 21$.

    (A) $(x + 1)(2x - 21)$
    (B) $(x - 1)(2x + 21)$
    (C) $(2x + 7)(x - 3)$
    (D) $(2x - 7)(x + 3)$

34. If you are making $10.00 an hour and get a 7% raise, what is your new hourly rate?

    (A) $10.07
    (B) $10.17
    (C) $10.70
    (D) $11.70

35. Solve the inequality: $-3(x - 9) > 15$

    (A) $x < 4$
    (B) $x > 4$
    (C) $x < 8$
    (D) $x < -14$

GO ON TO THE NEXT PAGE

PRACTICE TEST FOUR

36. A parking garage charges $4.00 for the first hour and $1.75 for each additional half hour. Which of these equations will predict the cost for any given amount of time (t)?

    (A) $(t-1)(2)(\$1.75) + \$4.00 = \text{cost}$

    (B) $\frac{1}{2}t(\$1.75) + \$4.00 = \text{cost}$

    (C) $2t(\$4.00) + \$1.75 = \text{cost}$

    (D) $\frac{1}{2}t(\$4.00) + \$1.75 = \text{cost}$

37. What is the value of x if

    $$x = 19 - (7-3)^2 + 2(3-1+5)?$$

    (A) 17
    (B) 21
    (C) 49
    (D) 64

38. Fred began work at 8:30 A.M. He took a lunch break from 12 noon for a half hour and then finished work at 5 P.M. How many hours did he work?

    (A) 7 hours
    (B) 7 hours and 30 minutes
    (C) 8 hours
    (D) 8 hours and 30 minutes

39. The National Weather Service has issued a storm bulletin stating that a storm is moving at a speed of 35 miles per hour. Its present location is about 100 miles from you, and it is moving in your direction. Approximately how long will it take for the storm to reach you?

    (A) 2 hours
    (B) $2\frac{1}{2}$ hours
    (C) 3 hours
    (D) $3\frac{1}{2}$ hours

40. Bert's company reimburses him at 55 cents a mile when he uses his car for company business. How much will he be paid for a trip that began with an odometer reading of 30,195 and ended with a reading of 30,640?

    (A) $24.48
    (B) $166.08
    (C) $168.52
    (D) $244.75

41. If you were setting up a trellis for growing green beans as shown below, how tall would the trellis be (x), given the other dimensions shown.

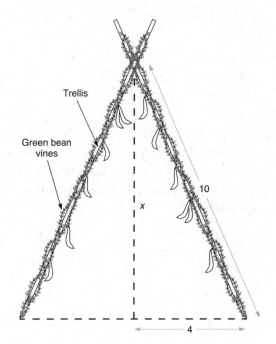

    (A) Between 8 and 9
    (B) Between 9 and 10
    (C) Between 82 and 83
    (D) Between 83 and 84

GO ON TO THE NEXT PAGE

42. Ralph uses his debit card at dinner at Outback Steak House. His bill is for $67.50. He wants to include a tip of 20%. How much will his card be charged?

    (A) $68.85
    (B) $71.00
    (C) $81.00
    (D) $87.50

43. Suppose that you are playing a game that uses a spinner. The spinner has eight colors that you could land on. The colors are red, blue, green, yellow, black, white, purple, and orange. What is the probability that any one spin will land on blue?

    (A) 2 in 3
    (B) 1 in 4
    (C) 1 in 7
    (D) 1 in 8

44. The speed of sound is 330 meters per second. The fireworks display is across the river valley from your home. If it takes 10 seconds for the sound to reach you, how many kilometers away is it?

    (A) $(10)(330)(1,000)$

    (B) $\dfrac{(10)(330)}{1,000}$

    (C) $(10)(330)(100)$

    (D) $\dfrac{(10)(330)}{100}$

45. How many cubic feet of water would it take to fill this pool to within one foot of the top?

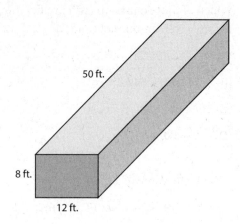

    (A) 3,773
    (B) 4,200
    (C) 4,400
    (D) 4,800

46. Calculate the slope of line CD in the graph below.

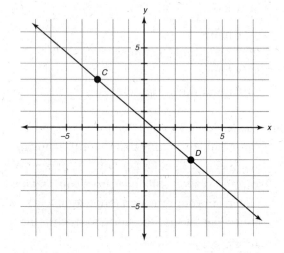

    (A) $\dfrac{5}{6}$

    (B) $-\dfrac{5}{6}$

    (C) $\dfrac{6}{5}$

    (D) $-\dfrac{6}{5}$

GO ON TO THE NEXT PAGE

PRACTICE TEST FOUR

47. From the graph below, which of these conclusions can be drawn?

SALES FOR AUGUST

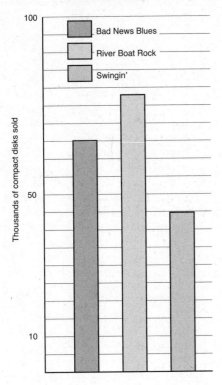

(A) Bad News Blues gained in popularity through the year.
(B) River Boat Rock outsold Swingin' by 3,300 copies.
(C) Forty thousand copies of Swingin' were sold in August.
(D) Sixty-five thousand copies of Bad News Blues were sold in August.

48. A survey in Hendersonville showed that three out of every five voting age citizens would vote again for the town's mayor. There are 20,000 people of voting age. If all of them voted, how many votes should the mayor get?

(A) 10,000
(B) 12,000
(C) 15,000
(D) 18,000

49. Which of these statements accurately describes the rainfall situation in Moose Creek, shown in the graph below?

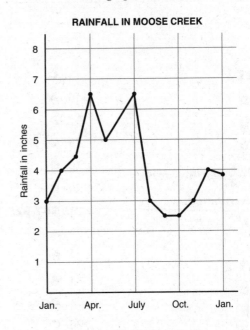

(A) April and July are equally rainy months.
(B) January is the driest month.
(C) There were 5 inches of rain in March.
(D) A flash flood occurs with $2\frac{1}{2}$ inches of rain in one hour.

50. Sally, age 46, wishes to buy a $100,000 life insurance policy. From the table below, what will this coverage cost her for a year?

LIFE INSURANCE PREMIUM COSTS	
Age	**Annual Cost per $1,000**
44	29.50
45	30.15
46	31.50
47	32.85
48	33.50

(A) $31.50
(B) $315.00
(C) $323.60
(D) $3,150.00

END OF EXAMINATION

PRACTICE TEST FOUR

Part 1

1. **D**
2. **D**
3. **D**
4. $-\dfrac{3}{2}$ **See Answers Explained.**
5. **A**

Part 2

6. **C**
7. **B**
8. **$36.50**
9. **D**
10. **D**
11. **C**
12. **D**
13. **C**
14. **D**

15. **C**
16. **A**
17. **B**
18. **C**
19. **D**
20. **B**
21. **$47,925**
22. **A**
23. **B**
24. **A**
25. **D**
26. **C**
27. **$40,800**
28. **75**
29. **B**
30. **B**
31. **B**
32. **D**

33. **D**
34. **C**
35. **A**
36. **A**
37. **A**
38. **C**
39. **C**
40. **C**
41. **B**
42. **B**
43. **D**
44. **B**
45. **B**
46. **B**
47. **D**
48. **B**
49. **A**
50. **D**

SELF-ANALYSIS

Did you get at least 35 correct answers? If not, you need more practice for the Mathematical Reasoning Test. You can improve your performance to Good or Excellent by analyzing your errors. To determine the areas in which you need further study, review the chart below. The question numbers from Practice Test Four appear in the column to the left. Circle the questions you answered incorrectly. (Unsolved problems are counted as incorrect.) Refer to the Chapter and Chapter Section indicated for each question for additional review.

WHAT'S YOUR SCORE?

Your rating	Number of correct answers	Equivalent GED® score
Outstanding	45–50	180–200
Excellent	40–44	160–179
Good	35–39	140–159
Fair	30–34	120–139
Passing (min.)*	25–29	100–119

*The acceptable passing score varies with each state. Your state GED® test sites can provide this information. If your score is low on this practice test, the explanation of the correct answers that follows will help you. You may obtain additional help by reviewing the self-analysis chart below.

SELF-ANALYSIS CHART

Question	Chapter	Topic
Part I		
1.	7	Probability
2.	7	Probability
3.	3	Measurement
4.	4	Identify graph parts
5.	6	Volume
Part II		
6.	4	Signed numbers
7.	4	Percent
8.	3	Addition/multiplication
9.	5	Conversion factors
10.	4	Percent
11.	4	Solve equations
12.	4	Interpreting graphs
13.	5	Time
14.	6	Similar triangles
15.	7	Average
16.	4	Scientific notation
17.	6	Slope
18.	3	Fractions
19.	7	Probability

Question	Chapter	Topic
20.	7	Charts
21.	4	Percent
22.	3	Multiplication
23.	4	Inequalities
24.	3	Rounding
25.	3	Multiplication/addition
26.	6	Area
27.	4	Percent
28.	7	Mode
29.	4	Percent
30.	4	Linear equations
31.	4	Exponents
32.	5	Conversion factors
33.	4	FOIL
34.	4	Percent
35.	4	Inequality
36.	4	Modeling
37.	4	PEMDA
38.	5	Time
39.	3	Long division
40.	3	Subtraction/multiplication
41.	6	Pythagorean relationship
42.	4	Percent
43.	7	Probability
44.	3	Set-up style
45.	6	Volume
46.	4	Slope
47.	7	Bar graphs
48.	4	Proportions
49.	7	Line graph
50.	7	Charts

ANSWERS EXPLAINED

Part 1

1. **D** Since there is only one K and 100 tiles, the probability would be 1 in 100.

2. **D** There are 2 of the B tiles. Since one has been selected already, one remains. The remaining tiles are 100 – 28 or 72, so the odds are 1 in 72.

3. **D** As you read the chart, none of the other answers is true.

4.

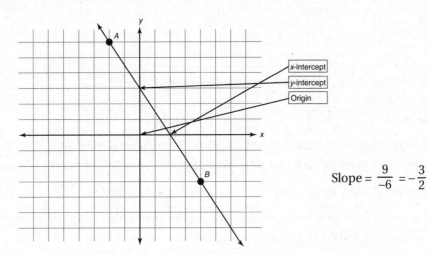

$$\text{Slope} = \frac{9}{-6} = -\frac{3}{2}$$

5. **A** It is not even necessary to calculate the volumes, but just to set them up to see the relationship. Remember that the radius is half the diameter.

   $V = \pi(5)(5)(4)$ for container A
   $V = \pi(2)(2)(10)$ for container B

   Not counting π, since it is common to both, you can see that A is 100, while B is 40, so A is larger than B.

Part 2

6. **C** To find the rate, think of the first time interval, which is two hours (from noon to 2). During this time interval the temperature rose 18 degrees (from –12 to +6). This gives a rate of 9 degrees in l hour. Applying this rate to the time from 2 P.M. to 4 P.M. gives 18° above the 6° at 2 P.M. Then 6 + 18 = 24.

7. **B** $64,000 × 0.12 = 7,680$ this year

   $64,000 + 0.04 × 64,000 = 66,560$

$$\begin{array}{r} 66{,}560 \\ \times\ \ 0.12 \\ \hline 7{,}987 \text{ next year} \\ +\ 7{,}680 \\ \hline 15{,}667 \end{array}$$

8. **$36.50** Sandra has invested in each craft item a total of $1.75. If she makes 2 per hour, she has a cost per hour of $3.50. If she can sell both of them, she makes $40.00 in income. The difference between $40.00 and $3.50 will be her hourly profit.

9. **D** If the pain pill is 1.5 grams, that would be 1,500 milligrams. 1,500 milligrams minus the 325 milligrams for the pain ingredient equals 1,175 milligrams.

10. **D** Since percent means "per 100," this is saying $\frac{0.08}{100}$. To get rid of the decimal in the numerator, multiply top and bottom by 100.

11. **C** $2x - 3 = \frac{1}{4}(7x - 4)$ Multiply both sides by 4.

$$8x - 12 = 7x - 4$$
$$\underline{-7x \qquad -7x}$$
$$x - 12 = 0 - 4$$
$$x = 8$$

12. **D** Start with $y = mx + b$. Calculate m (slope) $= \frac{3}{-3} = -1$. $b = -3$.
So, $y = -1x - 3$
$$y = -x - 3$$

13. **C** When you first start to add, $13 + 8 = 21$ hours. Then the total minutes is $43 + 24 = 67$ minutes, which is 1 hour and 7 minutes. So, the total time is 22 hours and 7 minutes.

14. **D** Remember in setting up proportions to compare similar parts.

15. **C** Adding all the temperatures gives 24. Dividing by the number of temperatures (5) gives an average (mean) of 2.4.

16. **A** When dividing by 2, the 5.5 becomes 2.75. Since 2.75 is still between 1 and 10, the exponent is not affected.

17. **B** In order to get 5% for the answer, using the formula works only for choice 2, where you would multiply 5 by 100 and then divide by 100.

18. **C** The regular part of the time would be 40 hours times $10 per hour for $400. The overtime part would be 12 hours at $15 per hour for $180. This would make the total pay $580.

19. **D** $\frac{1}{6} = 0.17$

20. **B** According to the chart, regular milk has 8 grams of fat and 2% milk has 4 grams of fat, or half the fat.

21. **$47,925** Take $6\frac{1}{2}$% of $45,000. $0.065 \times \$45,000 = \$2,925$. Rachel needs this much more just to stay even, so she needs to make $\$2,925 + \$45,000 = \$47,925$.

22. **A** $V = \frac{1}{3}$ (base edge)^2(height)

$$V = \frac{1}{3}(\sqrt{3,025})^2(40)$$

$$V = \frac{1}{3}(55)^2(40)$$

23. **B** $-4 > \frac{x}{3}$

$-12 < x$

Recall that multiplying by a negative reverses the inequality.

24. **A** The phrase "rounded to the nearest hundred" means that you would expect only zeros in the units and tens places. Since the 26 is less than halfway to the next hundred, it will be thrown out, leaving 900.

25. **D** Factoring the equation produces
$(x-4)(x-3) = 0$. Set each factor equal to 0 and then solve:

$$x - 4 = 0 \qquad x - 3 = 0$$
$$\underline{+4 \quad +4} \qquad \underline{+3 \quad +3}$$
$$x \quad = 4 \qquad x \quad = 3$$

26. **C** The area of the whole square minus the area of the circle will give the area of the striped part. The whole square has area $20 \times 20 = 400$. The circle's area is $(3.14)(10)(10) = 314$. Then, $400 - 314 = 86$.

27. **$40,800** $(60,000)(0.02)(34) = 40,800$

28. **75** The mode is the number that occurs most often, in this case 75.

29. **B** The increase is $150 and the old cost was $350. Percent is part divided by whole times 100, so 150 divided by 350 is 0.428. Multiplying by 100 gives 43%.

30. **B** $y = \dfrac{-2}{7}x - 3$

$$1 = \dfrac{-2}{7}x - 3$$
$$\underline{+3 \qquad\qquad +3}$$
$$2 = \dfrac{-2}{7}x + 3$$
$$14 = -2x$$
$$-7 = x$$

31. **B** $\dfrac{2(k^{-2})(k^3)}{k^{-1}} = \dfrac{2(k^{-1})}{k^{-1}} = 2k^{1-(-1)} = 2k^{1+1} = 2k^2$

32. **D** Divide the dimensions by 10 to see how many of the inch segments you will need for each side. Since there are 3 ten foot segments in 30, then 3 times $\dfrac{1}{2}$ will be $1\dfrac{1}{2}$. The other dimension is 100, for which there are 10 of the ten foot segments. Ten times $\dfrac{1}{2}$ is 5.

33. **D** Use the FOIL approach to see that this is the only factorization that works.

34. **C** Seven percent is 0.07 times $10 = $.70. This makes the new rate $10.70.

35. **A** $3(x - 9) > 15$

$$-3x + 27 > 15$$
$$-3x \qquad > -12$$
$$x \qquad < 4$$

Recall that dividing by a negative reverses the inequality.

36. **A** For each hour there are two half-hours, so the $1.75 must be doubled. Use $t - 1$ because one hour is covered by the $4.00.

37. **A** $19 - (7 - 3)^2 + 2(3 - 1 + 5)$

$$19 - 16 + 14 = 17$$

38. **C** From 8:30 to noon is $3\frac{1}{2}$ hours. He went back after lunch at 12:30 and worked to 5, which is $4\frac{1}{2}$ hours. The total hours is $4\frac{1}{2} + 3\frac{1}{2} = 8$.

39. **C** The distance formula can be used. Common sense will also do. 100 miles divided by 35 gives approximately 3 hours.

40. **C** The number of miles driven is the difference in the two odometer readings. Multiply this difference by the 55 cents per mile allowed. (The odometer is the dial on the dashboard that records miles driven.)

41. **B** Substituting in the formula for the Pythagorean relationship gives the following:

$$x^2 + 4^2 = 10^2$$
$$x^2 + 16 = 100$$
$$x^2 = 84$$

Since $9^2 = 81$ and $10^2 = 100$, the answer (the square root of 84) lies between 9 and 10.

42. **B** $\$67.50 \times 0.20 = \$13.50$
$\$67.50 + 13.50 = \$81.00$

43. **D** With eight colors, there is a 1 in 8 chance for blue.

44. **B** Distance = rate × time

$$\text{Distance} = \frac{330 \text{ m}}{\text{s}} \times 10 \text{ s}$$

Distance = 3,300 meters
Divide meters by 1,000 to convert to kilometers.

45. **B** From the formula page:

$V = \text{length} \times \text{width} \times \text{height}$
$V = 50 \times 12 \times 7$
$V = 4,200$ cubic feet

Note that the height is 7 feet, since the problem states that the pool should be filled to within one foot of the top.

46. **B** $\dfrac{\text{Rise}}{\text{Run}} = \dfrac{-5}{6}$

47. **D** This is the only correct response.

48. **B** Set up a proportion:

$$\frac{3}{5} = \frac{x}{20,000}$$

$5x = 60,000$
$x = 12,000$

49. **A** You could quickly eliminate choices 4 and 5 as having nothing to do with the graph. Choice 1 is the only true statement.

50. **D** The thing to notice about the chart is that the dollar amount given buys only $1,000 of insurance. There are 100 of these thousands in the $100,000, so the premium has to be multiplied by 1,000.

Getting ready to take the GED® Test?
Here's all the help you'll need!

How to Prepare for the GED® Test, w/optional CD-ROM
Christopher Sharpe and Joseph S. Reddy
ISBN 978-1-4380-0267-5, book only, paperback, $18.99, *Can$21.99*
ISBN 978-1-4380-7369-9, book w/CD-ROM, $29.99, *Can$34.50*

How to Prepare for the GED® Test, Canadian Edition
Chris Smith, Karen Sansom
ISBN 978-1-4380-0180-7, paperback, $23.99, *Can$23.99*

Essential Words for the GED®, 2nd Ed.
Langosch
ISBN 978-0-7641-2357-3, paperback, $10.99, *Can$12.99*

**Barron's GED®, Spanish Edition—Barron's GED® Examen
de Equivalencia de la Escuela Superior, en Español, 3rd Ed.**
Rockowitz, Brownstein, and Peters, trans. by Vendrell
ISBN 978-0-7641-4301-4, paperback, $24.99, *Can$29.99*

Math Workbook for the GED® Test, 4th Ed.
Holm
ISBN 978-1-4380-0571-3, paperback, $13.99, *Can$15.99*

Barron's GED® Writing Workbook, 3rd Ed.
Hogan
ISBN 978-0-7641-4205-5, paperback, $14.99, *Can$17.99*

Pass Key to the GED® Test
Christopher Sharpe and Joseph S. Reddy
ISBN 978-1-4380-0332-0, paperback, $9.99, *Can$11.50*

Barron's Pre-GED®
Koch, Bristow, and Miller
ISBN 978-1-4380-0110-4, Paperback, $21.99, *Can$24.99*

Barron's GED® Flash Cards
Battles, Villapol, and Vazquez
ISBN 978-1-4380-7149-7, 450 Cards, $16.99, *Can$19.99*

Available at your local book store
or visit www.barronseduc.com

Barron's Educational Series, Inc.
250 Wireless Blvd.
Hauppauge, N.Y. 11788
Call toll-free: 1-800-645-3476

In Canada:
Georgetown Book Warehouse
34 Armstrong Ave.
Georgetown, Ontario L7G 4R9
Call toll-free: 1-800-247-7160

BARRON'S

Prices subject to change without notice.

#96 R2/15

Really. This isn't going to hurt at all . . .

Learning won't hurt when middle school and high school students open any *Painless* title. These books transform subjects into fun—emphasizing a touch of humor and entertaining brain-tickler puzzles that are fun to solve.

Extra bonus—each title followed by (*) comes with a FREE app!
Download a fun-to-play arcade game to your iPhone, iTouch, iPad, or Android™ device. The games reinforce the study material in each book and provide hours of extra fun.

Each book: Paperback

Painless Algebra, 3rd Ed.*
Lynette Long, Ph.D.
ISBN 978-0-7641-4715-9, $9.99, *Can$11.99*

Painless American Government
Jeffrey Strausser
ISBN 978-0-7641-2601-7, $9.99, *Can$11.99*

Painless American History, 2nd Ed.
Curt Lader
ISBN 978-0-7641-4231-4, $9.99, *Can$11.99*

Painless Chemistry*
Loris Chen
ISBN 978-0-7641-4602-2, $9.99, *Can$11.99*

Painless Earth Science*
Edward J. Denecke, Jr.
ISBN 978-0-7641-4601-5, $9.99, *Can$11.99*

Painless English for Speakers of Other Languages, 2nd Ed.*
Jeffrey Strausser and José Paniza
ISBN 978-1-4380-0002-2, $9.99, *Can$11.50*

Painless Fractions, 3rd Ed.*
Alyece Cummings, M.A.
ISBN 978-1-4380-0000-8, $9.99, *Can$11.50*

Painless French, 2nd Ed.*
Carol Chaitkin, M.S., and Lynn Gore, M.A.
ISBN 978-0-7641-4762-3, $9.99, *Can$11.50*

Painless Geometry, 2nd Ed.
Lynette Long, Ph.D.
ISBN 978-0-7641-4230-7, $9.99, *Can$11.99*

Painless Grammar, 3rd Ed.*
Rebecca S. Elliott, Ph.D.
ISBN 978-0-7641-4712-8, $9.99, *Can$11.99*

Painless Italian, 2nd Ed.
Marcel Danesi, Ph.D.
ISBN 978-0-7641-4761-6, $9.99, *Can$11.50*

Painless Math Word Problems, 2nd Ed.
Marcie Abramson, B.S., Ed.M.
ISBN 978-0-7641-4335-9, $9.99, *Can$11.99*

Painless Poetry, 2nd Ed.
Mary Elizabeth
ISBN 978-0-7641-4591-9, $9.99, *Can$11.99*

Painless Pre-Algebra
Amy Stahl
ISBN 978-0-7641-4588-9, $9.99, *Can$11.99*

Painless Reading Comprehension, 2nd Ed.*
Darolyn E. Jones, Ed.D.
ISBN 978-0-7641-4763-0, $9.99, *Can$11.50*

Painless Spanish, 2nd Ed.*
Carlos B. Vega
ISBN 978-0-7641-4711-1, $9.99, *Can$11.99*

Painless Speaking, 2nd Ed.*
Mary Elizabeth
ISBN 978-1-4380-0003-9, $9.99, *Can$11.50*

Painless Spelling, 3rd Ed.*
Mary Elizabeth
ISBN 978-0-7641-4713-5, $9.99, *Can$11.99*

Painless Study Techniques
Michael Greenberg
ISBN 978-0-7641-4059-4, $9.99, *Can$11.99*

Painless Vocabulary, 2nd Ed.*
Michael Greenberg
ISBN 978-0-7641-4714-2, $9.99, *Can$11.99*

Painless Writing, 2nd Ed.
Jeffrey Strausser
ISBN 978-0-7641-4234-5, $9.99, *Can$11.99*

Prices subject to change without notice.

Available at your local book store or visit **www.barronseduc.com**

Barron's Educational Series, Inc.
250 Wireless Blvd.
Hauppauge, N.Y. 11788
Order toll-free:
1-800-645-3476

(#79) R4/14